THEBES

Paul Cartledge

THEBES

THE FORGOTTEN CITY
OF ANCIENT GREECE

ABRAMS PRESS, NEW YORK

Published in 2020 by Abrams Press, an imprint of ABRAMS. All rights reserved. No portion of this book may be reproduced, stored in a retrieval system, or transmitted in any form or by any means, mechanical, electronic, photocopying, recording, or otherwise, without written permission from the publisher.

Library of Congress Control Number: 2020932371

ISBN: 978-1-4683-1606-3
eISBN: 978-1-4683-1607-0

Printed and bound in the United States
10 9 8 7 6 5 4 3 2 1

Abrams books are available at special discounts when purchased in quantity for premiums and promotions as well as fundraising or educational use. Special editions can also be created to specification. For details, contact specialsales@abramsbooks.com or the address below.

Abrams Press® is a registered trademark of Harry N. Abrams, Inc.

ABRAMS The Art of Books
195 Broadway, New York, NY 10007
abramsbooks.com

To the Memory of Peter Mayer
(1936–2018)

Contents

Acknowledgements

Julian Alexander, my agent, and Georgina Morley, at Picador, my UK publisher/editor, are jointly most responsible for making this book happen. I am greatly in their debt, once again. The late great publisher Peter Mayer, to whom this book is dedicated (see Afterword), was also key to its conception and development, and acceptance by its US publisher. And it has also been a pleasure to work again with Tracy Carns (formerly with Overlook, now Abrams).

Dr Carol Atack (Newnham College, Cambridge) most generously volunteered to read the whole in draft. She proved yet again to be a quite seriously demanding critic, in all the best senses. Professor Robert Garland (Colgate University), my good friend of over twenty years, at very short notice read an early, very imperfect draft of the whole book and helped me clear up many unclarities and infelicities as well as eliminate many niggling slips, all with his usual tact. Dr Daisy Dunn (editor of the Hellenic Society's *ARGO* magazine) likewise kindly read all at a later stage and made several helpful corrections. Professor Fiona Macintosh (St Hilda's College, Oxford) helped greatly with the tragedy section and made some most helpful observations at a late stage. Professor Edith Hall (King's College London), another dear friend and colleague of long standing, unwittingly helped me fill a couple of major gaps by showing me the manuscript of her magnificent forthcoming work (with Dr Henry Stead, Open University, UK) on Classics and class in Britain and Ireland since the late eighteenth century. My Cambridge colleague Dr Yannis Galanakis was exceptionally helpful in discussing with me his exciting excavation at Prosilio, Boeotia. Paul Lay (editor of *History Today* magazine) put me on to Enescu's *Oedipe* late in the day. Finally, I have profited immeasurably from my collaboration over the past half dozen years with Professor Paul Christesen (Dartmouth College), with whom I co-direct and co-edit the *Oxford History of the Archaic Greek World* project.

Many years ago, I toured most of Boeotia by car with my late friend and former colleague (at the then New University of Ulster), Dr David Hardy (an alumnus of Clare College, Cambridge, at which I hold an A. G. Leventis Senior Research Fellowship). I have visited Boeotia and Thebes many times since, but that tour has stayed in my mind the most vividly.

Note on Spelling

I have generally used Latinized forms of Greek proper names, hence Cadmea rather than Kadmeia, but there are exceptions. There are always exceptions.

Timeline

(All dates down to 508/7 BCE are approximate and/or traditional.)
(B)CE = (Before) Common Era

BCE

Bronze Age

3000 (to 1000)	Minoan (Cretan) civilization
1600 (to 1150)	Mycenaean (or Late Bronze Age) period
1400	Destruction of Cnossus, Crete
1300	Palace of Thebes and Fortification of Cadmea (Kadmeia) acropolis
1200	Destruction of mainland Greek palaces: Mycenae, Pylus, Thebes
1150	Upheavals in eastern Mediterranean: marauding of the 'Sea Peoples'

Early Iron age

1100 (to 700)	Era of migrations (Dorian migration, Asia Minor settlements)

Archaic Age

800–700	Emergence of the *polis* state-form
776	Foundation of Olympic Games
750/720	Greek alphabet invented

700–650	Homer, Hesiod (*Theogony, Works and Days*)
750–	Greek Diaspora 'colonization' begins: southern Italy, Sicily, Black Sea, North Africa, southern France, eastern Spain (Thebes not a colonizer)
700	Introduction of hoplite fighting
550	Achaemenid Persian Empire founded by Cyrus II
525	First Boeotian federation, Boeotian coinage
508/7	Cleisthenes introduces democratic reforms in Athens
506	Boeotians defeated by democratic Athens
505 (–366)	Sparta's Peloponnesian League formed

Classical Age

490	Battle of Marathon: Athens and Plataea defeat Persian invaders under Datis and Artaphernes
480–479	Second Persian invasion, under Xerxes, defeated: Salamis 480; Plataea 479. Thebes fights with Persia against loyalist Greeks and serves as main Persian base
477 (–404)	Athens founds anti-Persian Delian League
467	Aeschylus (*c.* 525–456), *Seven Against Thebes*
463	Aeschylus, *Suppliant Women*
460–446/5	'First' (Atheno-)Peloponnesian War: Sparta and allies v. Athens and allies
457	Battle of Oenophyta: Athens conquers Boeotia
449	Peace of Callias (between Athens and Persia; existence disputed)
447	Thebes defeats Athens at Coronea, establishes oligarchic federal state (–386)

446/5	Thirty Years' Truce between Sparta and Athens (broken 431)
442, 430/29, 402/1	Sophocles's (497–406) Theban trilogy (so-called): *Antigone, Oedipus Tyrannus, Oedipus at Colonus*
431 (–404, with interruptions)	Atheno-Peloponnesian War: begins with attack by Thebes (Sparta's ally) on Plataea (Athens's ally)
429 (–427)	Siege of Plataea by Sparta
426	Destruction of Plataea by Sparta
424	Battle of Delium: Thebes defeats Athens; Thebes destroys Thespiae
423	Euripides (*c.* 485–406), *Suppliant Women*
421 (–414)	Peace of Nicias
421	Alliance between Sparta and Athens; Thebes remains loyal to Sparta when other Peloponnesian League allies defect
418	Battle of Mantinea: Spartan victory over Athens and defected allies
415–413	Athenian expedition to Sicily: Syracusan victory
413	Sparta occupies Decelea in Attica; flight of slaves to Boeotia; booty raids on Attica by Thebes
405	Dionysius (I) becomes tyrant of Syracuse
404	Sparta, with Persian aid, wins Atheno-Peloponnesian War; rejects Thebans' (and Corinthians') call for destruction of Athens, imposes Thirty Tyrants oligarchic junta backed by garrison of ex-Helots
404(–371)	Spartan hegemony
403	Thebes aids Athenian exiles to defeat and overthrow Thirty Tyrants; democracy restored in Athens

401/400	Proxenus of Thebes among the '10,000' mercenaries recruited by Cyrus the Younger
395 (–386)	Corinthian War: Sparta defeats Quadruple Alliance (Boeotia led by Theban Hismenias allied with Athens, Argos, Corinth)
386	King's/Common Peace: sponsored by Artaxerxes II of Persia and Agesilaus II of Sparta; Boeotian federal state dismantled; oligarchy maintained in Thebes; Thespiae occupied by Spartan garrison
382	Thebes occupied and garrisoned by Sparta; extreme oligarchy established; anti-oligarchic Theban exiles harboured in Athens
379/8	Thebes liberated by exiles led by Pelopidas; new, democratic *polis* founded
378	Thebes establishes democratic Boeotian federal state; Gorgidas founds 'Sacred Band'
378 (–338)	Athens founds anti-Spartan Second Sea-League: liberated, democratic Thebes a founder member
375	Battle of Tegyra: Thebes beats a Spartan force; Common Peace (of 386) renewed under Theban leadership
371	Battle of Leuctra: Thebans defeat Spartans; Theban ascendancy in mainland Greece (to 362), Common Peace renewed in Thebes
370	Athens allies with Sparta against Thebes
368 (–365)	Philip of Macedon held hostage in Thebes in house of Pammenes
367	Death of Dionysius I of Syracuse
366	End of Sparta's Peloponnesian League
364	Battle of Cynoscephalae, Thessaly; death of Pelopidas

362	Second Battle of Mantinea: Theban victory, death of Epaminondas; Common Peace (of 386, 375, 371) again renewed
361	Theban intervention in Peloponnese to shore up Arcadian federation
359 (–336)	Accession of Philip II of Macedon
357	Thebes advocates punishment of Phocians and Spartans within Delphic Amphictyony; Philip takes over Amphipolis
356 (–346)	Third Sacred War: Thebes and allies v. Phocians; Phocians defeated by Thebes's ally Philip
355	Battle near Neon, Boeotia: Thebans defeat Phocians. Pammenes in Asia Minor supports rebel Persian satrap
354/2	Thebes records funds received for war on Phocians
352–1	Invasions and counter-invasions of Phocis and Boeotia
351	Theban Cephision aids Megalopolis against Sparta
350	Thebes receives Persian subsidy from Artaxerxes III
346	Athenian Peace of Philocrates with Philip II; Philip destroys Phocis, joins Delphic Amphictyony, celebrates Pythian Games
345	Theban Lacrates sent to support Artaxerxes III in Egypt
340	Theban alliance with Athens procured by Demosthenes
338	Battle of Chaeronea, Boeotia; foundation of League of Corinth; Thebes garrisoned and placed under an oligarchy
336	Assassination of Philip II, accession of Alexander III

Timeline

336–323	Reign of Alexander III (later 'the Great')
335	Near-total destruction of Thebes ordered by Alexander

Hellenistic Age

316	Thebes rebuilt
146	Sack of Corinth; 'Achaea', including Boeotia, becomes Roman protectorate
86	Further Battle of Chaeronea: Sulla defeats Archelaus (general of Mithridates VI of Pontus)
31	Battle of Actium, NW Greece: Octavian (later Augustus) defeats Cleopatra (and Antony), becomes ruler of Greek east (as well as west)

Early Roman Empire

27 BCE (–CE 14)	Octavian/Augustus reigns as First Roman Emperor; Achaea becomes Roman province

CE

Later Roman Empire/Early Byzantine Age–Modern Age

324	Foundation (8 November) of Constantinople by Emperor Constantine
330	Dedication (11 May) of Constantinople
530	Silk industry established in Thebes during reign of Emperor Justinian (527–65)
1147	Raid on Thebes by Roger II of Sicily
1205	Duchy of Athens and Thebes founded
1453	Fall of Constantinople to Ottoman Turkish Sultan

Mehmet II 'the Conqueror' (May 29): Thebes becomes Istefe

1744	Handel, *Semele*
1906 (–29)	Excavation of Mycenaean Cadmea/Kadmeia by A. D. Keramopoullos
1936	Enescu, *Oedipe*
1952	'Linear B' deciphered as earliest Greek script/language
1963/4	Linear B tablets first excavated in Thebes
1966	Henze, *Bassarids*
1980	Byzantine Cadmea excavated
1992	John Buller, *BAKCHAI*
2004	M. H. Hansen and T. H. Nielsen (Copenhagen Polis Project) publish *An Inventory of Archaic and Classical Poleis*

List of Illustrations

1. A marble relief stele marking the appointment of Timeas as the Thebans' official representative. (Photograph of 1987.297 © 2020 Museum of Fine Arts Boston)

2. Part of a clay tablet incised with 'Linear B' from the Theban palace archives. (From: *Thebes: A History*, Nicholas Rockwell, Copyright © 2017 and Informa UK Limited. Reproduced by permission of Taylor & Francis Group)

3. Ivory cosmetics container of the thirteenth century BCE. (From: *Thebes: A History*, Nicholas Rockwell, Copyright © 2017 and Informa UK Limited. Reproduced by permission of Taylor & Francis Group)

4. Wine-mixing bowl from Thebes, depicting a warship with a warrior firmly taking in hand a woman. (B.M. 1899, 0219.1 © Trustees of the British Museum)

5. A small bronze statuette dedicated by Manticlus to the archer-god Apollo. (Photograph of 03.997 © 2020 Museum of Fine Arts Boston)

6. One of over one hundred marble statues representing either an idealized version of the dedicant or a vision of the honorand, Apollo. (Ángel M. Felicísimo from Mérida, España [CC BY-SA https://creativecommons.org/licenses/by-sa/2.0])

7. A stone stele showing a Boeotarch of the early fifth century BCE making an offering. (From: *Thebes: A History*, Nicholas Rockwell, Copyright © 2017 and Informa UK Limited. Reproduced by permission of Taylor & Francis Group)

8. An Athenian cosmetics jar illustrated with the myth of Theban king Pentheus. (Musée du Louvre, Photograph public domain [https://commons.wikimedia.org/w/index.php?curid=688480])

9. Frederic Leighton's *Antigone*, painted in oils on canvas in 1882. (Frederic Leighton, 1st Baron Leighton, Public domain [https://commons.wikimedia.org/w/index.php?curid=198450])

10. An elaborate Athenian-made wine-mixing vase showing an entire chorus with the god of drama, Dionysus. (Museo Archeologico Nazionale, Naples. Photograph courtesy of François Lissarrague.)

11. A grave stele from Tanagra, Boeotia. (From: *Thebes: A History*, Nicholas Rockwell, Copyright © 2017 and Informa UK Limited. Reproduced by permission of Taylor & Francis Group)

12. A silver coin bearing on the obverse a Boeotian-shape shield. (akg-images / Liszt Collection)

13. The stone victory monument marking the Thebans' victory over the Athenians at Leuctra. (From: *Thebes: A History*, Nicholas Rockwell, Copyright © 2017 and Informa UK Limited. Reproduced by permission of Taylor & Francis Group)

14. A burial stele inscribed with the names of three of the seven Boeotarchs who fought and died at the Battle of Leuctra. (From: *Thebes: A History*, Nicholas Rockwell, Copyright © 2017 and Informa UK Limited. Reproduced by permission of Taylor & Francis Group)

15. Lively, coloured statuette depicting a fully clothed woman. (Photograph of 01.7922 © 2020 Museum of Fine Arts Boston)

16. The stone lion marking the spot where many Thebans fell at Chaeronea. (From: *Thebes: A History*, Nicholas Rockwell, Copyright © 2017 and Informa UK Limited. Reproduced by permission of Taylor & Francis Group)

17. A stele inscribed and erected to record Thebans' gratitude for the

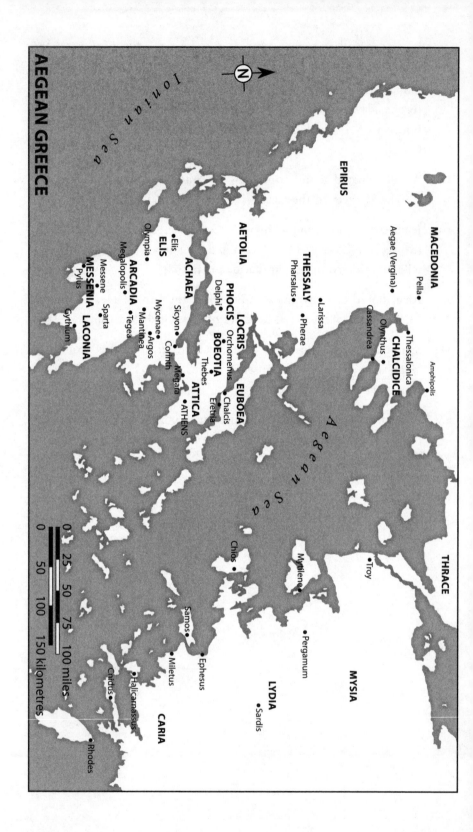

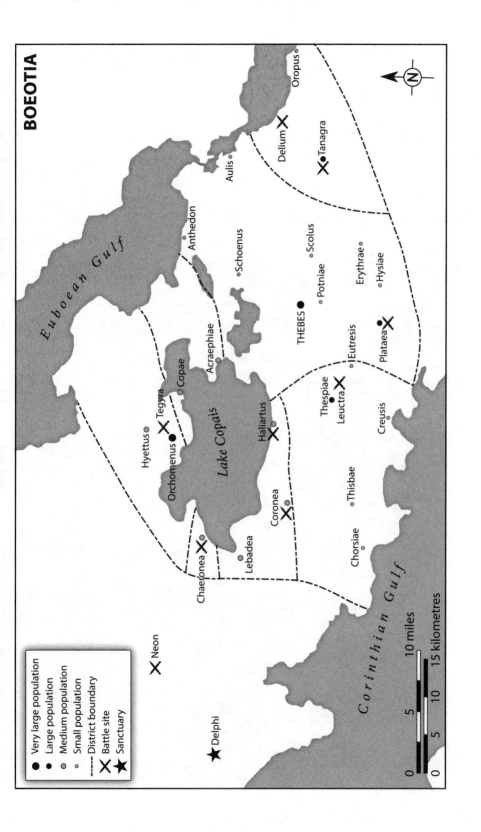

BOEOTIA

Very large population
Large population
Medium population
Small population
District boundary
Battle site
Sanctuary

Euboean Gulf

Corinthian Gulf

Lake Copaïs

Oropus
Delium
Tanagra
Aulis
Anthedon
Schoenus
Scolus
Potniae
Erythrae
Hysiae
THEBES
Eutresis
Plataea
Acraephiae
Copae
Tegyra
Hyettus
Orchomenus
Haliartus
Thespiae
Leuctra
Creusis
Coronea
Thisbae
Lebadea
Chaeronea
Chorsiae
Neon
Delphi

0   5   10 miles
0   5   10   15 kilometres

N

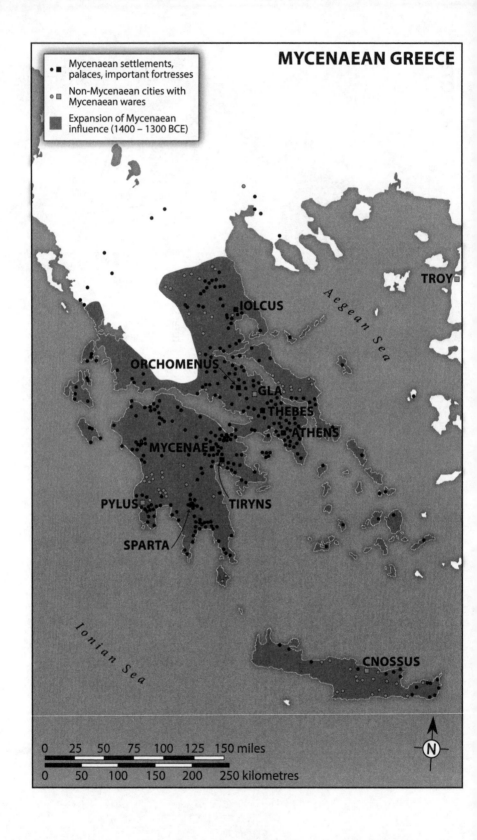

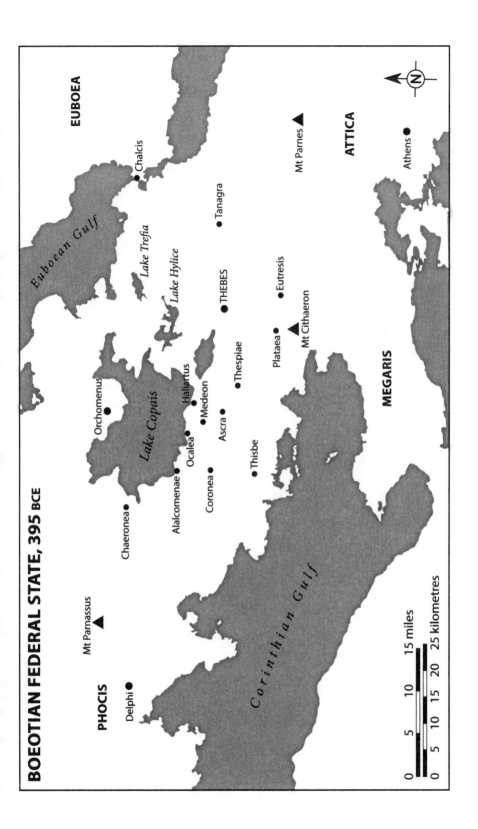

BOEOTIAN FEDERAL STATE, 395 BCE

Preface

History versus memory, and memory versus memorylessness.
Rememory as in recollecting and remembering as in
reassembling
the members of the body, the family, the population of the
past . . .
the struggle, the pitched battle between remembering and
forgetting . . .

(Toni Morrison, from *Mouth Full of Blood*)

A place's meaning is not set in stone – or its stones. Certain sites seem especially liable to becoming the objects of contested meanings. The ancient Greek city of Thebes is undoubtedly a prime example, or indeed exemplar. This is a history not only of ancient events and processes but also of social and cultural memory, over a very long run indeed: from the Late Bronze Age to our own day, more or less.

Almost continuously inhabited for five millennia, and at one point the most powerful city in all ancient Greece, Thebes has often been overshadowed by its two better-known rivals, Athens and Sparta. (Not to mention being confused with the Egyptian city of the same name, which is mentioned in the earliest extant work of Greek and European literature, Homer's *Iliad*.) Among other indignities, we find that the ancient Thebans were the butt of ethno-political jokes directed at them by other Greeks, especially by snooty Athenians (who called them 'Boeotian swine'). Undeservedly so, on many counts. The city has even been, literally, lost – and not just forgotten – on more than one occasion.

But why and how has ancient Greek Thebes been 'forgotten'? And how can we best rescue it, permanently, from oblivion? From the very beginnings of Greek literature in Homer, Thebes was a rich source of myths: traditional tales of origins, of cultural development, both progress and regress, and of psychological and moral insight into the human condition. But the city's history and indeed prehistory and protohistory are every bit as rich as its mythic origins. An important stronghold in the prehistoric Late Mycenaean (or Late Bronze) Age – the ultimate real source of all that Theban heroic mythology – Thebes emerged into the light of history centuries later in the pages of Herodotus as one of the two major contending powers, alongside Orchomenus, of its ethno-geographic region of Boeotia. Sometimes allying with and sometimes fighting against Sparta and Athens, its course as a member of Greece's fateful triangle was set from the late sixth century BCE on. From siding with the Persian invaders, who under Emperor Xerxes set out to conquer Aegean Greece, to being defeated by Pericles's democratic Athens, to allying with Sparta – like Thebes at that time, an oligarchy – and triumphing over Athens, to becoming for a decade the single greatest power and power broker of mainland Greece, to being utterly destroyed on the orders of Alexander the Great: this was a chequered and turbulent history.

In this book, therefore, I shall be aiming to maintain throughout some sort of balance between the twin cities of Thebes: the Thebes of Myth and the Thebes of History. Indeed, it is precisely the interaction between these two conceptual and intellectual registers that makes Thebes so interesting, so different, and so eminently studiable. Or so I shall argue.

But, as someone once wrote, there is nothing new under the sun. Painful though it is to me to cite words attributed to a bloodthirsty and bloodstained tyrant, Cassander of Macedon already made this point. Some 2,300 years ago, in 316 BCE or thereabouts, when he was about to restore Thebes after its near-total destruction in 335 (see Chapters 11 and 12), Cassander reportedly described Thebes as 'a city widely known for its achievements and for the myths handed down about it'.

The goal of this book, however, is not merely the recuperation of Thebes and its restoration to a high level of academic consciousness – my multinational academic colleagues across the world (H. Beck, D. W. Berman, S. Gartland, D. Knoepfler, E. Mackil, N. Rockwell, and N. Papazarkadas prominently among others: see Sources and Further Reading) have been doing their very best in their various ways to achieve that. My goal here is more to bring the ancient city of Thebes vividly back to life, and to make good the claim that it is not just an adjunct or a footnote, an also-ran, but actually central to our understanding of the ancient Greeks' multiple achievements – whether viewed politically or culturally – and thus to the wider politico-cultural traditions of western Europe, the Americas, and indeed the world.

Trumpington, Cambridge, November 2019

PART ONE

PRE-HISTORY

CHAPTER 1

Introduction: From Myth to History

The chief purpose of this first part of the book is to set the scene, to establish the backdrop against which any history of historical Thebes may and must be essayed and assayed. It aims above all to make clear both the differences and the interconnections between the Thebes of Myth and the Thebes of History, the twin cities that are our inspiration and objective.

'Historical' Thebes may be taken to begin at around 700 BCE. But as noted at the beginning of Part II, all periodization is at least somewhat arbitrary and rough. My 'Pre-History', for example, includes what I have called 'protohistory' as well as what I and others call the 'Dark Age' or 'Early Iron Age'. 'Prehistory', strictly, should be text-free, but historians of prehistoric Thebes have both the 'Linear B' tablets and the poetry of Homer to factor in, so the term has to be interpreted and applied rather liberally. To set the scene, a brief review of nomenclature and geography is followed by a survey of the available ancient sources of evidence, both written (including epigraphy) and unwritten (archaeology, including art history and numismatics).

The origins of the name 'Thebai', a plural form – hence the English transcription 'Thebes' or the German 'Theben' – are lost in the mists of time. But no self-respecting historical – and indeed historic – Greek city could be without a foundation story or myth (the Greek word *muthos* meant simply a traditional tale), or more than one if need be. The ancient Greeks (who called themselves

'Hellenes' – 'Greeks' is a legacy of the Romans, and not an entirely benign one) were myth-makers par excellence. Thebans, exceptional Greeks in many other ways, were no exception in this regard, and invented traditions with the best of them. In some ways, far better than most, as we will discover in Chapter 2, when we explore the stories of the city's foundation.

There was, however, no ancient Greek 'country' nor a 'state' of 'Greece'. Hellas, the Greeks' own term, meant the ancient Greek world, a cultural as well as geographical space that embraced all areas of permanent Hellenic occupation where Hellenic mentality and social practices predominated (see map 1). The heartland – Old Greece – was the southern Balkan peninsula and adjacent islands, which is sometimes referred to as Aegean Greece. From there many Greeks emigrated permanently, beginning by settling in Cyprus in the Late Bronze Age, and moving thereafter ever further afield: to Asia Minor (western Turkey today) from the eleventh century BCE on; to the northern Aegean, the Black Sea approaches, southern Italy and Sicily from the eighth century; to all round the Black Sea itself and to North Africa (Cyrenaica, in today's Libya) from the seventh; and to southern France and eastern Spain from the very beginning of the sixth. New Greek settlements were still being founded in the fifth and fourth centuries BCE, when Plato amusingly wrote that the Greeks lived like ants or frogs around a pond (actually two 'ponds': the Mediterranean and Black Seas), and that was before the massive further expansion eastwards in the wake of the conquests of Alexander the Great (reigned 336–323).

Thebes lay firmly in the centre of Old Greece, in the region known as Boeotia (see map 2), but Boeotian Thebes was not the only mainland Greek Thebes. Not far to the north, in the region of Thessaly called Phthiotis, lay another; this was an altogether lesser affair. To complicate things further, there was also an ancient, non-Greek Thebes, a Nilotic town, lying within the Egyptian region of Waset. It was mentioned in Homer's *Iliad* and visited by Alexander the

Great in the late 330s BCE, after his conquest of Egypt from the Achaemenid Persian Empire – that Egyptian Thebes sits within today's Luxor.

Our Thebes lies in the fertile 'Teneric' plain in central mainland Greece, north of the Isthmus of Corinth, midway along a chain of hills running in a natural ridge from Mount Helicon (home of the divine Muses, although Homer also locates them on Mount Olympus) to Boeotian Tanagra (site of more than one major battle). Its prominent acropolis, known since antiquity as the Cadmea (Kadmeia), is a vast plateau measuring 700 metres in length by 400 in width. On all sides except the south it is blessed or cursed with steep slopes, making it difficult to access; moreover, it is flanked on the west and the east by two deep gullies. The ancient city where most inhabitants lived spread out to the north and east of this acropolis site. Another point of topography is hugely relevant: Thebes lies west-north-west of Athens, about 90 kilometres by today's roads. A fast walker can get from one to the other in some twelve hours. Thebes and Athens, so often enemies, were far too close to each other for comfort.

Boeotia (see map 2) was mainly flat, relatively fertile and strategically crucial. It occupied around 3,000 km² of central mainland Greece, with East (Opuntian) Locris to its north, Attica to its east and south, and Phocis and the Megarid (territory of Megara) to its south. Just as the history of Athens can be properly understood only within its overall regional context of Attica (Attikê in Greek), and ancient Sparta within its regional context of 'Lacedaemon', that is Laconia and Messenia combined in the southern Peloponnese, so the city and settlement of Thebes can be properly understood only in the wider context of Boeotia.

That context must, however, be both political and geographical, since, although Boeotia was bounded to the east by the sea, to the north, south and west there are no 'natural' fault lines determining its limits. The Boeotia visited by the Asiatic Greek traveller-pilgrim Pausanias in the third quarter of the second century CE was not the

Boeotia of the geographer Strabo (also Asiatic Greek) in the late first century BCE/early first century CE, nor was Strabo's Boeotia the same as that of Theban Epaminondas in the fourth century BCE, and Epaminondas's again was not that of Boeotian poet Hesiod (from Ascra near Thespiae) in the late eighth/early seventh century BCE.

The eastern border district around Oropus often changed hands: in the years *c.* 500–411, *c.* 375–366, and 338–322 it was under Athenian domination. The town of Eleutherae was originally Boeotian, but became Athenian. And so on. Moreover, one major feature of the physical geography of ancient Boeotia that did play a determining – in the sense of decisively influential – role in the region's ancient political history has simply disappeared: Lake Copais has been drained, even more drastically than the Fens of East Anglia. Finally, ethnic status, always to some extent a matter of self-ascription and self-identification, was liable to fluctuate: Orchomenus, for example, at its earliest mention in extant literature was described as 'Minyan', whatever exactly that meant, but in all historical periods was firmly Boeotian.

'The Boeotians' therefore are a bit of a moving target. But one way to begin to get a handle on those ancient Thebans and other Boeotians is to consider the work of a fourth-century BCE Athenian historian, formally anonymous to us, who owes his name (or names: the Oxyrhynchus Historian, or the Papyrus Historian, or simply plain P) to the fact that chunks of his work have been recovered not on parchment (vellum) but on papyrus – from rubbish dumps in an Egyptian town known in antiquity as Oxyrhynchus or (roughly) Sharp-Nosed Fishville. In a chapter of his *Hellenic History*, modelled quite closely on the masterpiece of his immediate predecessor Thucydides, our – to us – anonymous author most helpfully sets out in detail the political components, the member polities, of the Boeotian federal state (*koinon*) as that was constituted in, precisely, 395 BCE:

As regards the governance of Boeotia, all the inhabitants had been divided [since 447] into eleven districts, each of which provided one Boeotarch. Of those eleven Boeotarchs the Thebans by themselves accounted for and controlled four: two Thebans, and two representing [collectively] the citizens of Plataea, Scolus, Erythrae and Scaphae. Two Boeotarchs were provided by the citizens of Orchomenus and of Hysiae. Two [collectively] by the citizens of Thespiae, Eutresis and Thisbae. One by the citizens of Tanagra. One by [collectively] the citizens of Haliartus, Lebadea and Coronea. One by [collectively] Acraephiae, Copae and Chaeronea.

Seventeen places mentioned in all, sixteen of them dependent *poleis*: that is to say, more or less dependent on the one superordinate *polis* of Thebes (see map 4). They show both the fact that for a town or habitation in ancient Greece to have *polis* status it did not have to have full autonomy or political independence (see Chapter 5 for more on this), and the fact that geography by itself was not a sufficient condition of a settlement's achieving *polis* status. Some of the 1,000 or so ancient Hellenic *poleis* did indeed owe their origin and existence as such to geography: the island-*poleis* of Chios and Samos are obvious examples. But the island of Lesbos boasted five, originally six, separate *poleis*, and on the broad, unencumbered Boeotian plains there was no intrinsic geographical reason why as many as seventeen (and at other times more) *poleis* should have emerged.

However, it was Boeotia's principal geographical feature, Lake Copais, that led directly to the principal geopolitical division of the territory in historical – and possibly even prehistoric – times between its two largest towns or cities; Orchomenus to the north-west and Thebes to the south-east. The political distribution of federal power in 395 BCE represented therefore the triumph of Thebes over Orchomenus, a triumph the Thebans were to translate thirty-one years later into something far more literally destructive and total. Likewise their treatment of Plataea even sooner.

In Classical and post-Classical times there were local Boeotian historians – Daemachus of Plataea, for example – but they were not judged worthy of preservation and presumably could not stand comparison with the likes of Thucydides or even Xenophon of Athens. However, Xenophon, despite a personal connection to a Theban comrade in arms, was an out-and-out Thebophobe, and cultural Athenocentrism yielded the soubriquet 'Boeotian swine' referred to by Pindar, a Boeotian and Theban by adoption, as early as 500 BCE. And although the ancient adage 'an Attic [Athenian] neighbour', meaning a seriously unpleasant neighbour, was not coined by Thebans, it could well have been; it nicely brings out the longstanding rivalry, if not hostility, between the two adjacent cities.

Apart from Homer's *Iliad* and Hesiod's didactic epic *Works and Days*, in terms of written/literary evidence we have to make do, paradoxically, with generally very much later writers, mythographers such as (Pseudo-)Apollodorus (first century CE) and travel writers such as Pausanias (second century CE). The so-called Archaic period, which means formatively and temporally pre- or proto-Classical rather than backward or old-fashioned, is best if sketchily covered in the *Histories* of Herodotus – Greece's and indeed the West's first proper historian – who was writing in the mid-fifth century BCE. 'History' for him meant enquiry or research, and what he enquired into principally were the oral traditions handed down officially or unofficially in families or through public remembrancers and priests and still vibrant in his own day.

Herodotus's main subject was the Graeco-Persian Wars, the series of military encounters between 499 and 479 which occupied the last four of the nine books into which later scholars and librarians divided his huge prose work. But on top of and around those narratives he wove a vast and enormously rich and varied tapestry extending back as far as the eighth and seventh centuries, and ranging as far east from his native Halicarnassus (modern Bodrum) in south-west Asia Minor as Babylon in what is now southern Iraq, and as far north and north-east as the northern shore of the Black Sea and beyond into the Eurasian, Caspian Sea hinterland; as far west as southern France, southern Italy, and Sicily; and as far south into Africa ('Libya' to him) as the Nile delta and Cyrenaica in eastern Libya (to us).

Thebes and Thebans do not feature as prominently in Herodotus as we might ideally wish, probably in large part because he found in Athens a culturally and politically far more congenial mainland Greek base. But nor does Herodotus disguise the fact that in the epochal conflict between (pitifully few) Hellene resisters and vast hordes of Persian invaders, as played out in the immortal land battles of Thermopylae and Plataea (the latter actually on Boeotian soil), Thebans fought, mostly, on the wrong side – that is, for the Persians.

Thucydides took up the stylus where Herodotus laid it down, beginning his narrative in 478 BCE, but really focusing on the events of what is often referred to largely in his honour as 'the' Peloponnesian War (431–404). Actually it was not just one war, but two, and those two bouts of continuous fighting between Sparta and Athens and their respective alliances (431–421, 413–404) were repeats of earlier flare-ups that would soon enough flare up again. By 431, moderately oligarchic Thebes had sided enthusiastically with Sparta, not least because in the interim between the Persian and Atheno-Peloponnesian Wars democratic Athens had insulted as well as injured the city by somehow occupying and controlling it and most of Boeotia for a whole decade (457–447), and Thucydides correspondingly opens his narrative with a typically Theban demarche – an attack on Boeotian Plataea, hated by Thebes for being a steadfast ally of Athens for some nine decades – rather than with the first systematic invasion of Attica by the Peloponnesian alliance, led in summer 431 by Sparta.

Unfortunately, Thucydides's brilliant account breaks off in mid-sentence in the summer of 411 BCE, leaving a further seven years of his war undescribed and unanalysed – seven whole years in which Thebes seems to have spectacularly profited, literally as well as figuratively, from the occupation of northern Attica since 413 by a permanent Spartan garrison. It would have been good, too, to have had

Thucydides's account of how Thebes responded to Sparta's eventual victory. As it is, Thucydides has left us valuable accounts of major fighting within Boeotian territory, and tantalizing hints of how the Boeotian federal state was constituted and managed by Thebes.

Those hints are happily fleshed out for us by the so-called Oxyrhynchus Historian, whose systematic description of the federation's structure in 395 BCE was quoted above. This very good Athenian historian, who may well have been Cratippus, was one of the four writers known to us who resumed Thucydides's narrative where he had perforce abandoned it, and the probability is that he continued his account from 411 down to the conclusion of a watershed peace sworn between Greeks and the Great King of Persia in 386: the Peace of the King (Great King Artaxerxes II) or Peace of Antalcidas (the Spartan chief negotiator), as it was alternatively known in antiquity; being also the first of a series of such 'common' peace treaties that came to a close first in 362 before being resumed by Philip of Macedon some twenty-five years later.

362 BCE was the end point chosen by Xenophon of Athens, one of several authors to continue the history of Thucydides. Xenophon, an upper-class adherent of Socrates, was by no means only or merely a historian: he covered the waterfront of the available literary and intellectual genres, writing philosophy, biography, economics and technical military manuals as well as his misnamed *Hellenica* or Greek History. Actually, it was more of a 'Peloponnesian' than a Greek History, as seen though the eyes of Xenophon and his pro-Spartan friends.

It was something of a comment on that work's quality and range that the much later Sicilian Greek historian Diodorus, writing in the first century BCE, preferred to follow not Xenophon but the Oxyrhynchus Historian and his fourth-century successor Ephorus when it came to writing up the course of Sparta's post-Peloponnesian War supremacy between 404 and 371. For that was precisely the problem: Sparta, led by one of its two kings, Agesilaus II, did exercise a very controversial hegemony during those three-plus decades, and Xenophon was not only heavily pro-Spartan but also very anti-Theban.

The battle fought at Leuctra in Boeotia in 371 and won hands-down by Thebes and its allies over a fading Sparta and its labile alliance was as decisive as almost any other battle ever waged on mainland Greek soil. Yet Xenophon somehow both failed to mention two of its principal Theban architects (Pelopidas and Epaminondas) until *after* the battle and – more heinous still – omitted to describe possibly its single most important consequence: Sparta's loss of control of half its domestic *polis* territory (Messenia) and with it more than half its subjected Greek workforce (the Messenian Helots). It would be wonderful if we could say that Diodorus's surviving *Library of History* (so called because it was cobbled together into a chronologically ordered, annalistic account from other authors' books) did full justice by way of compensation for those gross Xenophontic flaws – but it does not. It is selective, inaccurate – and dull.

Herodotus, Thucydides, Xenophon, and the Oxyrhynchus Historian were 'Hellenic' as opposed to local historians. Local Greek history – horography – seems to have sprung up as an intellectual exercise and pursuit during the last quarter of the fifth century. Hellanicus, a native of Lesbos noticed and criticized by Thucydides, included among his output a *Boeotian Histories*. He was followed by local Boeotian writers: an Armenidas, and an Aristophanes, of no specified town, and by Daemachus of Plataea. It's been strenuously argued that these all wrote in and about the last quarter of the fifth century and/or the first half of the fourth, but their extant 'fragments' are both few and uninformative.

After 362 BCE we are largely reliant on a very different kind of literary source – the speeches either delivered and written up by the Athenian orator-politician Demosthenes (384–322) or attributed to him in the collection put together by later grammarians and literary critics in Athens and Egyptian Alexandria (founded in 332 by Alexander of Macedon). These speeches are represented as more or less faithful renditions of what Demosthenes had once actually said either in the Assembly on Pnyx hill below the Acropolis of Athens or in the law courts down in the Agora, the Athenian civic centre.

Demosthenes did not come from an established political family, but he was seriously rich and went to great lengths to equip himself to serve as a *rhetor* (orator-politician). He began to come to public notice and make an impact in the mid-350s, in a quite conservative way; but around 352 he seems to have experienced a Damascene conversion – to a radical brand of democracy and, connectedly, an unremitting hostility to Philip of Macedon. Hence his four 'Philippic' orations – and our English noun 'philippic'. He stirred up controversy throughout his exceptionally long career.

The year 362, as we shall see, marked the apogee of Theban power and influence way beyond the borders of Boeotia. The nadir was still a fair way off, but, with the rise of Macedon to pre-eminence under King Philip II (reigned 359–336) and his hegemony ever spreading southward into and through Thessaly and then, by 346, over all Phocis, Thebes found itself confronted again, in 340 as in 480, with a decision on whether to resist or to give in to the encroaching superpower. Thanks in significant part to Demosthenes's persuasiveness – which was owed not only to his silver tongue but also to the fact that he served as the Thebans' official diplomatic representative in Athens – the Thebans opted this time for resistance, united with resolutely anti-Philip Athens. It did not, however, go well.

In 338, the first of several major battles fought over the centuries at Boeotian Chaeronea resulted in total victory for Macedon and Philip – and his late-teenage son Alexander. Two years later, Philip was assassinated, and one way in which Alexander attempted to shore up his controversial accession at home and controversial rule over mainland Greece was to take on and take out rebel Thebes in 335. More of that anon. So far as our narrative historiographical evidence for Alexander goes, it is generally conceded that the best of a not particularly distinguished and very much non-contemporary and split source tradition is the account by the Graeco-Roman soldier-politician of the second century CE, Arrian of Nicomedia (another Asiatic Greek), who rightly highlights the 335 Thebes episode, which will mark for us a major hiatus.

For the historian of ancient Thebes, Chaeronea has another very particular resonance. It was the birthplace of one of the ancient world's most distinguished intellectuals and littérateurs, known to us as Plutarch. In Greek he was Ploutarchos, in Latin L. Mestrius Plutarchus, for he was both a citizen of Chaeronea and a *civis Romanus*, a citizen of Rome and the Roman Empire – and a priest at Delphi into the bargain. At two vital moments of Theban history he becomes a major source of our evidence.

Born in about 46 AD/CE and living until about 120, he became one of the greatest ornaments of the movement known as the 'Second Sophistic' – second, after the 'first' Sophistic half a millennium earlier, exemplified by such *sophistai* (wise men) of the fifth and fourth centuries BCE as Herodotus and Aristotle. Those two had both engaged in what has been called 'second-order reflection', that is, an intense concentration on the nature and status of their own arguments and discourse. Plutarch did likewise.

His voluminous and well preserved oeuvre is divisible into two broad halves: on the one hand, his essays on diverse subjects – philosophical, scientific, mathematical and other, often lumped together as 'moral' essays; and, on the other hand, his biographies. We shall be drawing from works on both sides of the ledger.

Plutarch himself made it absolutely clear that he was not writing 'history' as that term might be applied to the works of Herodotus, Thucydides, even Xenophon, or even Diodorus. Of course he drew heavily on such works, but his own interest was rather in the characters, especially the moral characters (and quirks and foibles), of the illustrious Greeks and Romans whose lives he chose to write up. Conversely, when he did turn to 'straight' historiography, or historical criticism, as in his juvenile essay 'On the Meanspiritedness of Herodotus', he frankly did not make a very good fist of it. One of his key modes of critical appraisal was comparison, hence his composition of twenty-three sets of what in English are referred to as parallel – or paired – lives. One of those lives is that of Pelopidas of Thebes, a key actor in Theban and Greek politics during the first half of the fourth century BCE. It is one of the enduring sadnesses of the extant tradition that his biography of Pelopidas's great Theban contemporary and coadjutant Epaminondas has *not* survived.

For Aristotle, according to his brief treatise *Poetics*, 'history' is intrinsically inferior to 'poetry', on the ground that the latter was more 'serious' and dealt in universals, the sorts of things that 'could' or 'might' happen, whereas history – merely – told 'what Alcibiades did and what happened to him'. We shall, for once, ignore Aristotle here. For there is another, very different kind of 'literary' evidence available to us, and that is poetry. Though it lacks any overt historio-graphical intent or ambition, poetry is nevertheless a source of crucial information for reconstructing a cultural history of Thebes and Boeotia. Not all Boeotians were mere 'pigs'. Hesiod of Ascra and Pindar of Thebes conspicuously and rather magnificently were not. They operated in very different genres – and metres.

Hesiod achieved the universal Hellenic acclaim of being coupled with Homer (whoever he was, or how many), both of them composing in the same dactylic hexameter epic form and being jointly credited by Herodotus with inventing, or at any rate giving definitive form to, nothing less than ancient Hellenic polytheism, for they together

> *were the first to compose for the Greeks an account of the gods' and goddesses' genealogy, to award them their cult-titles, to allot them their honours and particular talents and to signify their – anthropomorphic – forms. (Herodotus:* The Histories, *2.53, trans. T. Holland, slightly modified)*

Herodotus was thinking particularly of Hesiod's *Theogony*, or 'Birth of the Gods and Goddesses', which is a sort of Greek equiv-alent to the biblical Book of Genesis. But Hesiod also composed – or was credited with composing – several other verse works, of which at least the *Works and Days* is without a doubt authentically Hesiodic.

The latter poem, composed around 700 BCE, is ostensibly a didactic treatise on good farming practice, but it also includes matter of a precisely political nature, dealing as it does with the distribution and exercise of political power in the early Greek city. (We shall return to Hesiod in Chapters 2 and 5, to Homer in Chapter 3.)

Pindar too was a highly politicized and political poet, but – rather in contrast to sour and surly seeming old Hesiod – he was above all in the business of praise, encomium, of both individuals and cities alike. And I do mean – as he too meant in another sense – business: he got into trouble – from people he had not praised – for being altogether too sordidly mercenary, for prostituting his very considerable verbal facility to the highest bidders, regardless of their moral or political worth. Pindar's greatest claim to fame – huge fame – was the four sets of his 'epinician odes': four because they were written about and for victors in the four major panhellenic (all- and only-Greek) religious festivals; 'odes' from the Greek for 'song' (*odê*); and 'epinician' from the Greek meaning 'as applied to' (*epi*) a 'victory' (*nikê*). It was a fame from which his descendants were rather unexpectedly, if also rather tragically, to benefit five or so generations later.

We shall return to Hesiod and Pindar in their appropriate chronological and cultural contexts below. Nor must we forget that ancient Athenian drama, both tragic and comic, was also poetry, *poiesis*. Both in its contemporary context (Chapter 7) and in terms of its modern reception (Chapter 13) we shall attempt to bring out how far, in what ways, and why Athenian dramas such as the *Antigone* of Sophocles or the *Bacchae* of Euripides can be used to illuminate a cultural history of Thebes.

Another, albeit rather more mundane source available to us can be found in the modern scholarly study of texts inscribed on non-perishable materials (usually stone, bronze or fired clay). Epigraphy is a highly developed and highly prized subdiscipline within the field of ancient Greek historical studies. One monograph on the 'local scripts', or regional dialectal variations of Archaic (*c.* 750–500/479

BCE) and early Classical (479–400) Greece, lists some fifty such 'Boeotian' texts of very varied kinds. More recent finds include a seventh-century graffito on a pot from Kommos, Crete, mentioning Boeotian individuals, and a Thasian-made wine amphora found in the Athenian Agora of the later sixth century BCE with a Boeotian owner's mark scratched underneath.

Other recent discoveries and renewed scholarly attention to inscriptions found in Thebes and elsewhere in Boeotia have illuminated the history of ancient Thebes in ways that go well beyond the ancient literary sources' preoccupation with great battles. The examples that follow illustrate this beautifully, but they are only three of many.

In the suburb of Thebes called Pyri, something over a decade ago a *kioniskos*, that is a mini-column, made of whitish poros (limestone) was found in a well-built, tomb-like cist. It bore an inscription relating to the near-immediate aftermath of Sparta's failed invasion of Attica in 506. Happily, this confirmed in a general way the account we already had in Herodotus, and from a Boeotian point of view.

A fifth-century example was discovered in 1965 through regular excavation by the German Archaeological Institute at Olympia (where its members have been digging since 1875): a bronze tablet bearing the inscribed text of a judgement passed in the years 476–473 by the Eleian judges (who presided over the management of the Olympic Games) regarding a dispute between Athens and the Boeotian federal state. An interesting pointer to the bad blood then running especially hot between those two states, which was to give rise to further negative encounters throughout the ensuing century (Chapters 6 and 8).

Finally, a fourth-century text that comes from Thebes itself; it is inscribed on a stone stele bearing a decree of *proxenia* (honorary consulship) conferred by the revamped, post-378 Boeotian federal state (*koinon*) in the early 360s (see figure 1). The honorand was one Timeas, son of Cheiricrates, a 'Lakon'. 'Lakon' could mean either a Spartiate (full Spartan citizen) or a Perioecus (*perioikos*), that is, a citizen of one of the fifty or so dependent *poleis* of Laconia and Messenia that went to make up the *polis* (state) of Lacedaemon ruled by Sparta. But, if he had been a Spartiate, he would more likely have been described either as 'Spartiates' or 'Lakedaimonios'. The scholarly consensus is that he was a Perioecus – not the first Perioecus to be so honoured by a foreign power, but an excellent example of the way that Epaminondas in particular deployed diplomacy to divide and weaken the Spartan state.

We are often being told that new archaeological discoveries, whether on an Aegean island or in a cave in the Mani peninsula of the Peloponnese, are 'rewriting ancient Greek history'. But what's new, really, under the sun? It was apparently Plato who coined the term *arkhaiologia*, from which is derived the English word 'archaeology', but Plato of course did not mean and could not possibly have meant by the former what we understand by the latter. *Arkhaiologia* was *logos* (talk, discourse) about *arkhaia* (ancient things), so tales of olden times – allegedly something that the Spartans were particularly fond of, as they liked to hear about the deeds of the great heroes of the past. Not necessarily all that distant a past, of course – the heroes of Thermopylae and Plataea (see Timeline) would do nicely for the Spartans of Plato's day (*c.* 427–347).

For us, however, in its sense first developed in the eighteenth and nineteenth centuries, archaeology concerns the recovery, classification, analysis and interpretation of mute material remains of the more or less distant past, often brought to light through excavation, but, since excavation is also inevitably destructive, by various non-destructive methods too. Historical as opposed to text-free prehistoric archaeology is both more and less difficult: less difficult, because the availability of texts in the form of good, reliable, ideally documentary contemporary evidence can sometimes settle questions that the absence of such texts leaves necessarily open; more difficult, because archaeology and history do not always tell the same sorts of stories; or rather archaeology may be better at telling some sorts, e.g., of long-term historical and especially economic development, than others.

One very current example might be the recent findings by members of the British School at Athens on the islet of Dhaskalio, located in the Aegean Sea some 125 miles north-east of Athens. The finds are many and complex – marble statues broken and unbroken, copper daggers, spearheads, axes and other tools manufactured on the islet. The trouble is – from the point of view of their interpretation – that these finds date to the Aegean's Early Bronze Age, the beginning of the third millennium BCE, long before the invention of any form of Aegean script. The spade may never lie, but of course it cannot speak; it has to be made to speak since it is mute. Moreover, archaeology can deal only with *surviving*, non-perishable remains: how wonderful it would be, for instance, to be able to view still the cedarwood statue of Apollo said to have been carved in Thebes by the Sicyonian sculptor Canachus (Kanachos) in the latter part of the sixth century BCE.

The archaeological record for the history – and prehistory – of Thebes has been assembled in a number of ways. At the outset, it is important to remember two things: first, that overall archaeology has probably done rather more for the prehistory than for the history of Thebes; and second, that the archaeological evidence should never be used solely or mainly for illustrative purposes, merely to add colour as it were to the picture to be gleaned from the written sources.

Before 1900, only sporadic excavations took place in Thebes and its surrounds. But between 1906 and 1929, with enforced interruptions, A. D. Keramopoullos excavated remains of the Mycenaean palace and fortifications on the Cadmea as well as several Mycenaean-period chamber tombs. He also investigated the Temple of Apollo Ismenius. A small museum was opened in Thebes to house these finds, together with those made elsewhere in Boeotia, and a catalogue of its collection was published in 1934. In the early 1960s, the Cadmeum and the Cabeirion were excavated. Excavations have continued in the decades since, and the findings are now housed – and fully catalogued – in a brand-new museum.

Excavation is not the only way to increase the archaeological record, and especially not the only way to diversify it. Intensive field-survey – repeated walking over specially designated transects (tracts) of land surface, and minutely detailed recording and re-recording of visible surface objects and features – began vigorous life as an archaeological technique in the New World, but has since been widely practised in the Mediterranean and elsewhere. Boeotia occupies an honoured place in this new tradition of research, with successive teams of both professional archaeologists and undergraduates exploring the Boeotian Valley of the Muses, focusing on Thespiae, the ancient *polis* within which lay Hesiod's hamlet of Ascra.

There have been excavations of Haliartus and Tanagra, too, as well as intensive surface surveys of Eleon in eastern Boeotia, and of the Oropus borderland. What such surveys mainly contribute is a better, more fine-grained understanding of rural habitation and agricultural land use over the long, sometimes very long, term. In other words, they tell you more about the daily lives of the vast majority of an ancient population than they do about individual, potentially unrepresentative elites whose families could afford to have them buried in durable and lavish form, or whose deeds were more likely to be reported in a literary source.

Numismatics – the study of currency and coinage in their many forms – is another important aspect of the archaeological evidence. Image and superscription tell a lot at a glance. Composition and weight (including weight standard) require further, scientific testing. Barclay V. Head, who published in 1911 what is still a quite standard reference work on all ancient Greek coinages (*Historia Numorum*), first sought to establish a chronological sequence for Boeotian coins in the 1880s. What's really important about them, historically, is that they are precisely Boeotian – and not exclusively Theban or Orchomenian or otherwise. Ancient Greek coins – mainly silver in this case, though small bronze denominations followed for use as small change – were worth what they weighed; when stamped with a representative image and superscription, they asserted that they were authentic, and that there was a recognized, legitimate political authority both issuing and guaranteeing them. To some extent, therefore, they were both political and economic phenomena.

Scholarly controversy has arisen and to some extent persists over which kind of motivation – the political or the economic – was the more significant for the very origin of coining money in Greek cities. (Many states never did; some – e.g. Sparta – did so, but only much later than the pioneers.) It is at any rate clear that the non-Greek kingdom of Lydia got there first of all, so the question of origins is, in part, a question of why Greeks decided to follow suit. Since the earliest denominations were all rather large, small change for everyday economic use by ordinary individuals – most of whom were peasant farmers – was not the original motivation. Rather, coined money was first used by states, for example to receive payments of taxes or to make payments to mercenary soldiers. Coinage also served to advertise a state's status as a proudly independent and sovereign political entity.

The first Lydian coins were of electrum, a naturally occurring local alloy of gold and silver. Few if any Greek cities possessed natural deposits of either gold or silver, let alone electrum, so the raw materials had to be imported in exchange for other goods or services. The earliest Greek electrum coins were fashioned around 600 BCE, not surprisingly on the Asiatic mainland – near Lydia and its capital at Sardis on the gold-bearing River Pactolus. But quite soon the preferred Hellenic medium was more or less refined silver, as struck by the island-city of Aegina. Aegina is not far from the (Attic/Athenian) mainland, and via Athens and Corinth the idea of a silver coinage seized hold quite quickly. Hence the origins of the Boeotian coinage in the latter half of the sixth century.

Coins, in order to serve their 'nationalist' political function, required a distinctive stamp – an image and/or superscription that would unambiguously individuate their source and guaranteeing authority. What is interesting about the earliest Theban coins is that they were also Boeotian: the issuing authorities chose a symbol common to all Boeotians, namely a particular form of the heavy-infantryman's shield. We shall return below to this and other federal political developments of the Archaic era.

CHAPTER 2

City of Myth: the Theban Cycle

> *Cadmus rode out in search of his lost sister.*
> *His kidnapped kin.*
> *Fruitless in his search,*
> *he found distraction*
> *in slaying other dragons*
> *along his way, until his mission*
> *was but a memory. The world*
> *no longer wondered whether*
> *he would have wept*
> *when he wed his Harmonia.*
> *And so it goes.*

> – (Mark Brayley, from 'The Festival of Janus', in Anna Johnson ed., *My Europe*)

> *Tris kopelles ap' ti Thiva . . .*

> – (Words: N. Gatsos; Music: Manos Hatzidakis, 'Mythologia')

Here is a city with a foothold deep in mythic territory. It was the (adopted) birthplace of the god Dionysus and of the überhero-turned god Heracles, and – though his failure to realize it at first was to prove tragically fatal for him – of King Oedipus. It was also the residence of choice for famous Phoenician immigrant Cadmus, who was credited with actually founding it.

According to the Thebans' own mythic repertoire, the city was founded when Cadmus, an incomer from the Levant, sowed dragon's teeth into the ground and warriors known as the Spartoi or 'Sown-Men' sprang forth, ready not only to build the fledgling city but to defend it from all comers. There is an irony (good Greek word) here. Cadmus was a non-Greek, from Tyre in what the Greeks called Phoenicia (modern Lebanon). (What the Phoenicians called themselves, if indeed they had a collective name for themselves at all, is another – unknown – matter.) He was what Greeks from the time of Homer on would have called a 'barbarian', a non-Greekspeaker. Yet he was believed to be the founder of a Hellenic – Greek – city. Moreover, he had not made the journey across the east Mediterranean to central Greece in order to found a new city, but in order to rescue his princess sister, Europa, who had been abducted by – as any ancient Greek would have instantly guessed – the predatory lord high chief Olympian god, great father Zeus. A further irony: the continent that came to be known as 'Europe' was thus named after an Asiatic princess. Yet a further irony: when the modern state of Hellas/Greece joined the European single currency, and so abandoned the drachma of old, it celebrated its accession and new monetary union by striking a coin bearing the image of Zeus disguised as an eagle in the act of abducting (a polite way of masking the actual fact of rape) Europa.

Cadmus was later credited with many other inventions, not least that of writing (though he had at least one rival there: Palamedes). The historical Greeks called their alphabetic script either 'Phoenician letters' or 'Cadmean letters'. As we shall see, there may be some dim historical memory lying distantly behind that particular claim. His marriage to Harmonia, however, is the purest fantasy, in the twofold sense that it, like the sowing of dragon's teeth, is mere froth and gossamer, but also in the sense of extreme and passionate wish-fulfilment. Harmonia's name gives a clue. The myth-history of Thebes and the actual history of the real Thebes are alike riddled with disharmony, what the Classical

Greeks were to call *stasis* or a 'standing-apart', too often involving civil violence.

The wedding of Cadmus and Harmonia was said to have been attended by all the Olympian gods and goddesses of the Greeks' almost indefinitely flexible pantheon, one of the last times at which they condescended to mingle en masse with mere mortals. The Italian publisher-scholar Roberto Calasso not so long ago concocted the myths surrounding that marriage and wedding celebration into a heady bromide for our distressed times (see Chapter 13). Yet, like that of a certain Italian city (Rome), Thebes's early mythopoetical life was attributed more realistically with a peculiarly nasty piece of intrafamilial slaughter.

The Cadmus city-foundation tradition did not stand alone. Rather awkwardly grafted onto it is the myth-tradition explaining how Thebes came to have such massive walls with seven gates. They were built by twin sons of Zeus, Amphion and Zethus. The latter seems to have done all the heavy lifting, literally, while the musically gifted Amphion accompanied him on the lyre. A very late source of the Byzantine era noted the irony: Thebes was originally built to a musical accompaniment – but also destroyed (by Alexander) to one (see Chapter 11).

Thebes enjoyed a particularly close association with the shape-shifting, cross-dressing, gender-bending god of wine, metamorphosis and theatre: Dionysus. He was reputed to have originated in Asia somewhere to the east of the Aegean Sea (probably Lydia) but to have arrived in mainland Greece under mysterious circumstances, and made Thebes his principal mainland Greek residence. One favoured version of his birth has him blasted from the womb of his mother Semele, daughter of Cadmus, by a lightning strike from his father, Zeus, who vaporized the mere mortal Semele but brought her fetus to term in one of his thighs. This was for Dionysus a less painful puerperal exit, presumably, than that of his half-sister Athena, who was born from the head of her father Zeus *via* a blow from divine craftsman Hephaestus's axe.

The Thebans repaid Dionysus handsomely by worshipping him as their patron city god, ahead even of Apollo, who performed that patronal function for other cities, and with whom he presided at Delphi. Located not very far away to the west in neighbouring Phocis, Delphi (literally meaning 'Wombs') was the Greeks' most sacred spot, the supposed navel (*omphalos*) of the universe. But, according to the version preferred and dramatized by Euripides in his *Bacchae* tragedy, Dionysus's first arrival in Thebes did not go well. Royal filicide and suicide ensued. Cadmus's nephew, King Pentheus, was slaughtered and decapitated by his own mother, Agave, who on emerging from her Dionysus-induced frenzy and realizing her ghastly error killed herself. It's complicated. We shall return later (Chapter 7) to this other sense in which Thebes was a 'city of Dionysus' – that is, on the fifth-century BCE Athenian tragic stage at festivals in honour of Dionysus, as represented in the work of Sophocles and Euripides among others.

This latter bloodletting was woven into the remarkable fact that Thebes somehow all by itself generated an important branch of the earliest form of Greek literature, the epic poem. Originally composed and transmitted from memory and by improvisation by illiterate poets over the centuries between the fourteenth and the seventh BCE, the most famous and influential exemplars of the epic genre were the *Iliad* and the *Odyssey* attributed to 'Homer'. In their 'monumental' – whence our use of 'epic' to mean huge – and quite soon written form they were composed and/or transcribed in the decades on either side of 700 BCE. Probably independent of this Homeric epic tradition was the so-called Theban Cycle of four epic poems, now all 'lost', which between them related Thebes's mythical early 'history'.

They were not credited in antiquity to Theban authors, though Pindar, the great Theban poet of the first half of the fifth century, drew upon them (for example, in his Eighth *Pythian Ode*, lines 40–8). It was from this tradition that sprang the dark story of Thebes as the haunt of the Sphinx (sent by a vengeful Hera), whose riddle royal Theban Oedipus solved, but only at terrible cost both to himself and to his city. For by solving it – the desired answer to 'What is it that has one name that is four-footed, three-footed and two-footed?' or 'What goes on four legs in the morning, two in the afternoon, and three in the evening?' (and other variants) was 'A human being' – he won the Theban crown and the king's widow in marriage, but (too) little did he know and too late did he discover that the widow was his mother, Jocasta (Iokaste), that it was he who had killed her husband, Laius, his own father, and that he had thereby fulfilled the very Delphic prophecy – your son will kill his father and marry his mother – that his exposure (pinned at the ankles, hence his name Oidi-Pous or Swell-Foot) had been designed by his luckless parents to evade.

The would-be fatal exposure of the undesired infant – not itself something absolutely uncommon in the real ancient Greece – was botched through feelings of pity on the part of the herdsman, an ordinary 'working-class' palace employee, entrusted with carrying it out. Instead of leaving the as yet unnamed Oedipus to die of starvation or to be devoured by wild beasts on a mountainside, as ordered, he had handed him over to a fellow herdsman from another community operating beyond the borders further to the south and west. That herdsman too was a royal servant, in the service of the reigning house of Corinth, and he passed the baby to his royal employers, who brought him up as their own. Oedipus had therefore grown up believing himself to be the son of royal Corinthian parents and not knowing of his true, Theban roots. Ancient Greeks would have appreciated the irony that *oida* in their language meant 'I know'. Oedipus knew from nothing.

Likewise the tangled web woven by Oedipus that ensnared both his natal and his acquired family, even unto the third generation. Once the scales had fallen from his eyes as to his origins and early life, he blinded himself in horror, and his mother-wife Jocasta committed suicide. Oedipus and Jocasta's two sons, Eteocles and Polyneices, succeeded him jointly but fell out, leading to a great civil war in which both were killed – by each other. Athens' master tragedian Aeschylus had, in the 460s, composed a version of that grisly tale, his *Seven Against Thebes*, and thereby indirectly set in motion the plot of another great fifth-century Athenian tragedy, the *Antigone* of Sophocles. For, during the post-civil-war interregnum, Oedipus's brother-in-law Creon assumed the reins of kingly power, as a dictator more than as a legitimate monarch, and among his more heinous acts he punished Oedipus's daughter Antigone, who was also Oedipus's half-sister and affianced to his own son Haemon, by walling her up to starve to death. This was for breaking his *diktat* not to bury her brother, traitor Polyneices, one of the 'Seven Against Thebes' who had returned from exile seeking to wrest power from Creon and Oedipus's other son, Eteocles. Instead, Antigone committed suicide by hanging herself, thereby breaking Haemon's heart but dying nobly according to Greek standards. One can only wonder what it was about Thebes that so attracted these Athenian creatives and their Athenian audiences.

Oedipus's snares proved fatal even unto the third generation because his own father was not without all mythological stain. Exposing an unwanted child as Laius had did not necessarily incur any stigma, especially given the terrifying nature of the Delphic prediction that prompted it. Pederastic rape, however, was another matter. *Paiderastia*, passionate desire (*eros*) of a male adult for a *pais*, an adolescent male, was not in itself stigmatized, at least not in all sections of every Greek society, and certainly not in the society of historical Boeotia and Thebes, where it was fully integrated into the rituals of maturation and adult sexuality – as we shall see in more detail when we come to discuss the famous Theban 'Sacred Band' (Chapter 9). In such a world of value and practice, a claim to being the originator of *paiderastia* might normally have chimed with the general Greek admiration of the 'first discoverer' (*protos heuretês*) of this or that positive invention, scientific or otherwise. However, in so far as Laius could claim to be – or be claimed as – the *protos heuretês* of *paiderastia*, this was not at all something to be unequivocally proud of, since he fulfilled his lust for Chrysippus by main force, by a brutal rape.

Sad to say, had he raped a female, even an underage female (as did, for example, Theseus of Athens, who was said to have raped a very young Helen of Sparta/Troy), he might have been given the benefit of the doubt by a largely sexist, indeed misogynistic, male Greek culture. But raping a desired boy implied by definition both a lack of self-control and a failure to persuade the victim. Laius's primacy and originality in the field of *paiderastia* were therefore very much a mixed blessing for him – and for Thebes.

Although the Theban epic tradition was probably independent of the Homeric, that very fact was likely a cause of intense rivalry among the Homeric and other epic bards, and a highly original recent study has suggested that one of the main functions of the Theban references direct or indirect to be found in Homer was precisely to appropriate them in a negative way: that is, to use them to show that somehow the heroes of Homer and their world were much superior to those of heroic-age Thebes.

Take, for example, the great high king Agamemnon's disparagement of Diomedes of Argos in Book 4 of the *Iliad*, for failing to live up to the high military and moral standards of his father, Tydeus. Tydeus was one of ancient Greece's Magnificent Seven, the 'Seven Against Thebes' (see below for more on that myth), yet Agamemnon's praise of the individual hero Tydeus sits uneasily with the *Iliad*'s overall concern to privilege the collective over the individual. Such examples can be built up to form a picture of how the poem emulously and systematically exploits and appropriates Thebes's and the Thebans' mythical pasts the better to subordinate, occlude and ideally obliterate them.

A similar reflection might be prompted by consideration of a remarkable passage in *Iliad* Book 9 (lines 381–4). Here Achilles is still skulking in or outside his tent rather than fighting; he is utterly disgusted that Agamemnon has unjustly robbed him, as he sees it, of his cherished female prize of war, Briseis, and has therefore withdrawn himself and his men from the Greeks' battle to rescue adulterous Helen and destroy Troy. He is made to compare with

Egyptian Thebes not Greek Thebes, but . . . Orchomenus, even though one of the stimuli to the comparison must originally have been the fact that both Greek Thebes and Egyptian Thebes were famed for being multi-gated. The latter was exuberantly said to have as many as 100 gates. Mythic-heroic Thebes more modestly but no less famously had seven, as built by Amphion and Zethus, and indeed they are mentioned earlier in the *Iliad* (4.406): Borrheae to the north, Proetides and Homoloedes to the east, Electra and Onca to the south, and Creneae and Neistae to the west. Very few actual traces of any of them remain on or in the ground. It is perhaps too the number of the gates that explains why, when Polyneices, son of the self-blinded Oedipus, attacked Thebes in rebellion against his co-regent brother Eteocles, he brought with him precisely six fellow champions, including Tydeus of Argos, thus the *Seven Against Thebes*.

That odious Homeric comparison with Orchomenus, and broader suppression of Thebes, arguably reflected the rivalry in seventh-century BCE Boeotia between the two would-be top-dog regional cities, though it might also preserve memory of a much earlier antagonism, even a Late Bronze Age/Mycenaean contention of the fourteenth or thirteenth century. At any rate, as we shall see, the real Orchomenus of that prehistoric epoch did have physical monuments that could stand comparison with those of contemporary Thebes.

It was not until the fifth century BCE, in probably 467, that the myth of the magnificent ancient Greek Seven Against Thebes received its most famous literary expression in Aeschylus's tragedy of that title; it is the only one of his Theban trilogy of that year – the others were *Laius* and *Oedipus* – to have survived.

Finally, as if that mythography and mythopoeia were not rich enough, Thebes was also the reputed birthplace of arguably the greatest – certainly the most colourful – of all ancient Greek heroes, Heracles/Hercules. Born as a half-divine hero to great Zeus, mightiest of the Olympian gods and goddesses, and his then latest paramour, the mortal Theban Alcmene, Heracles was destined by virtue of his great philanthropic deeds (the famous 'Twelve Labours') to be received up onto the summit of Mount Olympus itself, as a full-blown god.

With Dionysus and Heracles firmly ensconced in their pantheon of official deities, and, as we shall see, Apollo not far behind them in esteem and veneration, the Thebans might well feel that they were peculiarly divinely blessed.

However, although 'Herculean' has entered the English language, usually combined with 'effort', in a positive sense, the ancient Thebans might not be so thrilled to learn that the modern botanical name for giant hogweed, also known as giant cow parsley, is *Heracleum mantegazzianum*. They would surely be far more cheered, though, if they could watch any version in any format on any platform of Disney's blockbusting *Hercules*. Countless other versions have followed.

As it happened, but surely it cannot have been pure happenstance, it was a Boeotian, Hesiod from Ascra, who in the years around 700 BCE reinforced the Thebans' self-confidence by literally putting those gods and indeed all other Greek gods and goddesses in their place, in his epic poem *Theogony*, or 'Genesis of the Gods and Goddesses'. Herodotus's summation some two and a half centuries later of Hesiod's – and Homer's – definitive role in the making of Greek religion has already been quoted. Actually, though, Hesiod was himself only half-Boeotian by birth: his father was an immigrant incomer originally from Ionian Cyme in Asia Minor. But he composed and fulminated from a wholly Boeotian perspective, as well as commenting rather beautifully on the human condition:

> *All men when awake are in one common world, but each,*
> *when asleep, is in a world of his own [fragment 219]*

Hesiod has been described as a peasant poet, because in his other great hexameter poem, the *Works and Days*, he sets out in verse a peasant farmer's rather than a great landlord's almanac of annual, season-by-season agricultural tasks. Moreover, he rails from a sub-aristocratic standpoint against the 'bribe-swallowing lords' of his native Ascra, a village within the *polis* of Thespiae: in the scenario he paints they have been bribed by his feckless, work-shy brother Perses to allocate their father's disputed inheritance in Perses' exclusive favour. Hence there follows Hesiod's insistent refrain of the absolute necessity of constant labour – that is physical, manual agricultural labour – and his constant emphasis on its virtue. But did this Perses really exist, or, if he did, did he really behave as Hesiod claims? And was Hesiod really as humble and ill-starred – and upright – as he paints himself? His assumption that he will have labour, unfree labour, at his disposal to command in the field tends to suggest otherwise. So too does the undoubted fact of his poetic skill, sophistication, and general air of learning. Methinks he doth protest a little too much.

Like Homer, Hesiod invokes the Muses as his indispensable inspiration. They are according to his genealogy the daughters of Zeus and Mnemosyne, goddess of Memory. What a wonderful culture that puts such inspirational figures on a pedestal – or on top of a mountain! For Hesiod, they lived on Boeotia's Mount Helicon adjacent to Boeotia's Valley of the Muses; for Homer their abode was even more elevated, on Mount Olympus itself.

Whatever the truth of Hesiod's personal circumstances, he is an invaluable witness as we try to reconstruct the political life of Thebes and Boeotia in the early Archaic period. But first we must track back five or more centuries, to the late prehistoric era of the Late Bronze Age, known in local Greek terms as the 'Mycenaean' era (*c.* 1600–1100 BCE).

CHAPTER 3

City of Prehistory and Protohistory: Archaeology, the Linear B Tablets and Homer

Greek Thebes was and alas still often is confused with – or obliterated by – Egyptian Thebes, an altogether separate and quite different place. Confusion is not eased by what seems to be the fact that the earliest recorded mention of Greek Thebes is possibly in an Egyptian document: a geographical list inscribed on the funerary temple of Amenophis/Amenhotep III (reigned 1391/88–1353/51 BCE) at Kom el Hetan. Whether that inscribed presence of Thebes, together with that of Greek (Peloponnesian) Mycenae, signifies that the Egyptian court rated Thebes as a great power cannot be ascertained, but the archaeological record, such as it is, would certainly place Thebes in the Premier League of Mycenaean entities.

Were the modern town of Thebes (population: about 37,000) not directly on top of the ancient – prehistoric and historic – cities, we would know an awful lot more about the prehistoric city built upon the Cadmea (Kadmeia) acropolis, the most extensive acropolis in Mycenaean Greece (see map 3). As it is, more than a dozen Mycenaean sites within the city's curtilage have yielded Late Bronze Age remains, some very substantial and significant. Thus we know enough to be sure that in the thirteenth century Thebes's citadel possessed a striking Mycenaean-era palace that has yielded a substantial haul of (some 250) Linear B texts. The palace's origins possibly go back to the fifteenth century, or perhaps we are dealing with two successive palaces of different dates and orientations, the first of which was somehow destroyed towards 1300 BCE.

'Linear B' is the unromantic name for the earliest known script – of some 200 signs and symbols – designed to inscribe versions of the Greek language, though in syllabic and not yet alphabetic form. These clay tablets were preserved only accidentally; that is, they were burned in a violent, probably human-inflicted conflagration *c.* 1225 BCE – such as are attested elsewhere in thirteenth-century Mycenaean Greece. The name 'Thebans' occurs here in Greek for the first time (see figure 2). There are also Linear B signs painted as markers of origin and contents on oil jars of 'stirrup-amphora' shape, which were widely traded from as far afield as Crete (source of the earliest Linear B tablets, *c.* 1375 BCE at Cnossus).

The deciphered texts scratched on these bureaucratic palace-accountants' clay tablets reveal the existence of what looks like a professional warrior elite. They include forms of the Greek words for 'Thebes' and 'Theban female', but also more remarkably the use of a word that looks something like 'Lacedaemon', the name of the region of the southern Peloponnese that Sparta came to dominate. That find, together with an exceptional cache of Babylonian cylinder seals (used for marking documents written on clay or papyrus) also from the palace, has for some scholars given a whole new salience to the much much later Greek – originally of course Theban – view that it was Cadmus who somehow invented and/or at least introduced the writing of the Greek language. However, 'Cadmean letters' were also (known and referred to as) 'Phoenician letters', which more accurately reflects the historical facts of the original inspiration, source and model of the Greek alphabetic scripts, which were first devised sometime during the second half of the eighth century. The 'Cadmean' label was a later, false derivation from the coincidental origin of the anyhow mythical Cadmus in what the Greeks called Phoenicia.

The decipherment of Linear B as Greek (by architect Michael Ventris and Cambridge Classical philologist John Chadwick in the early 1950s) added up to six centuries to the known history of the Greek language and its dialects, which is really quite remarkable.

But as well as raising the issue as to whether there might even be some contemporary documentation, and so proof of the historicity, of the 'Trojan War' (or at least *a* Trojan War; the tablets have, so far, yielded proof of neither), this and other finds of tablets have also prompted questions about continuity not just of language but of politics, society, culture and above all Hellenic religion. As to the politics, the answer seems to be unambiguously clear: between the world of the (Mycenaean, Late Bronze Age) palace and the world of the (historical) *polis* there was an – unbridgeable – gulf fixed. The tablets did, moreover, seem to show that palatial Thebes had controlled the island of Euboea (as it did not in historical times) and had a harbour at Aulis (as in a way historical Thebes did, *via* the various iterations of the Boeotian federation).

A fundamental difference of political organization seems to presuppose fundamental differences in society (the type of unfreedom, the nature of the family unit) and high culture (no poetry?) – but what of religion? Several divinities worshipped in historical Greece have been identified, or so it has been argued, on the Thebes Linear B tablets: Demeter and Kore, Hera, Hermes, Potnia ('Lady' or 'Mistress'), and Zeus. But not all those identifications have been universally accepted, and there is as yet no Apollo, no Heracles, and no Dionysus attested – all cardinal objects of worship in historical Thebes (see Chapter 4). This could be just a matter of the accident of survival; or it could mean that the Hellenic – and so Theban-Boeotian – religion somewhat codified by Homer and local poet Hesiod was at least partly, and maybe in crucial part, a post-palatial creation.

Little remains of the 'Cadmean' walls: only some Mycenaean-era traces near what was later named the Proetides Gate. Even the alleged fact that Thebes, prehistorical or historical, ever had seven gates cannot be verified archaeologically. It has been estimated that at its maximum the city of Mycenaean Thebes may have encompassed an area of about 28 hectares, and accommodated at its height a permanent resident population of some 5,500–6,000 souls. Mycenaean-period cist graves containing weapons have been excavated in and around Thebes. A cache of bronze spearheads was excavated in one of the main palatial buildings; this was after all the Bronze Age, so labelled because bronze (a copper alloy with tin and/or zinc) was the material of choice for edged and pointed weapons and implements, its main two components necessarily imported from far afield: from Cyprus (copper – 'Cyprus' actually is the Greek word for 'copper') and from the Near East or from far-off Cornwall in Britain (tin).

On the hill of Kastelli nearby is one of several elaborate Mycenaean chamber tombs built outside the Cadmea; this one boasts two dromoi (entrance approaches) and is decorated inside with frescoes representing (Egyptian) papyrus flowers and well-dressed female figures, perhaps priestesses. Also thirteenth-century is a finely carved elephant ivory *pyxis* (cosmetics container) bearing a heraldic image of two confronted sphinxes (human male head above the body and wings of an eagle) (see figure 3). The sphinx motif is another Egyptian decorative borrowing, but one destined for a bright, Theban future. This luxury item came from a clearly elite, female burial.

Outside Thebes the other major fulcrum of Mycenaean Boeotia was Orchomenus. A large tholos (beehive) tomb was excavated here in 1880–1 and 1886 by Heinrich Schliemann, the fabled excavator – or fabulous inventor – of Homeric Troy. In 1914, architect-archaeologist A. K. Orlandos partially restored the tomb's side-chamber, and further restoration works have since been undertaken by the Greek Ministry of Culture in 1995–6 and again in 2009.

True to form, Schliemann – a true believer in the historicity of Homer – had to give a suitable name to the occupant of the tomb, so he fastened upon King Minyas, in myth the son of Chryses ('Goldie') and grandson of Poseidon. But as at Mycenae earlier, he rather spoiled the effect by labelling it the 'Treasury' of Minyas. It had indeed once contained treasures (looted in antiquity) – and treasure was mainly what Schliemann was after, apart from 'proving' to his own satisfaction the historicity of the Homeric and other legends, of course – but its function was as a burial-chamber.

Schliemann did not get there first, of course; far from it – he had been anticipated by some seventeen centuries by ancient Greek religious traveller and memorialist Pausanias. The tomb was approached by a dromos 30 m in length leading to an entrance measuring about 5.5 m high by 2.5 m wide. The entrance was built of local Boeotian stone (from Livadhia), the lintel over the doorway alone weighing several tonnes and measuring over six metres long. The main chamber had a diameter of 14 m; like the entranceway, it was decorated with bronze rosettes, and the small side-chamber on the north-east side with floral motifs in relief and with spirals. The Mycenaean palace, built *c.* 1250, lay to the east of the tomb. It had three wings, partially decorated with frescoes. Orchomenus was burned and the palace destroyed in the later thirteenth century.

Orchomenus was crucially dependent for its prominence upon its location along the edges of the Copais basin, wherein lay Lake Copais, famous in antiquity for its eels but since the nineteenth century – like formerly eel-ridden Ely in East Anglia, England – drained. It's thought that the Mycenaeans had already attempted to drain the lake, partially, in the basin's northern portion, by diverting part of the Boeotian Cephisus and Melas rivers towards already existing sinkholes along the basin's banks. Mycenaean engineers were skilled and could have reduced the water level and area of the lake there, and so rendered it available for the cultivation of crops (above all, barley, the grapevine, and the olive – the Mediterranean triad of dietary staples). These engineers would have been working, one assumes, under the direction of the Orchomenus palace.

Not far from Orchomenus is the site now known as Gla, just off the main road between Athens and Greece's second city Thessaloniki. This was most likely also under the control of palatial Orchomenus. It is located on a limestone hill jutting into and forming an island within Lake Copais. The simply massive stone fortification walls, about 3 m thick and typically some 2.8 m long, enclose an area of almost 20 hectares – more than ten times larger than contemporary thirteenth-century Athens or Tiryns (in the Argolis, not far from Mycenae). Equipped with four gates and elaborate ramps, the site's military purpose and function are undeniable. But the relative lack of identifiable structures within the circuit walls has prompted the hypothesis that this was largely an emergency refuge site for local farmers, to be used in times of external attack. A large L-shaped building on the north wall probably served as some kind of military HQ, rather than as anything much like the 'palaces' identified at Orchomenus and Thebes. The fact that the site was abandoned c. 1200 and never reoccupied argues for some intimate connection with the type of (palatial) culture and civilization that also went under, never to be restored, in the years around 1200, that is, the Mycenaean.

Also not far – c. 3.5 km – from Orchomenus is a huge, fourteenth-century BCE chamber tomb at Prosilio ('Towards the Sun'), which is currently being excavated and interpreted by a team from Cambridge University led by Dr Yannis Galanakis. Its area of 42 m² makes it the ninth-largest out of the 4,000 or so Mycenaean chamber tombs excavated during the past 150 years. The original – and sole – occupant was a man in his forties. He had been accompanied into the afterlife, however, by a vast assemblage of grave goods: different shapes and types of jewellery (recalling the grave of the so-called 'Griffin Warrior', more than a century older and only very recently revealed at Pylus, Messenia); clay vessels of various shapes (but only two painted pots – stirrup-jars designed to hold aromatic oils); a pair of horse bits, arrows, pins, combs, a sealstone, and a signet ring. The ring, sealstone and horse bits mark him out as a man of distinction, and wealth.

'Homer' is a catch-all title used today almost exclusively to refer to the author or authors of the *Iliad* and *Odyssey*, the two 'monumental' epic poems that were created in the decades around – probably after rather than before – 700 BCE. The ancient Greeks themselves credited Homer with many more works, including some that have also survived, but they couldn't agree on who exactly he was, or how many, or where he/they was/were originally from. That vague indeterminacy is a bit of a giveaway: we are not dealing with an authentic, unique individual poet-artist such as – apparently the earliest on record – Hesiod, or the somewhat later, seventh-century Archilochus of Paros and Thasos, or Callinus of Ephesus, or Tyrtaeus of Sparta. The latter, an elegist, shows especially clear signs of Homeric influence, but it was Archilochus who set a new trend of non-epic, 'lyric' composition in metres other than the dactylic hexameter.

Self-conscious followers of 'Homer', however, focused on the preservation and recitation of the master's works rather than on original composition, and their project received a considerable boost when competitive recitation of Homer was introduced as a standard item on the programme of the revamped quadrennial Great Panathenaea Festival in Athens in the mid-560s. Then, if not before, written texts of some or all of Homer began to circulate widely. But although writing might well have been involved somehow in the original composition of the 'monumental' epics as such (it was the genius of the monumental poet or poets to select and embroider a single guiding theme – the rage of Achilles, the wanderings of Odysseus), their antecedents were premised precisely on the absence of literacy, on total illiteracy. Homeric epic is – as comparative research has demonstrated beyond peradventure – traditional, *oral*, formulaic poetry.

At some point the vastly long *Iliad* and *Odyssey* – they would take some three days each to perform more or less continuously – were divided up into 'books', or lays, for convenience of reference; a sure sign of a literate culture. In the second book of the *Iliad*, as so divided up in the Hellenistic period (see Chapter 12), there is featured what is conventionally known as the 'Catalogue of the Ships'. The action of the *Iliad* is concentrated into little more than about nine weeks within the tenth year of a ten-year siege – of Ilion, another name for Troy (Troia in Greek), hence 'Iliad'. So it's formally a bit absurd to list only now – when the War for Troy (fought ostensibly to rescue abducted, adulterous Queen Helen of Sparta) is almost over – the fighting forces of the united Greeks under the grand command of King Agamemnon of Mycenae (brother of cuckolded King Menelaus) as they were at the outset of the campaign. Clearly the Catalogue originally had a separate, independent existence, before it was spatchcocked onto the separate and originally subordinate 'Anger of Achilles' motif, in order to give that some extra heft.

From the literary, compositional point of view the Catalogue poses some other problems; the fit with the rest of the poem – for example, regarding the areas of old Greece controlled by Agamemnon, Odysseus and Achilles – is not always as seamless and tight as it might have been. Historically, however, our main question has to be whether, and if so how far and when, the political geography of the Catalogue corresponded to the real-world political geography of Greece. Chronologically, the outer limits are roughly 1250 BCE, when archaeologists would say that something like the basic Iliadic scenario of (Mycenaean) palace-kingdoms was in place and not yet seriously weakened, and roughly 700, when the monumental *Iliad* was originally composed. A whole book could be – and several have been – devoted to answering that question. It's particularly salient for us, since in the Catalogue the Boeotian contingent is listed first of the twenty-nine 'Achaean' or 'Danaan' or 'Argive' contingents (Homer never uses 'Hellene'), and in more detail and with larger crews than those of any other region. Thucydides, who can often be taken as a model of the critical historian, was not at his finest on Homeric matters and was surprisingly confident that 'the Boeotians' existed as an entity before Homer, before the (or his) Trojan War. Historians of today have to be a little more critical and cautious.

In the Catalogue itself the poet begins by drawing a very big breath and praying for aid to the Olympus-dwelling divine Muses, since even with ten tongues, ten mouths, an unbreakable voice and a heart of bronze – even with them, the poet pseudo-modestly disclaims, he couldn't name the vast numbers of men that he is in fact about to enumerate. Altogether he names thirty 'Boeotian' places: Hyria, Aulis, Schoenus, Scolus, Thespiae, Graea, Mycalessus, Harma, Ilesium, Erythrae, Eleum, Hyle, Peteum, Ocalea, Medeon, Copae, Eutresis, Thisbe, Coronea, Haliartus, Plataea, Glisas, Lower (or Under) Thebes, Onchestus, Arne, Midea, Nisa, Anthedon, Aspledum, and Orchomenus.

It is interesting to compare and contrast that list with the only seventeen towns listed for 395 BCE as constituting the then Boeotian federal state. The spellings also differ in some cases from their later, historical spellings, and it is strikingly odd that instead of 'Thebes' we are given in the Catalogue 'Lower Thebes' or 'Under Thebes'. Homeric epithets are sometimes just window-dressing or metrical conveniences, but Haliartus is distinguished as 'grassy', Onchestus as 'holy' (sacred to Poseidon), and Mycalessus as having broad dancing-spaces, and those could all be pointed references, as Poseidon's Onchestus certainly is.

But most telling of all is the separation of the first twenty-eight place-names, which include (Lower/Under) Thebes, and the last two – Aspledum and 'Minyan' Orchomenus. The first contingent numbered fifty ships, each with a crew of 120 'young men', some 6,000 in all in round figures, commanded by four nobles of unspecified origin. Orchomenus and Aspledum between them mustered as many as thirty 'hollow' ships, under two semi-divine leaders (sons of Ares, no less), but the size of the crews is not given. 'Hollow' sometimes means rounded, that is, sail-driven merchant ships built for cargo capacity and much smaller crews, rather than warships dependent on raw oar-pulling power. It is not hard to infer that the poet here is doing his very best to exaggerate the claims to pre-eminence of Orchomenus, as against those of Thebes.

It is also possible to infer that, as with much of the rest of the *Iliad,* when it comes to talking about institutions and artefacts, there is a strong tendency towards anachronistic *aggiornamento* at work, that is, a constant updating of the tradition in order to harmonize it with the reality experienced by contemporary listeners. It has been demonstrated conclusively, for example, that from the material-cultural viewpoint the era which is the most densely represented in the final product of several centuries' poetic transmission is in fact the most recent, the eighth century (c. 800–700 BCE).

This is also the era that archaeologists and art historians label the Middle and Late phases of the 'Geometric' era. The term 'Geometric' cannot of course capture or represent an entire aesthetic, let alone a broader cultural thoughtworld, but it does nicely convey a basic component of the decorative repertoire that had dominated the Aegean Greek world since about 900 BCE. It was applied both to 2-D abstract figures – circles, triangles, squares, what 'geometry' instantly conjures up – and to what in nature is 3-D, non-human animals and – increasingly during the eighth century – humans. The most commonly depicted figural representation of this epoch was the horse, a classically aristocratic emblem, since horses require the sort of extensive pasturage that only the very richest Greeks could afford to own and maintain. In the Getty Museum near Los Angeles is the lid of a clay horse *pyxis*, a kind of toilette box with a lid surmounted in this case by three moulded horses, of the period; it very likely came from a grave mound at Kamilovrysi about thirty kilometres east of Thebes, the richest source of Boeotian graves of this period.

For a long time after the Late Bronze or Mycenaean period (c. 1600–1100), human figures and indeed 3-D figures of any kind were eschewed altogether in the one artform with a continuous history – painted ceramics. Exceptions such as those from Lefkandi on the island of Euboea in the eleventh or tenth century stand out like the proverbial sore thumb. From the tenth century onwards, however, craftsmen working in the medium of bronze (copper alloy, typically combined with tin but also zinc, sometimes lead) who manufactured figurines to be dedicated to the gods – such as Zeus at Olympia or Apollo at Delphi – found themselves ever more heavily employed. A 'Boeotian' style of 'Geometric' bronze horse figurine has been identified, examples of which were dedicated in numbers at Olympia and elsewhere. Boeotian craftsmen also produced in large quantities a kind of large, clothes-fastening safety-pin known as a *fibula*; a fine example, depicting a waterbird on its catchplate, is on display in the Metropolitan Museum, New York. By the dawn of the eighth century other materials than clay or bronze, such as elephant ivory imported from the Near East, began to be used to represent figures from the divine, the human and the animal spheres.

This was all part of an era of experiment and expansion which of course could not have been possible without shipping, both merchant and military. Thebes itself took no part in any official overseas settlement (*apoikia*), but even stay-at-home, inland-bound Hesiod from Ascra had a little boat and at least once took to the sea. Book 8 of the *Odyssey*, set among the Phaeacians of the never-never-island of Scherie (identified with modern Corfu), contains a memorable scene in which Odysseus, travelling incognito, is vilified by Phaeacian landed aristocrats for being – as they spitefully lambast him – merely a professional sea-trader. So, the very frequent representations of ships and crew on Late Geometric vases, especially those produced in Athenian workshops, were very much a sign of the times. One particularly well-preserved example of these – now on display in the British Museum – is a handsome *krater* (wine-mixing bowl) acquired in Thebes and quite possibly therefore originally from a tomb in Thebes (see figure 4). Its good state of preservation guarantees that it was originally deposited as a funerary offering.

One side recognizably depicts a woman, with long hair, shown holding a circular object in her right hand. A man, also recognizably such, grasps her by the forearm and makes as if to take her on board the ship that occupies the main pictorial register. The ship is a warship, with two steering oars, to be rowed by a crew of nineteen or twenty: they are shown on two levels as if on top of each other, but presumably the painter intended them to be understood as seated in parallel on either side of a single-decked ship. 'Give me a ship of twenty oars' is a standard Odyssean Homeric formula. Near the stern a small shield of 'heroic' shape is depicted, to make the point that this is a warship.

On the other side of the vase is the earliest known horseman in the Athenian Geometric repertoire, placed behind two chariots, horses and charioteers wearing long robes (as did Greek charioteers in the Olympic and other festival chariot races, competitions which began in the early seventh century). Is the scene generic, of everyday life? Or mythical? If the latter, who are represented? The favourite identification seems to be Athenian hero Theseus together with Cretan princess Ariadne – but that encounter did not end as well as it started. More secure is the *krater*'s dating, *c.* 735–730.

Burials and their contents can also be used as markers of many other things – class, status, wealth, taste, demography, or gender distinction. During the 'Geometric' period, Thebans preferred to have themselves buried in *pithoi*, large terracotta storage jars, thereby differentiating themselves from, say, the Athenians, who were usually buried in cist or pit graves.

In the museum in Thebes there is a late-eighth-century example of a *pithos* from the Pyri (Thebes) cemetery, which is decorated both with standard items of the Geometric abstract repertoire (meanders, lozenges, parallel straight and wavy lines) and with human figures. The principal figured decoration is placed on both sides in the zone between the two handles. On the front side is a man with a lyre facing a line of six women, together with a smaller female and a smaller male figure. He may be a mortal human lyre-player, but he could equally be lord of the dance Apollo, who together with the small male figure is leading a women's chorus. The Greek word *khoros* (whence our chorus, choreography) originally meant dance before it meant song, and Greek choruses often danced as well as sang, as they did conspicuously in the Athenian plays we shall be looking at in Chapter 7. Behind the women there is visible a serpent, a reminder of the pot's funerary function, since serpents like corpses are earthbound and, as they shed their skins to acquire a new one, served as symbols of the hope of a post-mortem, underworld afterlife.

On the flip side, the *pithos* painter has depicted eight women in line, more dancers, with another woman facing them. This unusually handsome pot may therefore have served as a visible grave marker as well as the container of the deceased's remains.

PART II

ARCHAIC THEBES

CHAPTER 4

Religion

All periodization in terms of absolute calendar years is more or less approximate, more or less subjective and misleading. We tend now to divide up the past by centuries; but sometimes historians resort, in desperation, to speaking of 'short' or 'long' centuries. As the great French social historian Marc Bloch once famously said, the eighteenth century in French history began in 1714 and ended in 1789. When it comes to qualitative as opposed to quantitative terminology, the problem increases. 'Archaic' may suggest something old-fashioned, even backward, but, as used in this book, it is a term of historians, originally art historians, meaning inchoate or – more positively – formative. 'Archaic' in this order of discourse presupposes and foreshadows 'Classical'. But there lies of course another potential nominal trap. 'Classical' seems to imply a value judgement, indicating something like perfection in the sense not only of completion but of superior, possibly unsurpassable form and content. That, as we shall see, holds true only up to a point for ancient Greece.

Moreover – in the case of ancient Greek history – the thousand or so Hellenic cities on extant record inevitably moved in different ways and at different relative and absolute speeds in different aspects. For example, it might be wholly correct to say that for the powerful city of Sparta the 'Archaic' period in chronological terms was also its 'Classical' era in developmental terms.

Normally and normatively, the 'Archaic' period of ancient Greek history is taken to run from *c.* 700 BCE to anywhere between 500 and 479 BCE. That is what I too shall mean by 'Archaic'. There is no one blindingly obvious event marking the transition from proto-historic/early historic to Archaic Thebes, but Boeotian Hesiod from Ascra who flourished around 700 BCE can serve as a very fitting transition marker, since he was a pioneer for all Greece and Greeks in the most basic sphere of religion and also has some interesting things to say about politics.

During the Archaic seventh and sixth centuries, Thebes emerged as the most powerful of the several cities (*poleis*) that occupied the region of Boeotia in central mainland Greece. The Thebans were also integral members of the *ethnos* (a group linked by common descent, real or fictitious) of the Boeotians, and Boeotians all shared certain cultural features in common, for example, dialect and religious festivals. Archaic Thebes, as we shall see very clearly in Chapter 7, has its major points of cultural interest, notwithstanding that their snooty neighbours in Athens liked to sneer at the Thebans collectively as uncultivated boors. In the late sixth/early fifth century, Thebes produced the leading lyric poet Pindar (*c.* 518–447), as Boeotia had produced Hesiod two centuries earlier, and a century later still it was the birthplace of one of the leading Greek players of the instrument called an *aulos*, Pronomus, who was renowned – ironically – in Athens no less than in his native Thebes.

Thebes was politically pre-eminent in Boeotia and may already, before 500 BCE, have formed some kind of common 'all-Boeotian' entity – a flourishing federal state, which offered an original and alternative mode of political organization to the single *polis*. From this polity, the small town of Plataea, though Boeotian, preferred to stay aloof and opted to join in alliance with Athens instead. Neighbouring Athens, which by 500 BCE had already become a proto-democracy, had little or nothing in common with Boeotian Thebes ethnically, politically, or culturally – and, thanks to its alliance with Plataea, was its sworn enemy, facing and defeating it in battle in *c.* 506.

The other major power of mainland Greece at this time, identified as such by Herodotus, was Sparta, which was building up its power base within the Peloponnese. It had as yet few dealings with central Greece, though it was allegedly a Spartan king who advised Plataea to ally with Athens. In *c.* 505/4 oligarchic, royalist Sparta tried to overthrow the new Athenian democracy – something of which oligarchic Thebes would have approved. But failure here led to the formation under Sparta's leadership of Greece's first permanent multi-state military alliance, to which Thebes as leader of the Boeotians would in due course adhere.

The Archaic Age (*c.* 700–500 BCE), it has been plausibly claimed, was in the Greek world generally an era of religious sanctuaries (*hiera*). In no other ancient epoch did so many new sacred spaces or *temene* (literally 'cut-off' spaces) make their appearance, often enclosing a temple (*naos*, built to house the cult-image, not for worship) but always an outside, open-air altar (*bomos*, for animal blood-sacrifice). This was as true of Thebes as of any other *polis*. The ancient Greeks did not 'have a word for' religion, however. They had words for worship and for piety and for gods and goddesses, and other objects of worship and piety such as heroes and heroines, but religion as such was so much part of the air they breathed that they did not feel the need for a special word to pick out this as a unique human category, concept or activity.

In line with our emphasis on a regional, Boeotian context, we shall therefore begin our discussion below with the sanctuary that offered collective, region-wide Boeotian appeal before focusing on chiefly Theban Archaic-period sanctuaries. Theban religion was importantly Boeotian, and vice versa. Of the specifically Theban sanctuaries, the two most prominent were probably those devoted to Heracles and to Apollo Ismenius. Both Apollo and Heracles were universal Hellenic objects of worship, but, whereas Apollo was argu-ably more special to other Greeks (the Dorian Spartans, for example, or the Ionian Greeks of the Cyclades archipelago centred on the sacred isle of Delos), Heracles was Theban in a very particular – aboriginal, natal – sense. Likewise, as we shall see, Dionysus. In short, Thebes was in many ways very like most other Greek *poleis*, but in two ways it was different and distinctive, something of which the Thebans and their neighbours were very well aware. Thanks to assiduous modern research, we have a fairly good understanding of the wide range of religious cults observed in Archaic (and Classical) Boeotia.

'The Boeotians' were both an *ethnos* (ethnic group) and a *koinon* (federal state), and the ideal unity of the Boeotians was expressed and reinforced in the characteristic ancient Greek way, by regular concelebration of a common religious cult: the Pamboeotia ('All-Boeotia(ns) Festival'), which was held annually at Onchestus in honour of Poseidon. However, as was often the case in Theban history, Pamboeotia was or became more a dream or hope than a reality, at any rate in political terms – in sharp contrast to the Panathenaea of their all-too near neighbours in Athens, which did genuinely unite all Athenians. Plataea, as noted above, chose not to be Boeotian in a political sense, and the culturally Boeotian town of Eleutherae was reincorporated in the political structure of neighbouring Athens, where it had a role to play in the annual religious drama festival of the Great or City Dionysia (see Chapter 7).

Dionysus was Thebes's patron god and so Boeotian, but the Dionysus whom the Athenians worshipped in their Dionysia festival was more precisely surnamed or subtitled Eleuthereus, that is, Dionysus of (ethnically, geographically) Boeotian Eleutherae. His re- or mis-appropriation was duly recognized symbolically by the annual relocation of Dionysus's cult statue away from his regular Athens domicile, which was the shrine by his theatre at the southeast foot of the Acropolis, to a site halfway towards Eleutherae, well on the Attica side of the border with Boeotia. From there each spring he was brought back home symbolically in pomp – literally: the Greek word for such a religious procession was *pompe* – in time for the start of the annual festivities.

Onchestus, already so-cited in the Homeric 'Catalogue', was presumably chosen as the site for the 'All-Boeotia(ns)' Poseidon festival because of its geographical centrality. The choice of Poseidon as patron presiding god is perhaps not quite so obvious at first sight. Often he is thought of predominantly if not solely as the lord god of the sea – as his brother Zeus was lord of the sky, and their brother Hades lord of the underworld. But Boeotia, though seagirt on the east, is not significantly maritime. In Homer, however, and later Poseidon is also the 'earthshaker', the sender of devastating earthquakes, and in that role he was worshipped, for example, in Sparta. (Inland Sparta lay right on top of an earthquake fault. In c. 464, despite all the unusually pious Spartans' prayers and offerings, the town suffered a shattering earthquake, a direct hit, with major political and military consequences.) Mostly inland Boeotia was not too far from the fault that ran across the Corinthian Gulf. All the more reason for keeping Poseidon sweet. His association with fish will have been an added attraction, given the proximity of Lake Copais and its fabled eels. But most important of all, probably, was Poseidon's association with horses. Boeotia's plains were by Greek standards unusually amenable to proper cavalry warfare, and among the mainlanders the mainly Theban cavalry of the Boeotians was rated second only to that of the Thessalians to their north.

Thebes actually had at various times more than one protective patron or 'poliadic' divinity, but *primus inter pares* was Dionysus, on grounds of his being associated with the city's founding father Cadmus. Other patron deities include Demeter the Lawgiver (Thesmophoros), a divinity of fertility more particularly associated with worship by married women, Athena surnamed Onca (cited in Aeschylus's *Seven Against Thebes* – below), and Athena Pronoea ('of forethought'). Dionysus's sanctuary on the Cadmea signalled its antiquity by being blessed with a type of wooden cult-statue that was imbued with an aura of especial sanctity, since it had reputedly 'fallen from heaven'.

This probably means that the cult-statue was 'aniconic' in form, that is, not fashioned in the characteristic anthropomorphic shape that the Homeric gods (and goddesses) were assumed to possess, and so probably hewn somewhat roughly from a tree trunk. Compare the fact that the most ancient and venerated cult-statue of Athena on the Acropolis of Athens was not the gold-and-ivory statue by Pheidias located inside the Parthenon, nor the open-air bronze statue also by Pheidias just inside the monumental entranceway to the Acropolis, but the aniconic olive-wood image housed eventually in the Erechtheum. Pausanias specifically states that this was reputed to be 'heaven-fallen'. So too was the cult-statue of Artemis in the city of Ephesus, as the city recorder (*grammateus*) pronounced at the time of (St) Paul's visit there in the early 50s CE, as mentioned in the Christian New Testament's Book of Acts.

A sanctuary south of the Cadmea, outside the walls, was dedicated to Heracles Promachus ('Champion' or 'Front-rank fighter'). It was later equipped with an adjoining stadium for athletic contests, including the stade or 200-metre sprint race, and with a gymnasium (literally a place where one exercised – typically wrestled – stark naked, *gumnos*). Recent excavation suggests that the early seventh century BCE was a period of particularly intense cult activity here.

Heracles was actually a slightly complicated champion of standard Greek mass warfare, since, as one of his Labours demanded, he was associated as much with the bow (he is depicted on a fragment of a large bowl found in this sanctuary aiming one at the centaur Nessus) as he was with the spear, whereas in hoplite warfare bowmen were decidedly inferior to spear-thrusting hoplites, and cavalrymen did not shoot arrows. Nor did hoplites or cavalrymen think that a lionskin was sufficient body armour. (There is a sixth-century Spartan-made bronze figurine of Heracles, who was also a major divine power for the military-minded Spartans, which shows him as *both* a hoplite equipped with helmet and breastplate *and* as an archer sporting a quiver. That's what I call trying to have it both ways. It is now in the collection of the British Museum.) Pindar is the first to mention this Heracles sanctuary, in one of his Nemean Odes.

Apollo featured strongly in Theban worship, both individually and collectively. In the magnificent Museum of Fine Arts, Boston, there is among its many prize exhibits a 20 cm-high bronze statuette, missing both legs below the knees (see figure 8). Its original provenance is now unknown, but we may confidently assert that it was, as claimed, in or near Thebes (possibly the Ismenion shrine, below), since the writing scratched upon it is in the local Boeotian alphabet. Iconographically, and aesthetically, the statuette's date should be placed somewhere in the first quarter of the seventh century, making the inscription incised upon it – not its most aesthetically pleasing feature – among the oldest known in the new alphabetic form of writing in all Greece (see next chapter for more).

The text, composed in hexameter verse, may be translated as follows:

> *Manticlus dedicated me to the far-shooter, silver-bowed god,*
> *As a tithe. Phoebus, provide a gift [charis] in return.*

Manticlus, otherwise unknown to fame, clearly thought the honorand, 'shining' (Phoebus) Apollo, would be pleased and flattered to receive a miniature simulacrum of himself – Apollo, that is, not Manticlus: so, quite likely the statuette was originally depicted holding a bow in its left hand. Manticlus further wanted it to be known, and not just to Apollo the far-shooter of the silver bow (both are Homeric epithets of the god), that he had been successful in some economic enterprise, since the dedicatory inscription declares that this is a tithe-offering, notionally worth a tenth of a sum of money gained or of some agricultural product farmed (not necessarily by him in person; like Hesiod, he would have been able to exploit unfree labour). The inscription is engraved in the ancient back-and-forth, *boustrophedon* ('as the ox turns') style, beginning on the right thigh, moving up to the crotch area (the genitals are very sharply delineated), curving around to the left thigh, then curling back to the crotch area and ending back on the right thigh where it began.

The dedicant ends with a request that sounds in its clipped form more like a demand: 'You [Apollo, addressed in the familiar, vocative case] might give [back, in return] to me *charis*.' From *charis* come

English 'charity' and 'Eucharist', which in the form *efkharisto* is everyday Greek parlance for 'I thank you' or 'thanks'. I give – so that you may give back (ideally, more and/or better). You scratch my back – I'll scratch yours: I am here scratching yours, Apollo, so now please give me back in return something of equivalent – or greater – value.

Among its many other informative virtues, this small masterpiece of unknown manufacture goes to the heart of the ancient Greeks' vision of religion (for which, as discussed, they had no one word – the gods and religion were everywhere). It beautifully brings out the pragmatic, contractual nature of standard Greek attitudes to the gods. Another possible motivation for such a dedication or religious donation in a marked-off, consecrated sanctuary (*temenos, hieron* – *hiaron* in Boeotian Aeolic dialect) might be no less practical but rather negatively defensive: I give so that you may not deal badly with me; so that – if you are feeling nasty – you may at least leave me alone.

Yet a third motive for dedication might be a desire to express admiration or thanks, a visual token of worth-ship or worship. That might seem to fit the case of a rather engaging bronze figurine of a draped female said to have been found with the Manticlus bronze but anything up to half a century later in terms of stylistic date. She resides in the Walters Art Gallery, Baltimore, her hands now empty but originally perhaps holding an offering.

Or a combination of motives and reasons could have been in play. At any rate, such fine religious offerings did not come cheap. A sceptical and shrewd writer preserved within the Classical corpus of medical writings ascribed to Hippocrates of Cos later observed that the rich were in a far better place to enter into such contractual relationships with the divine, successfully, than were poor Greeks. 'Twas ever thus: the poor we have always with us. Very few of the ancient Greek poor – the majority of the population – escaped from their poverty, however, through this religious ritual route of dedication, votive or otherwise.

About the same time as Manticlus's dedication to Apollo, a fellow Boeotian called Pagon or Pagondas of Thebes was gaining fame while expending a small fortune in a quite different sort of religious context, and in a panhellenic context, not a local one. This fame (*kleos*) he achieved by winning the four-horse chariot race at the 680 celebration of the Olympic Games (founded, traditionally, in what we call 776 BCE). The fame was all the greater because this was actually the very first time that event had been included in the Olympic equestrian programme; in fact, it was the very first equestrian event ever held at the Olympic Games, and for it the Eleans who hosted the festival had had to create a separate *hippodromos* (horserace course) some distance away from the original stadium (*stadion*, the running track and field events arena) that lay close by the sacred enclosure (the Altis) where the leaves for the victors' olive crowns were grown. Not that Pagon(das) drove the chariot himself necessarily: like a modern jockey, the charioteer would have been a servant of the owner.

Exactly two centuries later, in 480, an invading Persian general was reputedly astonished that the Greeks – and the Olympics were a panhellenic festival, open to all and only Greeks – competed at Olympia merely for a symbolic token prize, an olive wreath. But, of course, the glory of winning was the whole point, since it marked out the victor as a special favourite of the Games' honorand, Olympian Zeus. Any economic benefits that ensued – and they could be very considerable – were strictly secondary, according to the Greeks' moral-religious value code. It was only a shame that Pagon(das) achieved this crowning victorious feat far too early for it to be celebrated in an ode by fellow-Theban Pindar.

Theban Apollo was worshipped publicly and collectively under a number of cult-titles. Apollo Ismenius was named for the River Ismenus. (Alternatively, he is spelled 'Hismenius', because in some Theban inscriptions the equivalent of an aspirate, or rough breathing, precedes the first 'i'; a like ambiguity applies to the name of the important early fourth-century Theban politician (H)ismenias. See

Chapter 8.) His important sanctuary, which included a place for oracular consultation, lay on the Ismenium hill, south-east of the Electra Gate, and is mentioned in an inscription as early as the sixth century. The original, eighth-century temple was made mainly of wood and mudbrick, but it burned down and was replaced in the sixth century by a poros-limestone temple in the peripteral Doric columnar order measuring 22.8 × 46.35 m, with six columns on the front and twelve on the long sides. The cella or sekos, wherein stood the cult-statue, measured 9.3 × 21.6 m and was fronted by a spacious porch (*pronaos*). In the fifth century Pindar referred to it as 'the temple of the golden tripods', and Herodotus was intrigued enough to visit it and report on what he saw.

As recently as 2005, his report was quite startlingly confirmed. In March of that year a rescue excavation uncovered a column drum under half a metre in height inscribed with two identical epigrams, one incised in *c.* 500 BCE in the local dialect and script, the other a later copy of the original in the Ionic not Boeotian script. The drum is now on proud display in the new Thebes Museum.

The drum was cut in such a way as to receive and display a 'shining shield', which Herodotus reports was dedicated by a 'Croesus' to honour the memory of one 'Amphiaraus'. The principle of Ockham's razor (don't multiply hypotheses beyond what is strictly necessary) suggests that Herodotus believed – as he was probably told by a local attendant or priest – that the shield had been dedicated by philhellenic king Croesus of Lydia (reigned *c.* 560–545) to honour god-hero Amphiaraus, a brave but tragic figure in the story of the Seven. (On his oracular shrine, see below.) In Pindar's eighth Pythian (Delphic) Ode, the poet makes Amphiaraus in his capacity as a seer (*mantis*) foretell the fate of Adrastus just before the second assault on heroic-mythical Thebes, the one conducted by the Successors (*epigoni*) of the first band of Seven.

It may indeed have been this very ode of Pindar that influenced both Herodotus's footsteps and his vision. However, even if the shield had been originally dedicated by the royal Croesus, the accompanying epigram could not have been carved in the king's lifetime; rather, it was done some fifty years after his death and probably at the insistence of some Theban temple official, as a memorial of Croesus as well as of Amphiaraus. Either way, this is one of those very rare pieces of extant evidence that bring us into near-direct, almost tangible contact with one of the great innovating geniuses of the fifth century BCE, Herodotus of Halicarnassus, and with his religiously inflected researches (*historiai*).

Recent American excavations in the area of the fourth-century BCE temple continue to bring to light new and interesting finds; one of those – an imported fourth-century BCE Athenian vase with a scene of two sphinxes – is discussed later.

Another major Apolline sanctuary that flourished in the sixth century BCE was the Ptoion, located not far from Thebes, on the south slope of Mount Ptoios (accessible now by a hairpinned motor route). The French School in Athens excavated it, at first between 1884 and 1892, but a definitive publication of their results appeared only in 1971. A temple was built here in the fourth century BCE, on the site of the sixth-century original. As many as a hundred lifesize marble statues of the *kouros* (naked youth) type were dedicated to Apollo, a sure index of great local wealth as well as piety.

One 'modest' example, 1.42 m high, though now faceless and partially legless, is a good representative specimen (see figure 6). He is made of the usual local grey-white Boeotian marble, and standing originally at about normal male human height he would have taken the sculptor the best part of a year to fashion. He is dated shortly before the mid-sixth century. His frontal stance, left leg forward, is that adopted since the origins of the *kouros* tradition in the Aegean marble islands (Paros, Naxos) and in Attica in the later seventh century; the formal schema was borrowed from Egypt, but minus any clothing and plus a very prominently muscular torso. This was the era of the elite *gumnasion*, gymnasium, after all, which gives a clue to the type of person who'd have wished and been able to afford such an expensive commission and dedication to Apollo: the sort of wealthy aristocrat who enjoyed the leisure and freedom from routine productive toil to devote himself to bodybuilding and other physical exercise.

The layered and beaded hair confirms that this is no plebeian or working-class image: as Aristotle was to comment in his *Rhetoric* treatise, wearing one's hair long was the outward sign of a Greek 'gentleman' – a *kaloskagathos* (fine/beautiful and morally good/brave citizen), as the phrase went, someone who could not and would not be seen stooping to perform degrading manual labour. We know that the Thebans had a peculiarly pronounced distaste for such manual work. In its aesthetic, but not in its sociocultural allure, this statue contrasts instructively with a rather later example from Thebes, from the 530s, of which only the head survives; this is carved from Parian island marble by an Athenian, not a Boeotian or Theban sculptor. The hair is still curled, but it is much tighter to the head: bound with a narrow double band, it forms a fringe around the forehead and covers but does not extend below the nape of the neck. Altogether more functional.

More specifically political is an Archaic dedication at the Ptoion donated by the Boeotian city/citizens of nearby Acraephnium. It is a white marble, monolithic (without individuated drums) column, 1.60 m high, in the Doric architectural order. It is inscribed with just eight words, written continuously without word division in the usual way: 'during the archonship of Simonidas [note the Aeolic dialectal 'a' – in Attic-Ionic dialect he would have been Simonides] the men of Acraephnium dedicated this to the hero Ptoios'. According to the Greek way of religious thinking, heroes stood halfway between man and god, between this mundane world and the supernatural or the infernal spheres; there they functioned something like Christian saints, in that they were there to help you out – to provide physical and psychological succour in time of individual or, as here, collective need. We know nothing more about Simonidas, but from this opening formula we know that it was the office of Archon (see further next chapter) by which Acraephnium dated its official public dealings, including the decision to make an offering at a non-local, Theban sanctuary, presumably to keep the Thebans as well as hero Ptoios onside. We know little more about hero Ptoios, except that his shrine was also the site of an oracle.

The sanctuary known as the Cabeirion was situated 8 kilometres west of Thebes. In the fourth century a four-column, prostyle temple measuring *c.* 23 × 7 m was built on the east side of the sanctuary over prehistoric, Archaic and earlier Classical remains, including a large peribolos or circuit wall. The Archaic-period finds include a bronze figurine of the second half of the eighth century BCE depicting a deer suckling her fawn and with a bird perched cheekily on her haunches, all on a rectangular base (now in the Boston Museum of Fine Arts). Quite charming, but very likely the pious dedicator was more of a deerhunter than a nature lover.

The Cabeiroi were originally oriental, non-Greek deities, introduced to Greece as part of the 'orientalizing' cultural movement that began in the later eighth century and flourished extremely in the first half of the seventh. As Dionysus too had oriental connections, some would say origins, a syncretistic fusion or confusion of a (singular) Cabeirus with him could occur in Thebes. The first excavation of their sanctuary was undertaken by the German Archaeological Institute of Athens in the late 1880s, just over a decade after its seminal excavations had started at Olympia – a sure sign of the high priority the Theban site was accorded. And quite rightly so, since some of the finds here, above all the *skyphoi* (drinking cups) of the 'Cabeiran' style of decoration, have achieved a far greater than purely local Theban distinction, and indeed distribution.

The cult itself, however, although the most important devoted to these deities in Boeotia (there was a second site at Anthedon, Thebes's port facing Euboea on the east coast), was by no means the most important in the Greek world as a whole. That was located in the sanctuary of the 'Great Gods', as they were known thereabouts, on the northern Aegean island of Samothrace (source of the famed Winged Nike or Victory statue, now in the Louvre). There was another Cabeiran-style cult in the same general area on the island of Lemnos. What devotees relished the cult for particularly were its Mysteries, that is, its secret rites, which to participate in one had to be enrolled as an initiate (*mustes*, plural *mustai*). Postulants were required to proceed successfully through a prescribed series of stages and trials in order to achieve final initiation; a new, spiritual birth.

The ancient Mysteries that we know most about (and that's not much, since the secrets were zealously and jealously guarded, especially from curious and hostile Christians in later centuries) were those celebrated at Eleusis in Attica in honour of Demeter and her daughter known as Persephone, Pherephatta or simply Daughter (*kore*). Initiation there was a two-stage process, first into the Lesser and then into the Greater Mysteries. Most Athenians, female as well as male, and indeed many other Greeks from elsewhere and many non-Greek 'barbarians' (slaves or ex-slaves) had themselves initiated, so long as they satisfied the basic criterion of being able to speak and understand the Greek language used in the ritual ceremonies.

It is thought that the Cabeiran Mysteries of Thebes, though far less 'international' in terms of those participating, were run along broadly similar lines. The overall aim and gain for initiates, it appears, was the prospect of a happy afterlife – or at least a posthumous existence of some tolerable sort in the underworld of Hades ('Unseen'), where one would not be subjected to the sort of perpetual tortures inflicted day in and day out on the likes of the mythical bogeymen, Tantalus, Sisyphus and Ixion.

Numerous cheap terracotta figurines were dedicated at the Cabeirion, as were children's spinning tops. Far more elaborate items of fired clay used as dedications were the *kantharoi* – goblets with two high-swung handles, a shape particularly associated with Dionysus – of which one extant example, entirely black-glazed, is inscribed in bold letters on one side KABIRO ('Of Cab(e)irus), and another bears the inscription (in local spelling) *hiaros*, or 'sacred'. Most elaborate of all were the above-mentioned Cabeiran *skyphoi*, also drinking cups for wine, but more precisely comic in their outer decoration.

The figure scenes are painted in the black-figure manner on a light background, with details incised by a scraper tool called a burin. One near-complete example in the Thebes Museum shows on one side two cranes and on the other, main side, a group consisting of the god Cabeirus, the divine child and a woman playing the *aulos* (a reeded instrument, something like an oboe). All three are caricatures; the posterior of the woman in the centre is particularly accentuated for comic effect. The scenes on both sides are crowned with another Dionysiac feature – vine shoots bearing enormous bunches of luscious grapes, hinting none too subtly at the source of at least some of the pleasure experienced by worshippers. This particular example is of the late fifth century BCE, but the series goes back to the sixth. Other scenes depicted include rather crude theatrical performances, banquets and dances, as well as other mythological or epic scenes.

The goddess Athena did not command in Boeotia or Thebes the respect and awe she received from the Athenians, but she had a considerable presence. Her epithets Onca and Pronoea have already been noted, but these were outranked at Boeotian Coronea, site of two major Classical-period battles (447, 394 BCE), where a major sanctuary was dedicated to martial goddess Athena Itonia. Although not as pan-Boeotian as the Onchestus sanctuary, this too had a regional, Boeotia-wide appeal. In the British Museum, there is a clay Boeotian-made, sixth-century BCE *lekanis* (offering bowl) painted in the black-figure technique. On one side is depicted a procession in honour of Athena consisting of seven bearded male figures, all nude, together with the sacrificial he-goat and a filler ornamental bird. It is said to have come from Athens. The nudity could be purely an artistic convention – or it could signify something in the real-world religious realm.

Aphrodite almost by definition was the non-military member of the Olympian pantheon, ridiculed as such in the *Iliad*. The Greek word for the sort of courage or bravery required in battle, *andreia*, meant literally manliness or masculinity. Women in ancient Greece, including citizen women, stereotypically were the non-military half of any population. *Aphrodisia*, the things of Aphrodite (a euphemism for sexual congress), were on the other hand available equally to both sexes. Aphrodite did have a sanctuary on the Cadmea, and she served as the divine patron of those Thebans holding the office of Polemarch ('war leader': see next chapter) at any time. But far more famous was the sanctuary at Boeotian Thespiae devoted to her son Eros, the divine embodiment of sexual desire – or carnal lust – both heterosexual and homosexual. The Thespians played a memorable military role at Thermopylae in 480, and male-on-male *eros* was to be most conspicuously enacted by the celebrated Theban Sacred Band of warriors in the fourth century.

The oracle of Amphiaraus, traces of which have been detected 2 km south of the Onca Gate, was famously consulted in about 545 by the aforementioned king Croesus of Lydia. Herodotus is again our source, but, unlike in the case of Croesus's (alleged) dedication to Apollo Ismenius, his consultation of the Theban oracle was on a matter of the utmost, almost world-historical significance: namely, what attitude or response should he adopt to the Persian Empire that had lately arisen under Great King Cyrus. Lydia had featured very early on in Herodotus's narrative, for two main reasons: first, because of the way in which Gyges (as Herodotus calls him; he was Gugu to the Assyrians of Mesopotamia) had acquired the throne of Lydia and founded a dynasty – of which Croesus was fated to be the last representative; second, because Asiatic Lydia and the Greek cities settled on the Aegean coast to the west, such as Miletus and Ephesus, were in close cultural contact (Herodotus devotes a whole section to Lydian social customs, comparing and contrasting them with Greek). Herodotus also notes that the Greeks borrowed from the Lydians in the cultural sphere, including, in his opinion, the practice of pederasty. But by no means all Greeks believed that that had to have been originally a foreign import.

Croesus, alas, made two fatal mistakes, one cultural, the other strategic. For all his obvious philhellenism he did not understand that, in order to consult a Greek oracle, you must not first set it a test to gauge how accurate or inspired it might be. You must take its inspiration, typically regarded as coming ultimately or directly from Apollo the god of prophecy, for granted and on trust. And then you must not assume that the god's message will be transparently unambiguous: it's up to you both to ascertain what the god is trying to say to you and then to decide whether or not, and if so how, to act upon his utterance.

Croesus's first mistake therefore was to test, competitively, as many as four different Greek oracular shrines. Only two of them passed, that is, they in some way confirmed to his satisfaction that they knew the solution to the – in fact impossible – test Croesus had set them. One of those two was the famous oracle of Apollo Pythius at Delphi, which had been going strong since at least the late eighth century, and it is on the Delphic response that Herodotus bases his ensuing narrative. The other successful oracle was the Theban Amphiareum, about which Herodotus says that, though he doesn't know what exactly it responded to Croesus, he does know that it got the answer right.

The second mistake was one of interpretation and consequent action. The typically ambiguous response Croesus received from Delphi went as follows: 'Cross the Halys River [the eastern frontier of his kingdom] and you will destroy a great empire'. Croesus so misread the oracle that he made a pre-emptive strike against Cyrus by taking an army across the River Halys and thereby succeeded only in destroying *his own* great empire. Herodotus believed on principle that all oracles told the truth, so that, for him, it was purely human error that had led Croesus into this fatal misjudgement. All the same, Herodotus was a good-natured fellow, and he liked to believe in the truth of a magic-realist fairytale he was told that put Croesus in a good light.

According to this version, Croesus, having been defeated and taken captive by Cyrus, was about to immolate himself, Hindu-like, on a huge funeral pyre, when Apollo sent down a great squall of rain to extinguish the flames. This not only saved Croesus's life but also enabled him to take up the role of wise (or wised-up) adviser – not only to his conqueror Cyrus (who in real life had no doubt had him executed straight off) but also to Herodotus's audiences of avid listeners. For Herodotus's character Croesus proceeds to deliver a succession of wise saws and modern instances: such as that there is a 'cycle' (*kuklos*) to the affairs of mankind, so that those great men or cities who are at the top of the cycle now will inevitably be brought low sooner or later, and vice versa. Or that, whereas in peace sons bury their fathers, in wartime fathers bury their sons, a reversal of the natural, good order – a reversal made even worse in a context of civil war (the Thebans knew all about that!). Herodotus, I'd like to think, was some sort of proto-pacifist.

The Amphiareum in Thebes consulted by Croesus is not to be confused with the one at Oropus on the borderland between eastern Boeotia and Attica. Control of that frontier sanctuary was contested and regularly exchanged between the Boeotians and the Athenians. Quite a lot was at stake. This Amphiareum was a healing shrine, and for Boeotians and Athenians alike it offered a potent local alternative to the major Hellenic healing shrine of hero-god Asclepius located at Epidaurus in the north-east Peloponnese.

Good fences are said to make good neighbours, but, as this brief survey of Theban and Boeotian religion and piety has shown, all too often neighbourliness increased rather than reduced political friction. Oropus was contested, Eleutherae was expropriated, and the 'all-Boeotia' religious cult of Onchestus was not quite all-Boeotian in fact. On the other hand, no other Greek city but Thebes could boast Dionysus and Heracles as in some sense native divinities, and few others could boast an oracular shrine with the appeal and authority of the Amphiareum.

CHAPTER 5

Politics

When did the Greek *polis* 'rise'? Was it an original Greek invention or was it – like the alphabet – a Greek spin on an originally Asiatic, Phoenician idea? The chief historiographical problem is that far and away the best source for the nature and functions of the *polis* as both power-unit and organ of self-government is an intellectual who was thinking and writing two to three centuries later: namely Aristotle, who composed his *Politics* ('Matters to do with the *polis*') in the 330s and 320s, based on research (*historia*) conducted by himself and his pupils into 157 Greek and one non-Greek (Carthage) polities. Oddly, although Aristotle was indeed a citizen (*polites*), he was not a citizen of the *polis*, Athens, within which he established his advanced research institute, the Lykeion or Lyceum.

He was by birth and affiliation a northern Greek from the Chalcidice region, specifically a native of Stagirus or Stageira. In 348, however, his home city was physically destroyed – on the orders of Philip II of Macedon (Chapter 10), whose father Aristotle's own father had served as personal physician. By then, Aristotle was thirty-six, and he had been a student at and then a member of Plato's Academy in Athens for almost twenty years. The following year, 347, Plato died, and Aristotle chose to spend much of the next dozen years in north-west Asia Minor, where he married the daughter of a local Greek ruler – ruling as a vassal of the Persian Empire. Aristotle nevertheless forgave Philip to the extent of agreeing in 343 to become tutor for a year to his son and crown prince, Alexander. It was thus as a *metoikos* or resident alien in Athens that Aristotle established his Lyceum institute there in 335 – somewhere near today's Syntagma (Constitution) Square. That was in the year after his former employer Philip had been assassinated, and succeeded by his former pupil Alexander – with whom Aristotle stayed in personal touch. Alexander was to die in 323, the year before Aristotle.

Aristotle's Athenian domicile is not the only anomaly about the *Politics*. His theoretical disquisition on the *polis* was composed when Alexander was in the process of transforming and diminishing the status of actual *poleis* in many parts of the expanded Greek world. A checklist of the conditions Aristotle considered necessary and sufficient for a polity's being properly designated as a *polis* is quite easy to compile: ideally, it must be 'free' (*eleuthere*) and 'autonomous' (*autonomos*), free to decide its own laws and administration of justice; and the indispensable human constitutive element, the *politeuma*, must be a corporation or community (*koinonia*) of *polis*-people, *politai* or 'citizens'. A citizen, according to Aristotle's fullest definition, was he (only males need apply) who – being free legally and legitimate by birth – has an active, participatory and controlling share in holding public office (*arche*) and in exercising public legal judgement (*krisis*). Physically, the *polis* is a dynamic, symbiotic combination of a centre or capital (*astu*) and a periphery (*chora*, 'countryside'), the latter being the territory that the *polis* in some sense owned or controlled both publicly and privately, a territory with more or less defined – and defensible – limits or borders.

Modern English translations of the word *polis* vary, not surprisingly since this is not an 'English' concept; for myself, I prefer 'citizen-state' to either 'city-state' or 'city'. In the world of ancient Hellas there were no nation-states, and the large-scale territorial state was a phenomenon largely arising only after the terminal date of the narrative portion of this book (335 BCE), in the 'Hellenistic' world of territorial monarchies (see Part V). In the historical period under discussion – *c.* 700–335 – there were at any one time anything up to 1,000 *poleis*, of varying size and nature but all satisfying – or claiming to – the criteria outlined above. Politically, they did not refer to themselves by a local toponym: so, it was not 'Thebes' that did X or Y, but 'the Thebans', i.e., the *politai* constituting the *polis* of Thebes (Thebai in Greek). Most of these *poleis* were small, tiny even. The modal size of a *politeuma* has been put at between 500 and 2,000 (adult male) citizens. In Aristotle's day most *poleis* had a constitution (*politeia*, also the word for 'citizenship'), that is, a way of allocating offices and making communal decisions including laws, that could be broadly classified as falling under one of two headings or rubrics: either *oligarchia*, literally 'rule of the few', or *demokratia*, more ambiguously either 'power of the People' or 'power of the masses'.

One of Aristotle's most brilliant contributions to Greek political thought was the application of his taxonomic scientific genius (he was primarily a biologist and zoologist as well as logician) to the analysis of those two broad genera or types of *politeia*, *oligarchia* and *demokratia*. In fact, he analysed each of them into four species, placing them on a sliding scale as it were, from the most to the least extremely oligarchic or democratic, according to which or how many citizens were fully empowered or disempowered, and to what it was that citizens were empowered to do, and how they did it. (All women and all unfree persons were automatically totally disempowered in formal political terms. Resident aliens of Athens such as Aristotle had some privileges, but more duties and obligations.)

So, when he wrote – on the basis of considerable comparative empirical evidence – that most *poleis* in his day (the 330s/320s) had either some form of *oligarchia* or some form of *demokratia*, it mattered a great deal exactly where on the spectrum a particular citizen's *politeia* fell. In Aristotle's day, Athens, for example, had what he called the 'last' or most extreme form of *demokratia* going. Thebes, on the other hand, although it had once occupied the extreme end of the oligarchic spectrum, had by then gravitated from a more moderate oligarchy to democracy, but probably occupying a more moderate, centrist position on the democratic spectrum.

Being conservative, and by nature as well as intellect predisposed towards the golden mean, Aristotle favoured an intermediate kind of *politeia*, containing both oligarchic and democratic elements, leaning perhaps just slightly more to the democratic than to the oligarchic side. He was therefore generally keen to suggest ways in which a constitution might either be improved or at least preserved, and above all preserved from falling prey to *stasis* – civil strife, even outright civil war and revolution. For there was one thing about the *polis* – each and every one of them – of which he was quite remarkably certain: that in essence and at bottom oligarchy was the rule of the rich (few), democracy the rule of the poor (masses) – and this meant rule over the other side internally, not just external rule; whence the alarming tendency for states to divide along class lines within each polity and for the two binary polarized sides to fight it out, all too often physically as well as metaphorically, for control: democrats for control over the rich, oligarchs vice versa over the poor. Aristotle's master, Plato, had said that an oligarchic city was really two cities, one of the rich, the other of the poor.

What Aristotle is not so helpful for, however, is analysing and explaining how and why the *polis* idea and system first arose, and how it became almost universal. Predictably 'the *polis*' did not arise as such, nor all in a rush at one time. Rather, it seems that the first *poleis* emerged in the Greek mainland concomitantly with a big movement of permanent emigration away from the Aegean heartland, first west (to Sicily and southern Italy), then north and north-east (to the Black Sea area and its approaches).

Phoenicians too (from modern Lebanon) were 'colonizers', settling in northern Africa and the western Mediterranean especially, where they often rubbed shoulders with or rubbed up against Greeks. It would not be at all odd if political ideas had been mutually exchanged as well as techno-cultural ones. Certainly that was the case at home, where regular interaction could be a powerful homogenizer and energizer. Military factors played a big role at home too, as *poleis* sought to control the maximum amount of farmland against rival claims by neighbours. This meant that the element of the citizenry that shouldered the lion's share of the military burden, sometimes referred to as the hoplite class (more below), significantly assisted in Thebes's case by a cavalry force, also tended to acquire the larger portion of political privileges and powers.

The poetry of Hesiod may be of particular interest and relevance here. His *Works and Days* was composed in hexameter epic metre around 700 BCE. It is a hortatory, didactic poem, a form of wisdom literature, formally addressed to his feckless, workshy and weaselly brother Perses, who has – so Hesiod bitterly reports – somehow 'persuaded', that is bribed, the 'gift-eating' big men of Ascra to disinherit Hesiod to his own exclusive advantage. Hesiod calls these powerbrokers *basileis*, and *basileus* in the singular could mean 'king', but, since the word is used here in the plural, these are not of course monarchs, let alone autocrats.

To judge from the contemporary Homeric epics, and from only slightly later non-epic poetry, these big men were citizens who called themselves 'the best', *aristoi*: best in birth (including descent from a god or hero), best in wealth, and best in general knowhow. Much later, the word *aristokratia*, source of our term 'aristocracy', was coined, to compete with the also much later coinages *oligarchia* and *demokratia*. In *c.* 700, however, it was enough simply to be – or at least to claim to be – an *aristos* or 'best man', and it was *aristoi* who presided over the emergence of their respective *poleis* and determined the initial distribution of political power.

Within a couple of generations, however, it was not necessarily any longer enough just to be one of 'the best'. Hesiod's text strongly implies that conspicuous injustice and especially material greed were likely to arouse serious internal opposition, as well as – he hoped – suffer the justice of Zeus. As soon as there were enough such dissidents both from within the elite and from those just outside the *aristoi* group, there was a risk that an individual champion might seek to overthrow the traditional aristocracy and replace it with extra-constitutional, non-responsible sole power – for himself.

This is at least part of the explanation for the rise of what came to be called in Greek, using a Lydian-origin loanword, 'tyrannies', of which some thirty are attested in Hellas between about 650 and 500. Another part of the explanation is the rise of a characteristic mode of inter-state warfare, known as 'hoplite' warfare after the shield (*hoplon*) that formed the major defensive item of the soldier's heavy infantry equipment or panoply. The Boeotians laid claim to devising the distinctive shape of such a shield, which was indeed named 'Boeotian', and was later used for the obverse device of Boeotian federal silver coinage.

There is an ongoing scholarly debate as to whether the hoplite 'reform' was a gradual, piecemeal affair or, as I prefer, a rather rapid replacement of the older, more open-order, more individualistic style of fighting. The rapid-change view is based chiefly on the adoption of a kind of shield – big and heavy, having to be held with two handles in an unvaryingly fixed position on the fighter's left arm – that worked best in – i.e., could have been invented only for – the close-order formation later known as the phalanx. As it happens, one of the earliest witnesses to the achievement of the 'reform' comes from Thebes, though it wasn't made there. About 650 a Corinthian potter-painter – or potter and painter (he has acquired the modern soubriquet 'the Boston Painter') – produced an *aryballos*, a small (under 7 cm high) container for the sort of perfumed olive oil that athletes might anoint themselves with after exercise.

The neck and spout of the pot are formed separately, out of a moulded terracotta male head in the so-called Daedalic style: frontal, with hair in the form of what looks like a layered wig framing a triangular face. The ovoid or piriform body of the vase is divided into four horizontal zones, the main decorative zone being the third up from the base. On this is depicted an unmistakable scene of hoplite fighting, one of the earliest known, since the pot can be quite precisely dated typologically and stylistically within the sequence of

what is called 'Protocorinthian' ware. It is 'Late Protocorinthian', or
c. 650 BCE.

As one looks frontally at the moulded head, two warriors in the
principal zone are shown confronting each other, with a third lying
supine, dead, between them. Each of the two wears what is conventionally labelled a 'Corinthian' helmet: made of bronze, raised from
a single sheet of cast metal, with a horsehair crest. Each warrior
carries a basically wooden, round shield with a blazon attached
demanding that the shield always be held in the same, unalterable
position on the left arm. The left-hand warrior holds his long, iron-
tipped spear underarm, defensively, the one on the right overarm,
aggressively – that might be just artistic convention and concern for
variation, but the poses do correspond also to actuality. In short,
this is a remarkably sophisticated and accomplished artwork. It was
also a prized import, since the reason it survives intact is that it was
buried in his tomb with its wealthy Theban owner.

Whichever view of the origins of hoplite warfare is right, the fact
that the cities which adopted it were living no longer in a Bronze
Age but in the early Iron Age is crucial. Edged weapons and implements – spearheads, swords, ploughshares – were now always made
from the cheaper, more widely accessible material of iron; the Spartans
were lucky enough to have plentiful local supplies within their own
home territory, which helps explain their early military pre-eminence.
Another fierce debate concerns the political implications and effects
of this hoplite reform, that is, whether it directly or only indirectly
caused the rise of tyrannies (see further below on Corinth's). Whatever
the truth, the period from *c.* 725 to 650 was one of major change
throughout Archaic mainland Greece, and Thebes was at the centre
of it.

We are unfortunately desperately short of detailed reliable, let
alone contemporary, information on what was going on politically
in Boeotia – and so in Thebes – between Hesiod's day and the later
sixth century. *A fortiori* we know even less about what had gone
on in Thebes and the rest of Boeotia between the twelfth and the

eighth centuries. There is no doubt that the destruction of the Bronze Age palace in Thebes, as at Mycenae, Pylos and elsewhere around 1200 BCE, brought with it a distinct fall in the quantity and quality of material civilization. There were fewer, smaller, more scattered and impoverished habitations; total illiteracy supervened; and there was a marked diminution of inter-regional exchange and communication. Some scholars are prepared even to speak of a 'dark age' – or dark ages – though they differ over how long that or they lasted, and on just how dark particular regions such as Boeotia really were. The post-Mycenaean occupiers of 'dark age' Thebes to begin with chose to live north of and no longer actually on the Cadmea, which seems a significant shift.

Boeotia is surrounded by mountains, but within it the two main plains don't offer much in the way of 'natural' boundaries. What is clear is that, when Boeotia emerges into something more like the light of day in the eighth century, it has become a land peppered or dotted with a relatively high number of *poleis*, some of them very small fry indeed. Altogether twenty-six Boeotian (in some sense) settlements are attested explicitly as *poleis* in the Archaic and/or Classical periods. Thebes and Orchomenus were the largest of them by some way. As noted, neither was very fond of the other.

According to a poem of about 540 BCE attributed to the Megarian elegiac poet Theognis, Thebes was then a fortified city. The city-ethnic term 'the Thebans' is attested on a dedication made at Olympia in the sixth century, and on coins struck in the fifth. Its immediate territory was known alternatively as Thebais or (same as the city) Thebes. The Asopus river marked the border of this territory over against Plataea. Presumably the Ptoion at Acraephnium (see previous chapter) somehow belonged to or was under the control of Thebes. After 479 (battle of Plataea), Thebes was deprived of much territory and may have suffered further losses during Athens's occupation of Boeotia between 457 and 447, but by *c.* 435 its civic territory had risen again to some 650 km² (compared with Athens's 2,400 or Sparta's 8,000).

The political fate of the majority of Thebes's population during the Archaic period, including even the majority of those counted as citizens, was to be subordinated to varieties of oligarchy, including at the very end of the era an extreme one. Hesiod's father had somehow immigrated to Ascra and been accepted as a member if not necessarily a full or equal member of that community, which was to form part of the *polis* of Thespiae. But one gets the strong impression that Thebes – with one notable exception, to be noted soon below – was not even so welcoming or open a community as Ascra: Thebes for the Thebans, was probably how most Thebans habitually thought.

Like some other early *poleis*, Thebes was proud to claim and proclaim an early 'lawgiver' (*nomothetes*), though he didn't rival in celebrity – and alleged sagacity – Lycurgus of Sparta, nor, unlike Lycurgus, was he a native-born lawgiver. (The Spartans attributed all or most of their laws to Lycurgus, although he was an at least partly mythical figure and received posthumous worship as a hero.) Philolaus ('he who loves the people, the folk'), about whom Aristotle was to write in his *Politics* many centuries later (based on his unfortunately lost *Constitution of the Thebans*), probably promulgated or wrote his laws for the Thebans sometime in the seventh century BCE. It has been inferred from the fact of his legislation and from what little we know of its content that by the mid-seventh century Thebes was facing acute demographic and economic problems. Possibly.

Aristotle tells us three very interesting things about Philolaus and his laws. First, that he was a member of the aristocratic and one-time exclusive governing family of Corinth, the Bacchiads or 'descendants of Bacchis'. They had ruled Corinth at its emergence as a *polis* and continued to do so until overthrown around 650 BCE by Cypselus, who founded a tyrant dynasty that lasted until the 580s. Second, that Philolaus not only made laws for Thebes but actually emigrated there permanently and died there – but not alone: he went with his beloved (*eromenos*) called Diocles, an early historical example of that partly ritualized pederasty for which Thebes became much more famous, or notorious, later on. Third, the one branch of Philolaus's presumably far more comprehensive legislative programme that Aristotle does specifically mention concerns family law: the laws enacted in his name aimed, by regulating legal adoption, at preserving unchanged the number of estates held in land.

Other cities' early legal regulations, such as those of Cretan Gortyn, were also preoccupied with regulating the inheritance of property, especially landed. This adoption provision of Philolaus, however, looks to be the sort of regulation that applied only to those Thebans who were pretty well off economically, to those who – as later Greeks put it – 'held the [landed] properties' (*ousiai*), or who 'had possessions' (*chremata*). It was only such wealthy families as these who risked losing their properties altogether or having them seriously diminished either through equal partible inheritance among (too many) sons or through failure to produce any legitimate adult son – and heir – whatsoever. We are, though, far less well informed on the demography of the early *polis* of Thebes than we would ideally wish. In Athens, for example, the relative number and type of burials at different periods have been used to illuminate or even explain the demographic transformation that underlay the emergence of the Athenian *polis* in the course of the eighth century BCE. The major relocation and expansion of cemeteries in Thebes, however, seems to have come later, after 600 BCE, and a similar trend is detectable elsewhere in Boeotia: at Tanagra, Acraephnium, and Mycalessus.

I rather cautiously said 'promulgated or wrote' above, but it is almost certain that Philolaus – always supposing him to be a genuine historical figure – did write down his laws or dictated them for others to write down. Having written laws was considered by later Greeks to be a major marker of civilizational progress, and Greeks tended to reckon alphabetic literacy among their highest cultural achievements. In Chapter 4 we have seen, *via* the Manticlus Apollo dedication, that the Boeotian sub-dialect of Aeolic was already being transcribed onto durable material as early as *c.* 700–675 BCE. When written down in the epichoric (local) script, Greek laws served also as a pre-eminent mode of local self-definition – in this case as Thebans, citizens of the *polis* of 'the Thebans'.

Why and how the Greeks recovered literacy after the total illiteracy of the dark age is a complicated question. In brief, someone somewhere at some time adapted the non-vocalic alphabet used to write Phoenician letters so as to create a fully phonetic alphabetic Greek script. It used to be thought that the Thebans might have had a special role in this brilliant innovation, since one way of referring to the alphabet was as 'Cadmean letters', but the scholarly consensus is now that the invention was made by a Greek or Greeks from within a different – Ionic, not Aeolic – dialect-group, probably by Euboean islanders, and that it had been made by *c.* 750. At least half a century, then, before Philolaus (himself originally from yet a third dialect-group, the Doric) put pen to paper – or rather before he or his paid scribes applied either the stylus to the surface of waxed wooden tablets or the quill pen to leaves of Egyptian-origin papyrus. (The English word 'paper' is derived from 'papyrus', though paper as distinct from papyrus is actually a much later Chinese or Arabic invention.)

Philolaus, then, wrote or had written down laws for Thebes, but how was such legislation enacted? What were the bodies that were empowered to pass and police such legislation? Lacking the Aristotelian *Constitution*, we are obliged to feast on scraps. The minimum necessary components of a *polis* from this legislative standpoint were a Council (*Boule*), officials (*archai, archontes*) and an Assembly (*Ecclesia* – and other terms). We do not learn of their existence explicitly in Thebes before the fourth century BCE – from the contemporary Xenophon and the much later Diodorus; and a Theban Council and Assembly of the 370s or 320s will have been composed differently from one in the 670s or 520s. But given that in the seventh and sixth centuries and indeed until – at earliest – the 440s the Council will have presided over an *oligarchia* of wealth and birth, we may suppose that access to it, probably through election to high office in the first instance, will have been restricted on grounds of birth, wealth, and possibly also occupation (see below).

The Assembly, in so far as it was called upon formally to pass or ratify legislation, or indeed make any other practical or policy decisions of state, will have also been confined to the 'few': in this case probably those citizens capable of supplying their own relatively expensive hoplite equipment. High political offices attested in Thebes – again, only later – include those of Archon ('Ruler' or 'Leader') and Polemarchus (War-Archon, possibly meaning commanding general in the field, but possibly only or also a desk job for administering and supervising the armed forces of infantry and cavalry).

The sixth century BCE was in at least one vital respect a major *krisis* or moment of decision for Boeotian collective identity. At some point in it the Thebans had to fight off a joint attack launched by Orchomenus in conjunction with some section of the Thessalian peoples to their north. Such intra-ethnic or intra-regional internecine warfare was by no means unique to Boeotia. On the island of Lesbos the originally six *poleis* became at some point in the Archaic period five, when the other five ganged up on Arisba, destroyed it utterly and sold the surviving population abroad into slavery. Nice. One solution to *polis* particularism and intra-ethnic internecine warfare of that sort was federalism.

Rather than existing in splendid isolation from each other, the *poleis* of some ethnically self-demarcated groups chose to band together into a higher-order political grouping known as a *koinon* (literally, 'common thing'): that is, elevating the principle of local *polis* community (*koinonia*) to a regional level. Such federalism was, however, then and indeed for quite some time to come a rare phenomenon: surrender, even partial, of autonomy by a *polis* did not sit well with a passionate desire for freedom in all its forms. It took some extra factors – such as a concern for or a heightened sense of ethnic solidarity, and desire for safety in numbers against an external threat, or the need to overcome sharp intra-regional division – to make it happen, and happen successfully over the long term.

So, political *koina* ('common things', in the plural form) – which are to be sharply distinguished from the religious consortia for managing major inter-regional shrines known as amphictyonies (e.g. the Delphic) – were, frankly, not thick on the Hellenic ground in the sixth century BCE (or indeed later). 'The Arcadians' of the Peloponnese look like one possible other example (although see Chapter 9), but a stronger case can be made for 'the Boeotians', since some sort of Boeotia-wide federation does seem to have been in existence before the last quarter of the sixth century.

A common silver coinage bearing the obverse device of an infan-tryman's shield attests a form of political unity, since coinage in Greece was always as much a political as an economic manifestation (and the shield was an armament worn for the good of the whole army, not only the individual soldier). That does not mean that religion had no role to play in the federation's formation, continu-ation or management – far from it. A Greek city – or federation – was a city of gods as well as, indeed often before, it was a city of men. The two principal religious centres of the Boeotian *koinon* were Onchestus and the sanctuary of Athena Itonia at Coronea, both discussed above (Chapter 4). A state requires officers: the term 'Boeotarch' meaning 'leader of the Boeotians' was probably coined early on, well before its attestation in the fifth century (see figure 7).

The existence of Boeotian *poleis* within the Boeotian federation (*koinon*) demonstrates that being dependent on and within a larger political unit (the Boeotian federal *koinon*) was not a reason for disqualifying an individual *polis* as anything less than a fully fledged *polis*. Lack of total external and internal freedom, in other words, was compatible with full *polis*-hood. Boeotian unity, however, let alone unification, was never complete. Indeed, such was the internal strife among the cities of Boeotia that fifth-century Athenian super-statesman Pericles – admittedly not a disinterested witness – likened the Boeotians to tall trees whose tops crash together in a storm and act as their own mutual executioners.

Within the federation a constant struggle was waged between the two major cities, Thebes and Orchomenus (another place with a significant Mycenaean past), each dominating its own region, that culminated in (spoiler alert) the outright destruction of the latter by Thebes in 364. Two Boeotian cities (Eleutherae and, below, Plataea) actually 'got away', in the sense that they became allied to, or even incorporated politically within the territory of, Thebes's main neighbour and – usually – enemy, Athens. The original – painfully bad – 'Attic [Athenian] neighbour' of the proverb or maxim mentioned earlier. But the normal fate of the majority of Boeotian cities, which were small, was to be subordinated to the nearest larger entity, supposedly for the greater collective good.

Theban foreign affairs between about 550 and 500 BCE begin almost inevitably with relations with Athens. In *c.* 546 the Thebans had thought it geopolitically prudent to lend financial support to the exiled Athenian aristocrat Pisistratus in his attempt to regain sole power at home. He had already contrived to make himself tyrant (sole, autocratic ruler) of Athens twice before, replacing the moderately oligarchic regime instituted by the reforms of Solon in the 590s, but neither venture had been at all durable. In 545, with much outside assistance (and not only from Thebes), he finally succeeded in establishing a lasting tyranny, significantly by respecting and to a considerable degree implementing the pre-existing Solonian laws.

Pisistratus died in his bed, though several of his opponents had not, and was succeeded smoothly by his oldest son Hippias in 527, who to begin with was able to conciliate members of the other leading Athenian political families and to continue the economic prosperity, domestic political stability, and cultural harmonization through religion (especially *via* the Great or City Panathenaea) that his father had successfully engendered. But in about 514, two aristocrats attempted a coup, resulting in the murder not of Hippias but of his younger brother Hipparchus. Hippias's rule thereafter became harsher, and he made the fatal mistakes of alienating not only his fellow citizens, by establishing a marital connection with another Greek tyrant who was a vassal of the rising Persian Empire (see next chapter), but also the Spartans, with whom his father and indeed he had previously been on good terms. It was the Spartans who did for his rule by an invasion led by one of their kings, Cleomenes I, in 510.

By then, Athens and Thebes were already at loggerheads – over Plataea. What an insult it was felt to be that the citizens of this ethnically and geographically Boeotian city should have chosen to ally with Athens, and thereby opt out of the relatively new and formative Boeotian federation dominated by Thebes. As Herodotus tells the story – and he had a special interest in Plataea, given its absolutely key geopolitical and military role in his overarching story of Greek–Barbarian (Persian) relations – Plataea was resisting Thebes's overtures and originally approached Cleomenes of Sparta for an alliance, not Athens. The absolute date, if we may trust a passage of Thucydides (who had his own reasons for being specially interested in Plataea too), was 519 BCE.

That date makes sense in terms of Spartan history, since, as Herodotus's prior narrative explains, Sparta was by then top dog in the Peloponnese as a whole, having sufficiently quashed its one main rival for that spot, Argos, in a major battle in the mid-540s, and Cleomenes had only recently succeeded to one of the two Spartan thrones (he belonged to the Agiads; the other royal house were the Eurypontids) in unusually fraught circumstances. (His father was considered a bigamist, who had thereby broken one of the Greeks' most basic cultural taboos – monogamy.) He was therefore enjoying his 'honeymoon period', and there is ample evidence from throughout his thirty-or-so-year reign (c. 520–490) that he was an exceptionally forceful, adventurous and activist personality.

Within a decade of his accession he was indeed going to intervene personally north of the Isthmus of Corinth, as we shall see, but in 519 he adopted a more prudent and rather more Odyssean strategy.

Rather than advocating to his fellow-Spartans that they should ally with Plataea, he advised the Plataeans to seek an alliance with Hippias's Athens. The Plataeans acted on that advice, and their request was accepted by Hippias. The Plataean envoys cleverly presented themselves as suppliants at the time of a major Athenian religious occasion. And it seemed likely to Hippias that the alliance would gain Athens and him advantage through the weakening of incipient Boeotian unity and so of Theban power. Divide and rule is a slogan and nostrum usually associated with the Romans (*divide et impera*), but Cleomenes's Sparta and Hippias's Athens had got there first.

Not unnaturally, the Thebans did not take their fellow-Boeotians' treasonous behaviour lying down, and proceeded to launch an attack upon Plataea, against which the Athenians, in honour of their treaty of alliance, sent a counter army. But according to Herodotus, some citizens of the Spartans' allies the Corinthians, who just 'happened' to be on the spot, intervened at this juncture and effected an arbitration which both the Athenians and the Thebans apparently accepted. No Boeotian town that did not wish to be 'Boeotian' in a federal political sense could thereafter be legally coerced into becoming so. However, when the Athenian army withdrew, the Thebans attacked it, but they lost, their defeat obliging them to accept the River Asopus (which was to play a big part in the decisive 479 battle) as the frontier between Theban and Plataean territory.

It was not until 506 that Thebes and Athens actually came to further, less opportunistic blows. The context is provided by the sharply deteriorating relations between Athens and Sparta within the preceding decade. Cleomenes's Sparta and Pisistratid Athens were reportedly in friendly relations down to about 513 or 512. But the Spartans then did a most unusual thing: they sent an expedition by sea to attack Athens and unseat Hippias. It was not quite unprecedented, because in 525 (before Cleomenes's accession), together with their strategically and geopolitically crucial ally Corinth, they had launched a naval expedition against another tyrant, Polycrates, ruler of the island-city of Samos, who had been a friend of Egyptian king Amasis but like Amasis was now being forced to kowtow to the rising – or rather the sharply risen – power of Persia.

Sparta, which never experienced a tyranny itself, acquired and carefully fostered an image of being a principled opponent of tyranny and a supporter rather of oligarchic governments. So the naval expedition of 512 led by the non-royal Spartan Anchimolus or Anchimolius could be fitted into one of two useful, ideologically driven narratives: either anti-tyrant or/and, since Hippias was showing pro-Persian tendencies, anti-Persian. All the same, sending a naval expedition was, for landlocked Sparta, pretty extraordinary, and it was no real surprise (to anyone probably) that it was a total failure.

At the same time, even the slight loss of face that the failure produced will likely have been a contributory motivating factor in the much bigger military decision that Cleomenes's Sparta took just a couple of years later. Herodotus's scenario is largely but not entirely plausible. The Spartans were very pious, or superstitious: they valued the things of the gods far above the things of mortal men, as Herodotus was careful to state more than once, since for him that attitude and outlook explained some major actions – or inactions – on the Spartans' part. One of these was their decision to send an invasion force to Athens in 510 to unseat Hippias and replace his tyrant regime with either a more pliant and acceptable tyrant or some other regime that would be suitably pro-Spartan. For what – or who – most of all persuaded them to undertake such a risky operation was Apollo, speaking through the medium of his priestess, the Pythia, at his oracular shrine at Delphi.

So important did the Spartans rate Apollo and the Delphic oracle that they attributed their entire *politeia* (constitution) to Apollo. They considered the laws of Lycurgus to be 'Delphi-prophesied' (*puthokhrestoi*). Each of the two kings, whose place in the Spartan constitution was literally enshrined by an oracular utterance they called a *Rhetra* or Ordinance, was entitled to appoint two permanent ambassadors or diplomatic representatives with the function of mediating between Sparta and the Delphic Oracle. The four were called Pythioi after Apollo's Delphic title as Apollo Pythios (a title derived from the myth that he had slain a great python in order to become lord and master, with Dionysus, of Delphi).

This particular oracular shrine had first risen to wide prominence in the Greek world in the later eighth century, in connection with Apollo's successful patronage of the great waves of emigration from old Greece to the new colonial world. By the 510s Apollo's authority was extraordinary, and for the Spartans it was enough – or was stated to be enough – to explain and justify their attack on Hippias and thus intervention in the internal affairs of another autonomous Greek *polis*. For, so the Pythioi reported, whenever they consulted the Oracle on behalf of Sparta on any matter whatsoever, they were getting back just the one response: overthrow Hippias!

And so the Spartans, led in person by Cleomenes, triumphantly did, eventually. Since about 515 Cleomenes had had a new royal colleague – or rival – in the Eurypontid king Damaratus, but either he was then in support of this aggressive anti-Athenian initiative or he did not yet feel able or bold enough to resist Cleomenes, as he later very successfully did. Cleomenes therefore took the credit for terminating the Pisistratid tyranny in Athens in 510, but it was a temporary triumph that was also quite dearly bought – by no means all Athenians were equally keen on being 'liberated' by a Spartan. The chief priestess of Athens, the priestess of Athena Polias ('Of the City'), is on record as wishing to deny Cleomenes entry to the sacred Acropolis on the grounds that it was not lawful for a Dorian Greek such as Cleomenes to enter it, let alone seize it with violent hands. To which Cleomenes's typically laconic – that is, brusque and pointed and quick – rejoinder (as recorded by Herodotus) was: 'Madam, I am not a Dorian – but an Achaean.' There may well have been a pun involved here, since the Greek for 'Dorian', Dorieus, was also the name of a half-brother of Cleomenes who had died abroad in unfortunate circumstances. But the main thrust of emphasis was on the 'Achaean', whereby Cleomenes was laying claim to the very ancient, Homeric usage of 'Achaean' to mean Greek of the heroic age of the *Iliad*, when Sparta had been ruled by King Menelaus, and when Menelaus's older brother Agamemnon of Mycenae was over-lord of all 'Achaean' Greeks. This was a neat mythological way of putting the Athenians – no great shakes during the War for Troy – in their place, especially as recitation of Homer was one of the fixed competitions during the quadrennial Great Panathenaea festival that tyrant Pisistratus had done much to promote in the interests of Athenian unity and patriotism.

Athena's priestess was by no means alone in her opposition, either. Enough Athenians were sufficiently more hostile to Cleomenes's takeover than to Hippias's continuing rule that they barricaded Cleomenes and his troops actually on the Acropolis for three whole days. This incident of 510 had such a lasting impact on Athenian consciousness that it could be referred to for the sake of raising a laugh almost a century later, in a comedy of Aristophanes. Finally, Cleomenes managed both to extricate himself and to have Hippias deposed. But a couple of years later he was back intervening in Athenian affairs, because the post-tyranny regime governing Athens was still not settled to his satisfaction; and he thought that another personal intervention, this time on behalf of a friend and client called Isagoras (with whose wife he was rumoured to be a little too friendly), would do the trick.

It did not. What seemed to many Athenians to be Cleomenes's utterly contradictory intention to install Isagoras as a puppet, pro-Spartan tyrant provoked some sort of popular uprising, which ultimately – after the temporary exiling of many anti-tyrant, anti-Spartan opponents – resulted in Athens's achieving for itself an entirely new form of independent polity, later to be labelled a *demokratia*. The guiding and presiding spirit of this new regime was an aristocrat and in his later career diehard opponent of Hippias called Cleisthenes; a later, even more prominent member of his same, Alcmaeonid family was Pericles.

This was the proto-democratic Athens on which Cleomenes tried, yet again, to impose his will in 506. On this third occasion he took the time and trouble to raise first a large, properly Peloponnesian land army, jointly commanded by himself and his Spartan co-king Damaratus, with which he passed again through the territory of Corinth and across the Isthmus apparently untroubled. But as the allied force approached Athens in the vicinity of Eleusis (Aeschylus, born in c. 525, was a native of this important religious centre), Damaratus kicked up. At just the worst moment – selected for that very reason – he, together with the troops provided by Corinth, refused to have any further part in what was clearly Cleomenes's pet project.

What exactly they objected to is not clear: was it on principle to any such military intervention in the affairs of another state? Or, pragmatically, to the imposition of tyrant Isagoras on a state that was not doing anything particularly anti-Spartan? Or was it just done in order to take the arrogant Cleomenes down a peg or two? The outcome of their dissent and withdrawal is, however, abundantly clear. The expedition broke up in disarray, to the great humiliation of Cleomenes, and to some extent also to the diminution of Sparta's authority over its allies. Thebes suffered collateral damage in the fallout, as we shall see, since, still smarting from its Plataean humiliation, it had nevertheless thrown its support behind the Spartans' ill-judged invasion in order to help them damage Athens.

A year or so later, in 505/4, Sparta is said to have proposed to its allies, in a formal conference of allied delegates convened at Sparta, a repeat anti-Athenian performance, with the same tyrant-imposition goal. But it was again the Corinthians (perhaps this time more secretly and silently supported by Damaratus) whose objection proved decisive. Thereafter the rules of engagement between Sparta and its allies were formalized and clarified into a permanent arrangement and structure that moderns call the 'Peloponnesian League'. Technically, this was a hegemonic symmachy, a full offensive and defensive alliance within which one member, Sparta, was the permanent *hegemon* or leader.

By its terms, which had religious sanction, Sparta alone could convene a conference of the League to decide policy. Sparta provided the overall commanders of any allied expeditionary force. Sparta determined how many troops each ally should contribute, and allocated a Spartan officer for each allied contingent; and so on. But the allies great and small formally decided collectively by majority vote of their delegations whether to accept or reject any proposal Sparta put to them. It was this Spartan-led, basically hoplite alliance that formed the backbone of the Hellenic resistance to Persia in 480/79, and which again took to the field, by then with the additional adherence of the Boeotians under Thebes, against Athens and its allies in and after 431. But what concerns us now is the military conflict between Athens and Thebes that followed immediately upon the failure of the Spartan-led expedition of 506.

Newly dynamized, proto-democratic Athens seized this moment to take on Thebes – and not only Thebes but also the city of Chalcis ('Bronzeville') just across the Euripus strait on the island of Euboea (which Thebes had once, many moons ago, controlled). The new model Athenian army triumphed twice over, leading Herodotus to eulogize the benefits of political equality, which made every man fight for his city as vigorously as if for himself. We have inscriptional evidence from both the Theban and the Athenian sides.

The inscribed Theban *kioniskos* has been cited already in Chapters 1 and 4. The Athenians, never backward in coming forward, officially inscribed a block of dark Eleusinian limestone and had it erected on the Acropolis where it was unearthed near the monumental marble entranceway known as the Propylaea. The text of the inscription is not completely preserved, but restoration is certain because the epigram is quoted in full by Herodotus:

> In miserable chains of iron they [the Athenians] subdued their pride,
> the sons of the Athenians, by deed in battle, when they crushed
> the Boeotians and Chalcidians, from whom these horses as a tithe
> they dedicated to Pallas [Athena].

This tells us that in accordance with normal practice the Athenians had dedicated – to Athena Polias – a tithe (formally, one tenth) of the sum realized from the booty acquired, out of which they had commissioned the fashioning in bronze of perhaps as many as four horse effigies, of the sort that went to make up a chariot team at the Olympics.

At an Olympic Games celebration somewhere around 500 BCE, however, the winner of the ultra-prestigious four-horse chariot race was none other than King Damaratus of Sparta. Take that, Cleomenes . . . But Cleomenes was far from finished in his intervention, or meddling, north of the Isthmus, as we shall see.

PART III

CLASSICAL THEBES

CHAPTER 6

Foreign Affairs

Old, unhappy, far off things / And battles long ago

(Wordsworth, 'The Solitary Reaper')

'Classical' in the conventional terminology regularly follows 'Archaic', as if the Classical age represented the full flowering of tendencies merely embryonic or adumbrated in the Archaic epoch. Some scholars dislike that supposed or implied evolutionary paradigm and claim that the 'Archaic' was the true age of ancient Greek experiment. Others observe that for at least one Greek city (Sparta) the 'Archaic' age chronologically was its 'Classical' age developmentally speaking. But Thebes seems to me to conform to the traditional periodization. Certainly it was in the Classical fourth century that Thebes reached its apogee in terms of political, military, and diplomatic power and influence. But that came at a cost, a huge cost.

The 'Classical' period opened with the Graeco-Persian Wars, in which Thebes played a distinctly unglamorous role, and it ended with the near-total destruction of the city at the hands of the then newly risen power of Macedon. There were, however, many compensatory high spots in between, the brightest probably being the years between 371 and 362 which are often referred to in the context of all ancient Greek history as the 'Theban hegemony'. It is important to remember, however, not only that Thebes then exercised a military-political hegemony of power, but also how, for what purposes, and to what effect it was exercised. Other civilizations and cultures have had their 'liberators': Bolivar, Sherman, Garibaldi . . . Thebes – and Greece – had Pelopidas and Epaminondas.

In about 550 BCE, Cyrus II, king of the Persians and Medes (the Greeks liked to diminish the Persians by confusing them with the Medes, a separate but related Iranian people), established both his kingship and the foundations of what was to become the largest and fastest-growing oriental empire of its day. The Achaemenid Persian Empire would last in one form or another for over two centuries, until conquered by Alexander the Great. This was the starting point of Herodotus's *Histories*, and the context within which the phenomenon of 'medism' – that is, unduly or even traitorously siding with the Persians against Greece or Greek interests – came to affect or even infect the history of Classical Thebes.

Greeks were absorbed into the Persian Empire of Cyrus (Kurash in Persian) as subjects from early on. Those Greeks who had been settled for centuries on the eastern Aegean seaboard all along the west coast of Asia Minor, from the Hellespont (Dardanelles) to what is now south-west Turkey, were all reduced to the status of conquered subjects within little more than a decade. The empire expanded from Asia (all of which it considered 'Persian') into Africa *via* the conquest of Egypt and Cyrenaica to its west, and later into Europe *via* the conquest of Thrace and Macedonia. But in the later 520s it suffered both an interregnum or usurpation and massive revolts, especially in Egypt and Babylonia, until order was restored by the empire's second founder, Darius I ('Daryaush' in Persian).

The East Greek subjects chose not to join in that widespread outbreak of rebellions; and cities such as Miletus in Ionia or Lampsacus along the Hellespont (with whose tyrant ruler Hippias of Athens contracted a marital connection, as we saw in the previous chapter) found themselves under the political thumb of local tyrants ruling them as vassals in the Persians' mainly economic and military interest. Culturally, and especially as regards religion, the Persians

– like the Ottomans later – were quite tolerant imperialists. But the deprivation of prized political independence increasingly chafed, and in 499 the Asiatic Greek subject cities together with non-Greek subjects of Persia both in western Asia Minor and on the island of Cyprus did rise up in rebellion, and their revolt was of sufficient organization and magnitude to last for six whole campaigning seasons until it was finally quelled and terminated after a great sea battle off Miletus in 494. Miletus suffered the usual Persian punishment in such situations; total physical annihilation coupled with the transportation of surviving Milesians far into the interior of Asia, there to languish in a virtual open prison. A tragic play on the subject performed in the theatre of Dionysus in 493 – Phrynichus's *Capture of Miletus* – reduced its Athenian audience to tears of pity, and rage.

The exact same fate was meted out four years later to one of the two non-Asiatic Greek cities that had had the temerity – or ideological enthusiasm – to lend military-naval support to the revolt of the 'Ionians' (actually, members of both the other two main ethnic-linguistic branches of Hellenism, the Dorian and Aeolian, had also joined in). That city was Eretria, the other major city besides Chalcis on the long offshore island of Euboea that lies athwart Attica to the east, and which maintained especially close ties with Athens, to the extent of imitating some of its democratic political reforms. But it was Athens, democratic Athens, that was the main target of the Persians' 490 campaign of retribution and reprisal under Datis (a Mede) and Artaphernes (a Persian royal).

This was because during the campaign year of 498 Athens not only had manned and dispatched twenty ships to aid the anti-Persian rebels, but had had the effrontery to march the seventy or so kilometres inland from Ephesus, right up to Lydian Sardis, capital of the Persians' satrapy (administrative province) of Ionia, and torch the citadel and some of its religious shrines too. The 490 Persian naval expedition was therefore a kind of crusade as well as a purely secular enterprise, and thus all the more galling for the Persians when it came to grief on the battlefield of Marathon in eastern Attica.

For reasons that will never be entirely clear, the invaders had failed to deploy their cavalry, and the 9,000 or so heavy infantrymen of democratic Athens, aided mostly symbolically by 1,000 hoplites from their gallant Boeotian ally Plataea, dealt the Persian forces a fatal blow, allegedly seeing off to Hades no fewer than about 6,400 enemy souls, as against Athenian losses of a mere 192. (Herodotus was quite sure of that non-rounded casualty figure: not 191 nor 193, but 192, precisely. He gives no figure for the Plataean casualties.)

The Plataeans were rewarded for their solidarity by being represented among the frescoes of the Stoa Poikile (Painted Stoa or Colonnade) erected officially in the Athenian Agora in the 470s. (See Chapter 12 for more on this important building.) Conversely, the fate of deposed Athenian tyrant Hippias, by then aged eighty or so, offers a quirky footnote to the battle. After his ejection from Athens by Sparta in 510 he had eventually made his way to one of the seats of Persian imperial power, the administrative capital of Susa in southern Iran. He had been admitted there to the small resident circle of expatriate Greek exiles whom Great King Darius consulted as advisers on 'Greek affairs' – and thereby committed the crime of what came to be labelled *medismos*, medism. (By patriotic Greeks the Persians were insultingly called 'Medes', who were actually a different, but related, people, or, as in Aeschylus's epitaph 'the Mede', just as the Romans insultingly called Hellenes 'Graeci', a Latinization of Graikoi, whence our Greeks.) To go over to the Persians, as Hippias had done, was to turn traitor not just to Athens but to Hellenism, 'Greekness', the Greeks' way of life, including – crucially – its political life.

In 490, Hippias accompanied the Persian expedition to Marathon in hopes or even expectation of a Persian victory, to be followed presumptively by his Persian-backed restoration to sole power in Athens. According to Herodotus, who of course knew how things turned out, he had had an ominously Oedipal moment shortly beforehand that had given him, at least, great encouragement: he had dreamed that he was sleeping with his own mother! No less colourfully, if rather more realistically, John Stuart Mill, utilitarian philosopher of the nineteenth century, opined in a review of George Grote's *History of Greece* that Marathon was a more important battle in *English* history even than the Battle of Hastings, meaning that, but for this Athenian-Plataean victory of 490 BCE, the course of ancient Greek and so ultimately all Western – including English – history would have been dramatically different. Something similar has often been said about a couple of the major battles between Greeks and Persians that were to follow a decade later.

For it was to be only a matter of time before the Persians would be back again in massive military force. The objective this time would be, at the least, to teach the Athenians and any others a lesson of non-intervention in the Persians' sphere ('Asia') that they wouldn't forget. But possibly too – of this the defending Greeks as represented in the entrancing pages of Herodotus were absolutely certain – an even more major imperial goal for the Persians would be to turn all mainland Greece (they already had Thrace and Macedonia under their belt and thumb in the north) and the Aegean islands into the empire's westernmost satrapy (apart from Egypt). There were, however, a couple of hiccups before the way was cleared for the assault: in the mid-480s Egypt and Babylonia revolted, again, and Darius I died before he could repeat his pacification act of the late 520s.

So it was left to his son and chosen successor Xerxes (though he was by no means the Crown Prince), having quashed those two rebellions, to turn his thoughts to conquering (some part of) 'Hellas', which he did in earnest from 484 BCE onwards. Planning what proved to be a massive amphibious operation – the biggest before the D-Day landings of June, CE 1944 – with the sort of ethnically and militarily heterogeneous forces that he and his Western satraps had at their disposal would have been immensely complicated. Small wonder that it was not until the spring and summer of 480 that Xerxes was ready to give the green light for his land forces to lumber westwards from where they had been assembled at Sardis to the Hellespont, and for his mainly Phoenician and Egyptian but also, significantly, subject Greek navy to meet him there and provide backup assistance of various kinds. Initially the campaign was both planned and executed as thoroughly amphibious.

The Greeks of the mainland who were not – yet – Persian subjects had therefore plenty of time, three or more years, to make up their minds: whether to resist outright (individually or, much safer, collectively), or to do a dirty deal with the Persians (what loyalist Greeks sneered at as medism), or to try to remain 'neutral'. The extreme loyalist historian Herodotus, himself too young to fight (he had been born a Persian subject at Halicarnassus, modern Bodrum, in the mid- to late 480s), did his bit for the cause retrospectively by writing up – both celebrating and explaining – 'the great and wondrous deeds accomplished by both Greeks and non-Greeks'. He had nothing but scorn for the would-be 'neutrals': *de facto*, he said, they too had medized. But for the outright medizers his disgust and contempt knew no limits. One of his chief targets, therefore, was the city of Thebes, both retrospectively (he was composing and publishing in the 440s and 430s) and prospectively.

As in the case of Argos, only more so, the Persian invasion of 480 seriously compromised Thebes's claims to Hellenicity. Whereas Argos feebly stayed neutral, the ruling hierarchy of Thebes actually opted positively for the Persian side – a sufficiently blatant and memorable act of treachery ('medism') to constitute a plausible justification, even a century and a half later, for the total destruction of Thebes at the hands of Alexander of Macedon in 335. A later generation of Thebans, during the Atheno-Peloponnesian War, allegedly sought to explain away their ancestors' vile act, on the grounds that Thebes had not then been ruled in a properly constitutional way, but had fallen into the hands of an extreme oligarchic junta, a *dunasteia* or collective tyranny. Whether that was strictly true or not, it reflected Greek political thought's careful attention to nice distinctions of a political-constitutional kind and degree –

though it did nothing to stay Alexander's imperial as well as imperious hand.

Thebes in 480 was indeed ruled by an oligarchy – a narrow, exclusive oligarchy, not a broadbased one, an oligarchy that was very much founded on landed wealth and that despised and excluded from full citizenship those Boeotians, no matter how free, who engaged in trade and craft-manufacture. This was the oligarchy – or even perhaps dynasty – that chose to side with Xerxes and his invading Persian forces rather than join the 'loyalist' Hellenic resistance. In his *Life* of the Athenian general Aristides, Plutarch – who was of course partly trying to exonerate most of his fellow-Boeotian ancestors from the crippling stigma of medism – explicitly distinguishes the role and attitude of the elite few of the ruling class, who were enthusiastic medizers, and the 'majority of the people' who were, he claimed, not.

For that medism, all the same, Thebes earned undying opprobrium. This was, however, somewhat unfair. Pretty well all Greek cities and peoples north of Attica did likewise – with a couple of notable exceptions. The Phocians were said to have remained loyal and not medized, but only because their hated Thessalian neighbours had medized, acting therefore on the principle that my enemy's friend is my enemy. Much more difficult for the Thebans, however, was the fact that not all Boeotians (and maybe not even all Thebans) medized: the Thespians and, pro-Athenian as ever, the Plataeans conspicuously did not. For their loyalty to the cause of Hellas they had their cities torched and razed by the invading Persians, which rather emphasized both the point that they were making, and the different point the Theban regime was making.

Marching up to the pass of Thermopylae ('Hot Gates', so named for its still active sulphur springs) between northern and central Greece, Xerxes found himself confronted by a Hellenic defence force numbering between 6,000 and 7,000, as against his perhaps as many as 200,000 land troops. The topography vastly reduced the practical significance of that apparent numerical disparity, and the morale factor was on the resisting Greeks' side to some extent. But this was a difficult time. In 481 and again in 480 just a handful of Greek cities and peoples, a little over thirty in all, had sworn an oath in a sanctuary of Poseidon at Corinth to do or die, to resist the Persian invasion come what may. The majority of those sworn resisters were allies of Sparta within its Peloponnesian League, and Sparta, even though it had no naval tradition and indeed virtually no navy of its own, was automatically chosen to be the leader of the resistance both by land and by sea.

So it was that one of the two Spartan kings, Leonidas, was in overall command at Thermopylae in August 480. But he had under him just a small, if elite force of only 300 specially picked full Spartan citizens (Spartiates), together with their unfree Helot servants (serving as batmen, cooks, armour-bearers, orderlies etc.), 1,000 Perioeci, plus 4,000 or so 'Peloponnesians' and – of special interest to us – small groups from two Boeotian cities: 700 men from Thespiae, and 400 from . . . Thebes. It is quite clear that these 700 men, probably the entirety of their hoplite army, had been sent by the Thespians because their city – like Boeotian Plataea – was determinedly on the loyalist Hellenic side. But what of the 400 Thebans?

Because of the bad odour in which Thebes was held later, all Thebans tended to be tarred with the same medizing brush as their political leaders, and so, according to one, negative interpretation, these Thebans were merely hostages taken by Leonidas to try to keep Thebes from too actively supporting the invaders, or at any rate to punish them somewhat for their medism. Alternatively, and far more positively, these Thebans were volunteers – and rebels, possibly even pro-democratic rebels, but certainly freedom-fighters willing to die for the cause of Greek liberty. In the end, of course, it made no difference either way, as, like the 700 Thespians, they all died at Thermopylae, even if in different ways and for different reasons.

Another cause of difficulty for Leonidas was the timing of the battle in August: the year we call 480 BCE was an Olympic year, and the Olympic Games were timed to coincide with the second full moon after the summer solstice, that is, sometime in August. That potentially affected all Greek cities and communities. Simultaneously, moreover, some Greek cities were holding their major annual religious festivals – in Sparta's case, the Carnea in honour of Apollo. So Leonidas either really meant what he said when he claimed that the Thermopylae taskforce was but a token, advance guard – or he used the timing as an excuse to present it as such. The outcome, in any case, was a nightmare, in more senses than one, as we shall see.

For three days, Xerxes waited outside the pass at its western end, hoping probably to stimulate further defections and anyhow to exacerbate the defenders' already jangling nerves. But the resisting Greeks were well dug in, at the so-called Middle Gate, and in the end it was Xerxes who had to make the opening moves. The evidence for what happened is of course dependent ultimately on survivors' testimony, which may well have been selective and retrospectively coloured, but there is no serious alternative to the account that has come down to us composed nearest in time to the actual events – that contained in the seventh book of Herodotus's *Histories*. Herodotus, being a non-Spartan and inclined to credit Athens rather more than Sparta for the eventual overall victory of the resisting Greeks, was not susceptible to swallowing any Spartan-generated myths whole. He gives the credit where he believes it to be due, and he is a sane and sober voice amidst the melee of postwar self-congratulation and self-delusion. That applies to his accounts of all the major battles of the Graeco-Persian Wars – to Artemisium and Salamis in 480 and Plataea and Mycale in 479, no less than to Thermopylae.

Briefly, for the first two days of fighting at Thermopylae Leonidas's Greeks held their own remarkably well. Not only were they not overrun and forced to surrender nor wiped out by sheer weight of numbers, but through a combination of cunning, skill and sheer bravery they inflicted serious damage on some of Xerxes's most elite Iranian troops, not least his crack force of 10,000 'Immortals' (as the Greeks erroneously called them – we happen to have Persian records from around this date, though none directly relating to the Greek campaign). But on the second day a local Greek from the Malis region, called Ephialtes, saw his opportunity.

Cynics will say that it was bound to happen sooner or later; that, if it hadn't been this Ephialtes, it would have been another man who, in hope of lucre and expectation of Greek defeat, turned traitor. Ephialtes at any rate it was who informed Xerxes of a tricky, mountainous back route, the Anopaea path, whereby a force of Persians could get round behind Leonidas's encampment to his east and so have him kettled in the pass and pincered. Actually Leonidas was, unsurprisingly, well aware of the Anopaea's existence and had posted a lookout detachment of local Phocians to guard it, ideally to block it off but at least to serve as an early warning system. But during the night after the second day of fighting, a force drawn from the Immortals succeeded in bypassing the Phocians and so caught Leonidas unawares. It was a game-changer.

Day three was the decider. Probably large numbers of Leonidas's troops had already agreed on day two to depart to fight another day, or had simply fled. If so, Sparta's later propaganda that Leonidas had deliberately let them go in advance was designed to cover up any wavering or disloyalty. Those who remained included: the survivors of Leonidas's original 300 Spartans plus Leonidas himself, and the survivors of the c. 1,000 Perioeci called up, of the 700 Thespians – and of the 400 Thebans. It was now just a matter of time before Xerxes triumphed and forced the pass.

It is too often said that the Spartans of 'the 300' died to a man in the pass: no surrender for Spartans. But actually, as Herodotus is very careful to record in contradiction of this Spartan-originated myth, two of the Spartans did survive Thermopylae, one inadvertently (he had been sent away on a mission by Leonidas and did not return in time), the other because he was so disabled by eye disease that he recused himself from the fray. Unfortunately for the latter, called Aristodamus, another Spartan had been in the exact same situation and still had gone in to fight, led by his Helot, and die. (Aristodamus compensated or over-compensated later, at the battle of Plataea, by in effect committing suicide. The other survivor, riddled with survivor's guilt, hanged himself upon his return to Sparta.)

What of those Boeotians who were fighting against as opposed to for Xerxes? The surviving Thebans, according to the black propaganda version, allegedly tried to surrender at the finish and pleaded with the Persians for their lives on the grounds that they hadn't wanted to fight against them in the first place – and were summarily killed none the less. The Thespians, however, went one better even than the Spartans. They did die – to a man. Belatedly, very belatedly, a Thespian memorial has been added to the modern (1950s), very Spartan memorial in the pass. It is deeply moving – as of course is the whole truly epic tale of the Spartans' and other Greeks' never-say-die derring-do. The Greek defenders were always going to lose the struggle for Thermopylae, in the end, but all the same the name of Ephialtes has gone down in infamy: not only in his own day (the Spartans tracked him down after the wars and had him executed), but even up until this very day, for 'Ephialtes' is the modern Greek word for 'nightmare'.

After exiting through the Thermopylae pass, Xerxes and his certainly 100,000-plus fighting land troops moved through Boeotia with impunity, torching Thespiae and Plataea en route to their main target and prize, Athens. They easily took over abandoned Athens and effected considerable destruction on and around the sacred Athenian acropolis – revenge, it was claimed, for the Athenians' desecration of Sardis in 498. Coincidentally with the Thermopylae affair, the loyalist Greek navy – dominated by Athens but commanded by a Spartan admiral – had been engaging with Xerxes's mainly Phoenician and Egyptian but also Greek and Cypriot navy, off the northern tip of Euboea.

The battle known as Artemisium (after a sanctuary of Artemis) was a draw, and the Greeks' fleet, which was both smaller in numbers and slower than the best of the Persians' warships, was fortunate that the weather – strong northerlies – intervened on their side to destroy considerable numbers of Persian ships. But off the islet of Salamis in the Saronic gulf in August 480 it was to do extraordinarily, almost incredibly, much better. Certainly, even the battle's chief Greek strategist was prepared to share the glory of the victory with the gods and heroes who had fought on the loyalist Greeks' side.

That strategist was Themistocles of Athens. He had anticipated the need for Athens to become a more naval than land-based power as early as 493, when he held a top elective office in the immediate aftermath of the Persians' great naval victory off Miletus and in the same year as Phrynichus's affecting tragedy was performed. Exactly ten years later, it was he who persuaded the Athenian democratic Assembly to divert a lucky strike in the state-owned silver mines of the Laureum area of south-east Attica to the building of a hundred or more of the state-of-the-art ships of the line which we in English call the trireme: a sort of glorified racing eight, pulled by 170 oarsmen seated in three superimposed banks (hence tri-reme), equipped with a bronze-sheathed ram, steered by a helmsman and captained at least notionally by the wealthy Athenian citizen who had paid substantially towards the costs of equipping and manning it. By September 480 BCE, Athens had well over 200 of these triremes available to contribute to the allied fleet, compared with the Spartans' paltry sixteen, and it was they – and Themistocles's strategy of luring Xerxes into narrow waters, where his own navy's superior numbers and skill would be neutralized – that won the day. As even the Spartans were prepared to recognize – they gave Themistocles the equivalent of an open-top-bus, tickertape parade in Sparta.

The hugely damaging and humiliating Salamis defeat, which Xerxes had watched in astonishment from a specially constructed lofty throne, caused him to return at once with part of his army and all his surviving ships to his Asiatic heartland *via* Sardis. But not to abandon the overall campaign, not by a long chalk. For he left behind in Greece Mardonius, by some accounts the prime mover of the whole campaign and certainly one of its most enthusiastic supporters, in command of a very substantial army to finish the job of conquest. Once again, in late summer 479, Athens was trashed, before Mardonius withdrew to Boeotia and set up his HQ in Thebes, there to await the final, decisive land encounter that was sure to follow sooner or later.

In fact, it took rather longer than one might have expected for the two sides to muster in huge force at Plataea, making this the largest battle yet fought on Greek soil, probably over 200,000 men in all, adding the numbers on both sides together. The outcome of the battle of Plataea was 'the fairest victory of those we know' (Herodotus), which rubs in the fact that the Persians had been actively aided throughout by the Thebans. The final encounter began after more than ten days of delay with a cavalry skirmish, but the outcome was decided essentially by the disciplined Lacedaemonian (both Spartiate and Perioecic) hoplites. Mardonius was killed, his defeated army retreated to Asia. Mainland Greece was thus free for the foreseeable future from the threat of Persian occupation, but a further amphibious mopping-up operation was required at Mycale on the Asia Minor coast by the island of Samos. That like Salamis was essentially an Athenian victory, though the admiral of the loyalist Hellenic fleet was formally the Spartan king Leotychidas.

One linguistic footnote to the battle of Plataea may be added: Plutarch's battle description in his *Life* of Aristides (the elected general who had commanded the Athenians' 8,000 troops) employed the word *sunaspismos*, referring to the characteristic way in which hoplites fought in serried ranks 'shield-with-shield'. The modern political party that governed Greece from 2014 to 2019 was known by its acronym as Syriza: the 'Sy' element was short for Synaspismos ('Battlefront') 'of the Radical Left'. With such unconscious ancient echoes is the history of modern Greece shot through.

The post-Plataea outlook did not promise well for those Greek cities which had decided to take the Persian side, none more efficaciously than Thebes. Moreover, two members in particular of the ruling Theban upper class, Timagenidas and Attaginus, seem to have been dedicated medizers well beyond the call of absolute necessity. At least, that is the impression Herodotus wished to convey, though it is possible he was excessively influenced by the testimony of Thersandrus from Orchomenus, one of his only three explicitly named individual sources in the entire massive work. Hence perhaps the broadly negative picture of the city as a whole ('enthusiastic medizers that they were') painted a little unfairly in Herodotus. This was the picture which many centuries later the Boeotian patriot Plutarch (*c.* 100 CE) still thought it worthwhile or even necessary to try to rebut in his juvenile essay 'On the Meanspiritedneness of Herodotus' (see Chapter 1).

Thebes was finally liberated from Persian control by the allied Hellenes in late summer 479, following a twenty-day siege. The young Spartan regent Pausanias, who had commanded the more than 100,000-strong Greek resistance force at Plataea, tellingly did not have Timagenidas and Attaginus executed on the spot, but at Corinth. Corinth, a key ally of Sparta, had also been a crucial member of the loyalist Greek resistance, fighting with exceptional bravery at Salamis in 480. Moreover, it was at Corinth in a panhellenic sanctuary of Poseidon that representatives of the – few – such Greek loyalist cities had first met in 481 and again in 480, to swear oaths of mutual fealty as 'Hellenes'.

A truly (pan)Hellenic 'national' consciousness was always something rather evanescent, appearing only briefly in terms of practical collaboration and only under the most extreme external pressure, and then quickly falling away again. Herodotus, a Hellene from Asia who had been born within and under the Persian Empire, was especially keen to make the most of any such exceptional moments. In a speech which he placed in the mouth of Athenian speakers, making a formal diplomatic reply to a Spartan expression of alarm that their most important ally might go over to the Persians during the winter of 480/479, the Athenians are made to say that there were many reasons, both specific to Athens and more general, why they could not possibly turn traitor. Most of all, they say, it was out of respect for 'the Greek thing', *to hellenikon*, the fact of being Greek, a compound of common blood, common language and common customs, especially religious customs and values. These are the same Athenians whom Herodotus, in what he explicitly acknowledged to be a controversial judgement, had earlier called out as 'the saviours of Hellas'.

If one were a Theban reading or hearing those ringing words, even if one were a Theban who only very reluctantly had been enlisted willy-nilly in the Persian cause, it is likely that they would have provoked either anger or shame, or both. For ancient Greeks, those were two of the most powerful emotions, and two of the most powerful motivators. What behaviour and actions they – or sentiments like them expressed both privately and in public forums by other Greeks – motivated in the Thebans post-479 we turn to now.

Having recovered first from the humiliation of medism in 480–479 and consequent punishment, Thebes then had to suffer the humiliation of occupation by Athens between 457 and 447. What happened at or to Thebes in the 470s and 460s is almost unknown, just as the nature of Thebes's constitution between 479 and 457 is unfortunately unclear. There is documentary record from Olympia of an arbitration by Elis involving Thebes in the 470s. One further Thebes-related incident of some import, datable a few years later to about 470, is recorded by Herodotus in his sixth book. The Persians' expedition to Marathon twenty years earlier had been a lamentable failure, but, setting an example later followed by great King-Emperor Xerxes himself, one of the Phoenician ships' crew had stolen a sacred Greek object, a gilded cult-statue of Apollo, as loot.

During the defeated expedition's return from Greece to Asia one of the two overall commanders, Datis – a Mede, not a Persian, by ethnicity – had allegedly discovered the theft and piously ordered that the statue be deposited for safekeeping on the isle of Delos, sacred to Apollo, for the Delians in due course to restore to its original home, the sanctuary of Delian Apollo on the east Boeotian coast opposite Euboean Chalcis. But the Delians for whatever reason had not complied with this request, making the Mede Datis look more properly pious than they, and it was the Thebans who after a delay of twenty years, prompted by an oracle, did finally restore it. Herodotus of course had his own, pious agenda here, but so too did the Thebans, keen to shake off the taint of impious medism and to emphasize both their concern for the god of Boeotian Delium and their ability to look after what they considered to be their own.

As for Thebes's post-Persian Wars constitution, we are reliant for our knowledge on a single passage in Book 5 of Aristotle's *Politics*. Here he is discussing changes or transformations (*metabolai*) of constitution and how to prevent them, at least where *stasis* (civil strife or war) is at issue; and he almost casually remarks that in Thebes 'the democracy' was destroyed owing to bad government after the battle of Oenophyta. This is puzzling. In 457, certainly, democratic Athens had elected to extend its imperial sway by land – at the expense of Thebes – and, in consequence of inflicting a heavy defeat on the Thebans at Boeotian Oenophyta, had made of Thebes an Athenian subject for the next ten years. But it is hard to see how, or why, Thebes would or could have become any sort of real democracy before the Athenian conquest – unless by *demokratia* Aristotle really meant only a more broad-based oligarchy than the one that had governed Thebes during the Graeco-Persian Wars. On the other hand, a democratic regime change *after* Oenophyta seems far more plausible, and we can well imagine that other Boeotian cities that were already pro-Athenian – Plataea and Thespiae most obviously – would now if not before have taken a democratic turn.

For Athens, the 450s were an extraordinary moment altogether in terms of its extra-territorial engagements. Early in the decade a publicly inscribed casualty list of just one of its ten tribes (political-administrative units, this one named after mythical king Erechtheus, eponym of the Erechtheum) records the names of 185 Athenian dead, including one seer (*mantis*) and two generals, who had died fighting in Cyprus, or in Egypt, or Phoenicia, or at Halieis (in the north-east Peloponnese) or on Aegina, or at Megara, all within just one campaigning season (probably 459). Not everything went swimmingly. In 458 or 457 the Athenians intervened in a struggle for control of the Delphic amphictyony – which had economic and symbolic implications but was not strictly a 'religious' war, despite its common title as a 'sacred war'. (See further, Chapter 10.) This brought them up against their erstwhile allies the Spartans for the first time in a direct conflict since the Graeco-Persian Wars, and the Spartans apparently had rather the better of it – and certainly claimed as much by dedicating a gold shield as a thank-offering on the new limestone temple of Zeus at Olympia. But the very next year, the Athenians won their great victory at Oenophyta and with it control of all Boeotia.

Diodorus – but not Herodotus or Thucydides – records a direct communication between the Theban authorities and the Spartans when at Tanagra, but he seems to have confused the 450s with the 420s, since Sparta was showing no intention of invading Attica at the earlier date, though it is possible that Sparta did in some way help the Thebans enhance their city's fortification walls. Also, although a handsome funerary stele for one Saugenes was found at Tanagra, and it is tempting to see him as a Boeotian casualty of this battle, scholarly consensus suggests rather that he is to be associated with a much later battle, the battle of Delium in 424 BCE between Athens and the Thebans, so discussion of this intriguing memorial is postponed until Chapter 8.

Sparta and Athens had already fallen out in a big way over a massive revolt by the Spartans' Helots which had started in about 464; the 4,000 democratic Athenian hoplites sent to help Sparta quell it, presumably in accordance with a treaty of alliance, were far too supportive, or so the Spartans perceived, of the Helots' liberationist cause. That and other aggravations had led to the outbreak in 460 or 459 of what is sometimes called the 'First' Peloponnesian

War, a sporadic war between Athens and some of Sparta's allies such as Corinth, rather than with Sparta itself.

The near-run loss at Tanagra in 458 or 457 was a relatively minor setback and had not prevented Athens from taking control of Thebes and Boeotia. Its overseas failure in Egypt, culminating in 454, was another matter altogether. Failure, indeed, is too mild a word – disaster, rather: for by intervening on behalf of a local Egyptian ruler in revolt from his Persian imperial overlords, the Athenians over-reached themselves and lost many thousands of men and many dozens of ships. Such indeed was the scale of the debacle that it forced the Athenians to rethink where and how they were to store the funds of the imperial allied treasury securely, and they decided, probably unilaterally, that for the future they would be better kept on the Athenian Acropolis rather than on the island of Delos. From 454 the Athenians' Athena (and no longer the Ionians' Apollo) could keep her beady eye on them, and in return one-sixtieth of all imperial tribute moneys received would be paid into her coffers under the watchful management of the annually elected Treasurers of Athena together with the – also annually elected – Athenian board of imperial treasurers, called Hellenotamiae, or 'Stewards of the Greeks'. The remains of the Athenian tribute-quota lists inscribed on stelae of local Pentelic marble are some of the most handsome as well as informative archival documents to have survived from all Greek antiquity.

Despite the Egyptian disaster, however, Athens continued to maintain its control of Thebes and Boeotia for a further seven years or so. Tanagra seems to have been treated with particular harshness, whereas both Orchomenus and Acraephiae seem to have been willing or to have judged it prudent to make monetary contributions to Athens. As happened often in Boeotian and Theban affairs, but not only theirs, it was political exiles who began the process of regaining independence from foreign domination. In 447 a bunch of them took control of cities in north-west Boeotia, including Orchomenus, and – supported militarily by other non-Boeotian Greeks who had an interest in taking Athens down, including Locrians and exiles from Euboea – they confronted the Athenians at Coronea, within Boeotia, and inflicted a significant defeat upon them.

So significant indeed was the Coronea defeat that the Athenians decided to withdraw altogether from their Boeotian land-empire, for good. Later, Thebans claimed a major share of the credit for the Coronea victory, but very likely that was a rewriting of history. Certainly, the Athenians' withdrawal left the Boeotians free to rethink and reorganize politically, and here the Thebans undoubtedly did take the lead. It was probably now, rather than ten years earlier, that they added an outer circuit wall around their city.

In 447, therefore, the Thebans established or re-established a Boeotian federal state on new lines, with their own city clearly in the driving seat from the start, that flourished down to 386 (see also Chapter 8). We happen to have an account of this remarkable federal constitution, preserved on a papyrus from Oxyrhynchus in the Fayum in Egypt, composed by an unusually well-informed and accurate (but anonymous) Athenian historian (see Chapter 1). But that description dates to 395, and in the half century between 447/6 and 395 an awful lot happened.

To begin with, the new, moderately oligarchic federal state served Sparta very well indeed as its ally against Athens during the Atheno-Peloponnesian War (431–404), before the Boeotians turned their coat in 395 and joined a multi-state coalition of which they were a moving spirit. In 386, however, the Thebes-led Boeotian federal state was disaggregated and destroyed by Sparta, which, however much it approved of oligarchy in its allies and indeed worked constantly to foster or even impose it, never much cared for multi-polity federal states that might compromise or threaten its domination over them.

The renewed and revitalized Boeotian federal state or *koinon* of 447 and following was oligarchic, but moderately so; high office and effective political and military power were confined to the top

30 per cent or so of wealthier citizens who could afford to equip themselves as cavalrymen or at least as hoplites. Citizenship of any sort was denied to traders and craftsmen, since such people were deemed to have soiled their souls as well as their hands by engaging in economic production and exchange other than agricultural. A complicated system of local representation on the governing federal Council gave disproportionate power and influence to Thebes from the start, a position which it only enhanced over the years by fair means and foul.

Political federation originated as a formalization of older patterns of co-operation and interdependence in the religious and economic spheres; in the case of pioneering Boeotia, the co-operation and interdependence were already adumbrated in the later sixth century. Shared religious practice and sentiment were not just a marginal add-on, but a vital mechanism for legitimizing the regional state and maintaining its cohesiveness – especially given the typically fissile nature of individual inter- and intra-*polis* Boeotian politics, which were by no means rendered obsolete or superseded by federal structures. Integration at the religious and political levels fostered economic integration, but such integration by no means ruled out the possibility or actuality of breaches in the federal bargain, and it was therefore a condition of the overall state's remaining strong and successful over time that there be legal means of rendering miscreant cities and individuals accountable to each other – both at the *polis* level and as citizens – through federal courts.

However, as we have noted, Pericles, Athens's leading democratic statesman, lawmaker and strategist between the late 460s and the early 420s, and always one for the memorable rhetorical phrase, likened the Boeotians in their intestine, often internecine relations to very tall trees which, when the wind blows strongly, crash together and knock off each other's tops and so act as their own mutual executioners or 'headsmen'. Pericles died in 429; in 427/6 and in 424 he was proved to be spectacularly foresighted.

By then, Athens was embroiled, thanks not least to Pericles's obdurate refusal to allow the Athenians to give an inch to the Spartans, in a major 'world' war among Greeks. Thebes and the Boeotians enlisted on the side of the Spartans, and Athens waged war fiercely against them. But for decades before this Athens had waged a propaganda war against Thebes, seeking to make out that all Thebans were less than highly cultivated, that – not to put a fine point on it – they were 'Boeotian pigs', always mucky and with their snouts buried deep in a trough of sordidly material existence. The truth was very different, but the culture wars did also help to produce some of the finest Athenian literature, as we shall now see.

CHAPTER 7

City of Song: Pindar and Athenian Tragedy

The 'Boeotian swine' canard is alluded to in the extremely compli- cated and sophisticated poetry of Pindar. Though perhaps not a Theban by birth, Pindar (Pindaros in Greek) was a Theban by adoption, by identification and by culture. A near-coeval of the Athenian poet Aeschylus, he lived from about 518 to about 448 or 447. The phrase appears in his sixth *Olympian Ode* (468 BCE?) and, less surprisingly, in a dithyramb (a type of choral hymn dedicated specifically to Dionysus) commissioned from him by the Athenians.

Sparta was known as the city of the beautiful women and the fine choirs and choral dances. Athens – as Pindar was willing to repeat – was 'the violet-crowned', a reference to the environmental effect of its purple atmospheric haze. But Thebes lay at the heart and the head of the 'dancing-floor [*orchestra*] of Ares' – the Greeks' brutish, uncultivated god of war, as Theban Epaminondas was to call Boeotia. Almost single-handed, or single-voiced, Pindar set out to at least dent and ideally to wreck that all too widespread image. The most travelled and cosmopolitan of poets, he also was always mindful of his Boeotian roots, harking back (*Pythian* 8.40–48, cf. *Olympian* 6.16) in myth to the famous anti-Theban Seven.

There's just one explicit mention in Pindar of his Boeotian predecessor Hesiod – in *Isthmian* 6.66–9, where he deferentially praises the father of the honorand, Phylacidas of Aegina, for contin- uing to give voice to and adhering to the wisdom of the old epic poet. But several inexplicit allusions have been detected. Far more striking, however, is how self-referentially autobiographical Pindar is: his own first-person voice and experiences are regularly foregrounded. As a victor-praising poet, his chief official goal was to achieve imperishable fame and glory for his commissioning victor-client, but it sometimes seems that he was as much concerned to do the same for himself too; and his chief method of achieving that goal was to place the victor – and by extension and implication himself – in a direct relationship to one or more gods or goddesses.

Oddly, perhaps, the only three adult Theban victors whose feats Pindar was commissioned to hymn and celebrate all won in the biennial Isthmian Games, held in honour of Poseidon near Corinth from 582, and the Nemean Games, founded in 573 for Zeus, rather than in either of the more prestigious quadrennial Olympian (also Zeus) or Pythian (Delphi – for Apollo) Games. (These four formed a *periodos* or 'circuit'.) One of the three Theban victors, Herodotus, won his crown (made of wild celery leaves) at the Isthmian Games not as a participant in person but as the owner of a horse-driven chariot, possibly in 458. Melissus at an unknown date won the chariot-race at the Nemean festival, but at the Isthmian Games, possibly in 477, he also – rather remarkably – won in the toughest combat event of all; the *pankration* or 'all-strength' contest (a combination of wrestling and judo with no moves barred except biting and gouging). His fellow Theban, Strepsiades – 'Mister Twister' – was also a victorious pancratiast, possibly in 454.

All four victories, of course, gave Pindar a chance to expatiate on Theban mythology, in which he is interested not so much for itself as for the chance it offers him to display his great learning, and to show how the present is informed by the past. And so it is that we learn of Heracles, 'that dauntless son', of his charioteer nephew Iolaus, of Onchestus (home of the Pamboeotia festival), of the vale of Minyas (mythical king of Orchomenus), of Oedipus's grandfather King Labdacus, of the seven gates of Thebes city, and of the Spartoi (Sown Men). But he wasn't above dragging Thebes and Heracles in where one might not consider them strictly relevant, for example in his ode in celebration of a victorious client from Cyrene in North Africa (*Pythian* 9). Elsewhere too – in *Olympian* 2 (in honour of Theron of Sicilian Acragas, chariot victor in 476) – Pindar tells of the birth of Dionysus to mortal Semele; and in *Isthmian* 7 he gives yet another version of Thebes's mythical history.

Onchestus was also the native place of Herodotus's patriotically named father, Asopodorus ('gift of the River Asopus'), and it's quite possible that this was the same Asopodorus mentioned by Herodotus as commanding the Theban cavalry at the battle of Plataea in 479 – on the Persian side. Pindar was not ashamed to write for non-Theban tyrants, so it seems he felt no compunction in pocketing the filthy lucre of a high-ranking, medizing Theban oligarch family. A case can be made that for some of his honorand-patrons Pindar was angling to lay the groundwork for their posthumous heroization – that is, religious worship of them as life-enhancing, benevolent semi-deities after their death. But that hypothesis cannot be substantiated from the specifically Thebes-related odes.

It does seem indeed to be the case that Pindar had a highly traditional rather than an opportunistically affected admiration for what we might call people with titles, members of the peerage, the self-appointed *aristoi*, 'best men', who claimed political power (*kratos* – whence *aristokratia*) simply and solely on the basis of their alleged natal superiority to the common herd. A late *Life* of Pindar preserved on a papyrus from Egyptian Oxyrhynchus (*Oxyrhynchus Papyrus* 2438) tells us the names of his wife, Megacleia ('of great fame', very aristocratic), and two daughters, Protomache ('first in the battle') and Eumetis ('well endowed with cunning intelligence'). This seems to confirm that inference. Once upon a time in Greece, such an outlook would have been considered natural and normal, even normative, but by the first half of the fifth century BCE it was beginning to look reactionary, at least from the standpoint of a more socially progressive state such as Athens.

On the other hand, from the standpoint of his clientele, democratic Athens might have seemed dangerously, even frighteningly too

1. In the 360s BCE a Laconian called Timeas was honoured by the city of Thebes by being made the Thebans' official representative (*proxenos*) in his home town. This marble relief stele marked and celebrated his appointment, which represented new-style Theban diplomacy reaching out to Laconians other than the recently defeated Spartans.

2. Part of a clay tablet, incised te-qa-jo-i, 'Thebaioi' as written in the 'Linear B' syllabic script, thirteenth century BCE. From the palace administrative archives, Thebes, burnt along with the palace. Linear B was deciphered in the early 1950s as recording an early form of the Greek language.

3. Ivory cosmetics container of the thirteenth century BCE depicting confronted sphinxes (human head, body of lion, wings of eagle). This was a widespread, originally oriental heraldic symbol, which acquired a peculiarly Theban association.

4. From a grave in Thebes, and now in the British Museum, this fine wine-mixing bowl (krater) made in Athens *c*. 725 BCE depicts a scene of a warship with a warrior, presumably heroic (Theseus? Paris?), firmly taking in hand a woman (Ariadne? Helen?).

5. Manticlus, a wealthy Theban of the early seventh century BCE, wished for Apollo to do him a favour, so he dedicated to him this small bronze statuette representing the archer-god Apollo and had it inscribed with a complex, curling message written in the local Boeotian alphabetic script.

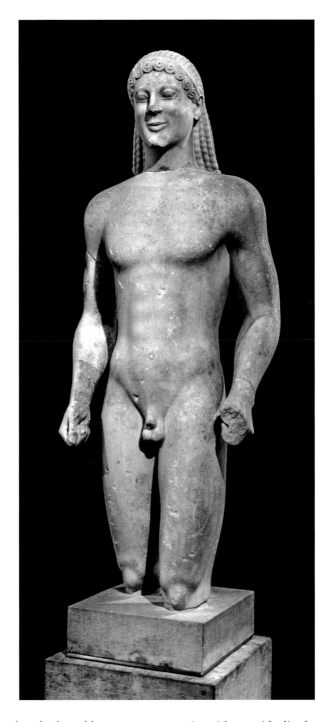

6. Over one hundred marble statues representing either an idealized version of the dedicant or a vision of the honorand, Apollo, were dedicated at the sanctuary of Apollo Ptoios not far from Thebes in the sixth and fifth centuries BCE. This example, now in the Museum of Thebes, has lost his legs below the knees. It was made of local marble and dedicated in the second half of the sixth century.

7. Boeotarchs were the chief executives both political and military of the Boeotian federal state. On this stone stele, held in the Museum of Thebes, a Boeotarch of the early fifth century BCE, the time of the Graeco-Persian wars, makes an offering.

8. This Athenian cosmetics jar, now held in the Louvre, Paris, is illustrated with the myth of Theban king Pentheus, a central character also in Euripides's late tragedy *Bacchae*, 405 BCE. Pentheus is here being shown rent asunder by his mother Agave and a fellow-Maenad/Bacchante (cf. Plate 22).

9. Frederic, later Lord Leighton (1830–1896) was like many of his contemporary artists enamoured of ancient Greek figures; his Antigone was painted in oils on canvas in 1882.

10. Probably celebrating the victory of a winning Satyr-drama, this elaborate Athenian-made wine-mixing vase is named for the celebrated Theban *aulos*-player Pronomus. An entire chorus is shown together with the god of drama, Dionysus. The vase was exported to south Italy and buried at Ruvo near ancient Taras (Taranto), now held in Naples, Museo Archeologico Nazionale.

11. Grave stele honouring dead Saugenes from Tanagra, Boeotia. Possibly killed at the battle of Delium, 424 BCE, in which the Thebans and other Boeotians defeated the invading Athenians during the Atheno-Peloponnesian War. Note the banquet scene in the top register.

12. The Boeotians were early federalists and struck silver coins bearing on the obverse (front side) the peculiar local symbol of a Boeotian-shape shield to mark their political union. The illustrated example, inscribed on the reverse with an abbreviation of the minting official's name Damo-, was struck in the fourth century BCE.

13. The stone victory monument marking the Thebans' famous victory over the Athenians at Leuctra, Boeotia, in 371, was possibly not erected until after the restoration and rebuilding of Thebes in *c.* 316.

14. The names of three of the seven Boeotarchs (see Plate 7) who fought and died
at the Battle of Leuctra, 371, are inscribed honorifically on this burial stele. The
Boeotian federal state, dissolved by Sparta in 386, had been reconstituted in 378.

15. Lively, coloured statuettes of fired clay depicting fully clothed women in both static and, as here, action poses were a speciality of workshops based in Boeotian Tanagra from the fourth century BCE on.

16. The stone lion, a funerary monument marking the spot where many Thebans fell in defeat against an invading Macedonian force at Chaeronea in 338, was possibly not erected – like the Leuctra tropaion (Plate 13) – until after the restoration and rebuilding of Thebes in 316.

17. The rebuilding of Thebes in 316 BCE followed the hiatus of twenty years since the city was destroyed on the orders of Alexander the Great in 335. Both individuals and cities made generous financial contributions towards the enormous cost, and the Thebans duly recorded their gratitude publicly by inscribing and erecting this stele.

18. The Latin poet Statius composed his *Thebaid* epic poem in twelve books in the first century CE. Illuminated manuscript copies were a prize possession in the Middle Ages (this handsome example was fashioned in Italy on vellum in the late fourteenth century), as also in the twentieth century (when it was bought by Mrs Chester Beatty).

19. Jean-Auguste-Dominique Ingres (1780–1867) was a painter in the Neoclassical style who produced *Oedipus and the Sphinx* in about 1826, now in the Louvre. Oedipus famously solved the riddle of the Sphinx but fatally failed to solve the mystery of his own true birth origins.

20. This elaborate clay rhyton (wine-pourer) in the form of a seated sphinx was excavated in the so-called 'Brygos Tomb' at Capua, Campania, in south Italy and is now in the British Museum. It was potted and perhaps also painted by Sotades *c*. 470–450 BCE. Around the neck are depicted in the red-figure manner figures from Athenian foundational mythology.

21. The house in north-west London where Sigmund Freud practised psychoanalysis as a refugee from Nazi-occupied Vienna is now a museum in Maresfield Gardens, Hampstead. On show, predictably, is his richly attired psychoanalyst's couch. Not far away was hung a copy of the Ingres illustrated in Plate 19.

22. In 1911 Ballets Russes impresario Serge Diaghilev (1872–1929) commissioned
philhellene Russian-Jewish artist and designer Léon Bakst (born Lev Rosenberg,
1866–1924) to stage his version of a Theban myth. *Narcisse* was the eclectic result,
featuring a chorus of Boeotian women, including the 'Beothienne' (sic) depicted here.

modern. The Athenians' inexhaustible taste for tragedy, arguably an inherently democratic genre (discussed below), was by no means universally shared. Coupled with Pindar's work for – and unstinted praise of – tyrants, especially those of Sicily, where the egalitarian protocols of the *polis* had not seemingly sunk such deep roots as in Old Greece, his philo-aristocratic persona makes him look quite the anti-democratic ideologue.

Besides the four festivals of the panhellenic circuit, Pindar quite often mentions local Boeotian festivals. One of these is the annual two-day Heraclea/Iolaea of Thebes, named for Heracles and his bosom-buddy nephew, Iolaus, who assisted him in some of his Labours besides serving as an Argonaut under Iason (Jason) of Iolcus. The prizes for the Heraclea/Iolaea were a bronze tripod or a symbolic myrtle crown. Pindar mentions the festival in each of an Olympian, a Nemean, and an Isthmian ode (*Olympian Odes* 7.83, *Nemean Odes* 4.20, *Isthmian Odes* 4.61).

Apart from his odes, Pindar also wrote a *daphnephorikon* – a song for a chorus bearing laurel branches to be sung at the sanctuary of, and in honour of, Apollo Ismenius. The late *Life* of Pindar mentioned above states that the *daphnephorikon* was composed for his son Daiphantus.

In the decades on either side of 500, the annual performance of tragedies, satyr-dramas and later comedies at religious festivals in honour of Dionysus was becoming an integral element of the Athenians 'doing' their brand of democracy. Democracy in ancient Greece was not just a matter of institutions, but also a matter of deep culture. By attending the theatrical performances – and the Athenians took many steps to ensure that poverty would not be a decisive obstacle to attendance for anyone – the citizens in the audience, no less than the actors and chorus members below them on stage, actively performed their democratic duty and roles.

At the same time they learned – especially but not only through the tragic suffering of others (*pathei mathos*, 'learning by/through suffering', a phrase used by Aeschylus in the *Agamemnon*) – what it was to be fully human in a fully political community, one in which direct self-government was a matter of daily life, not just occasional ritual. This, of course, raises a question. Why was it that the mythology – and almost all Athenian tragedies were set in the dim and distant, more or less fabled past – of ancient Thebes in particular held such an appeal as raw material for Athenian tragic dramatists in the fifth century, not least among the 'big three', later canonized by the Athenians themselves, Aeschylus, Sophocles and Euripides?

We have already encountered Aeschylus's version of the 'Seven Against Thebes' myth, performed probably in 467, and we shall return to Euripides's *Bacchae* of 405. By an accident of survival and preservation there also exist three Theban plays by Sophocles, three separate tragedies set in ancient Thebes, which are too often mis-described – or mis-sold – as his 'Theban trilogy'. This is doubly unfortunate. Ancient Athenian dramatists were indeed required to write sets of three tragedies for competitive performance at the annual Great or City Dionysia play festival held in late March/early April at the foot of the Acropolis. But only rarely was the set of three an actual trilogy in the strong, connective sense – Aeschylus's *Oresteia* trilogy of 458 is the sole classic, extant example. Moreover, they did not write only those three tragic plays: if chosen by the Athenian official responsible (the 'Eponymous' Archon, who was selected by random lottery and not for any special dramatic expertise), they also had to write and have staged a fourth play, a (more or less comic) satyr-drama, conceived and performed as a relieving, releasing coda.

In the tragedies, the identity of the chorus of twelve or fifteen members varied according to the play's plots, but in satyr-drama the chorus always by definition represented Dionysus's goaty-horsey (male) animal followers: the satyrs. They were conventionally sex-addicted and drink-sodden, hardly models of exemplary social behaviour. Only one satyr-drama, the *Cyclops* of Euripides, survives complete, and another, the *Trackers* by Sophocles, part-complete; neither has a Theban focus. But sometimes, as we shall see below, it was a satyr-drama that caught a contemporary vase-painter's eye, with an exceptional Theban performer at the centre of the drama.

Sophocles's three surviving Theban plays each formed a part of three quite separate sets of three tragic dramas, and they were written and performed over a period of some forty years, a very long generation: the *Antigone* in probably 441, the *Oedipus Tyrannus* in 430 or 429, and the *Oedipus at Colonus*, first performed posthumously (Sophocles died, in his nineties, in 405) in 401. Aristotle, who was not an Athenian and may not have been the Greeks' greatest theatre critic of all time, was convinced that the *Oedipus Tyrannus* was the perfect, the canonical, tragedy. Certainly it ticks all the familiar boxes – of unintended consequences, human (mortal, fatal) error of identification and judgement, of overall inscrutable, indefeasible divine power, of murder, incest, suicide, a catalogue of altogether horrifying death and destruction. Everything gone awry. And that, of course, is one part of the answer to the question about the peculiarly insistent appeal to Athenian poet-dramatists and audiences of specifically Theban mythical themes. How sweet (the ancient Greek metaphor of choice, sweet as honey) to revel in the spectacle and imagination of your enemies being under the cosh, and so often a self-inflicted cosh at that.

But there was more to it – and this can be best brought out by reference to another of Euripides's tragedies, his *Suppliant Women*, which was set in the famous sanctuary of Demeter and Kore at Eleusis just to the west of Athens. Athenians were fond of suppliant plays – Aeschylus's *Suppliant Women* happens to be extant, probably dated 463. In it he had been daringly quasi-anachronistic, and not for the first time. He has Pelasgus, who if historical would have been the hereditary king of Peloponnesian Argos, behave as if he were but a constitutional monarch, obliged to consult and abide by the wishes of the so-called people (*demos*) of Argos.

They duly meet in open assembly to express their opinion on whether Argos should or should not receive as suppliant-strangers in the midst of their community – and therefore to be protected under a religious sanction – a large number of foreign refugee women from Egypt, the fifty daughters of Danaus. By an overwhelming majority they vote 'Yea', which decision King Pelasgus quasi-anachronistically, and disingenuously, refers to as an act of the *kratousa kheir* of the *demos*, the 'decisively empowered/empowering hand of the people'. In 463, actual Athenians took some of their public political decisions by open majority vote, raising their right hands (*kheirotonia*), which were then either counted individually or more usually 'told', that is guesstimated. That was the *kratos* of the *demos* that together went to make up a very newfangled *demo-kratia*, hardly something in existence in supposedly prehistorical Argos.

Likewise, there is a famously democratic passage in the 423 BCE *Suppliant Women* of Euripides. A Theban herald – what we would call an ambassador or official envoy – has come to Athens from King Creon to demand officiously that Athens, that is to say, its sole ruler King Theseus, surrender to him a group of Argive suppliant women, whose cause is aided by the father-in-law of (dreaded, traitor) Theban Polyneices. Theseus of Athens, not to be outdone by Pelasgus of Argos, in fact outdoes him by a considerable distance – which for him was not difficult, since over the course of the fifth century he had been gradually transmogrified from a Bronze Age, monster-slaying hero into a pacific founder of nothing less than the Athenian *polis*. This foundation he was supposed to have effected *via* the mechanism of *sunoikismos* (synoecism), the literally 'housing together' of all the *demoi* (villages) of Attica into one unified and centralized political entity, 'the Athenians', with its capital in Athens focused around the mighty Acropolis, or high-city. Even the supposedly critical and rational Thucydides seems to have accepted that this city-founding Theseus had actually existed. Who better therefore than the stage character Theseus to respond, witheringly, to the Theban herald with a magnificent declaration of democratic, ideological intent?

The herald begins his pitch badly, in Athenian democratic terms the worst possible way. Who, he demands, is the *despotes* of this land? As if he didn't know who ruled Athens, he asks in effect who is the unaccountable lord and master, the despot, of the Athenians? To which Theseus replies that there is no such 'despot' here: that is not how our community, unlike your Thebes, manages its politics of self-government. The Theban royalist herald, however, will have no truck with the notion that the masses – the 'mob' – can possibly have any legitimate public political say. But they do, rejoins Theseus, and quite rightly so too. In John Davie's admirably sober and accurate prose translation:

> No enemy is more dangerous to a city than a monarch[!], for then, firstly, laws for all citizens do not exist and one man enjoys power, appropriating the law as his own possession. This means an end to equality. But when laws are written down, the weak and the rich man alike have their equal right . . . Liberty speaks in these words: 'Who with good counsel for his city wishes to address this gathering?' Anyone who wishes to do this gains distinction; whoever does not, keeps silent. Where could a city enjoy greater equality than this?

Freedom and equality were the watchwords of fifth-century Athenian democracy, a suitable counterpose and counterpoise to the herald's 'foolish words'. Theseus's speech will have gone down very well, at least with the Athenian members of the perhaps 15–17,000-strong audience, seated in the open air in the architecturally still quite basic Theatre of Dionysus located immediately underneath the Acropolis. For in 423, democratic Athens and oligarchic Thebes were on opposite sides in the midst of the Atheno-Peloponnesian War that had broken out in 431. Just three years earlier, in 426, Sparta had physically annihilated relatively small Boeotian Plataea, Athens's ally since 519 and gallant fellow-fighter against the Persians in 490 and again in 479. Plataea – the site of an annual festival of panhellenic remembrance and celebration commemorating the victory and the human and other losses of 479.

Moreover, in 424, just a year before the *Suppliant Women* was first performed, Thebes had visited some sort of destruction also upon pro-Athenian Boeotian Thespiae, before soundly trouncing an Athenian army at Delium, in Boeotia, after a badly mismanaged Athenian invasion. Besides the relief of laughing at Aristophanes's Socrates-guying *Clouds*, one of the three offerings in the Comedy (*komoidia*) section of the Dionysia festival in 423, the audience could thus vent their spleen upon Thebes and all its anti-democratic works in tragic vein.

We cannot leave Euripides without a close look at his final play, the *Bacchae*; this too was Theban not only in its personnel but also in its plot, setting and dynamic. It was moreover partly autobiographical, but in a different sense. Euripides was born in about 480 BCE and on the very islet of Salamis by which that year's famous eponymous battle took place. By the last decade of the fifth century BCE, he had been suffering not only the many failures of his plays in competition – it was rare that the plays he submitted were not accepted by the authorities for performance, at both private and public expense, but equally rarely did any of his sets of three tragedies plus satyr-drama win first prize – but also the hardships, the miseries, the hunger, the plague, and the lack of sanitation that afflicted all residents of Athens between 431 and 421, and again after 413. So in 406, by then in or around his mid-seventies, he decided to accept an invitation to be court poet to Macedonian king Archelaus, far up north at his new capital of Pella.

Macedon, once a Persian vassal, had not exactly been a good friend and ally continuously to Athens throughout the Atheno-Peloponnesian War. Some of the more refined – or snobbish – Athenians affected to consider all Macedonians, not excluding the kings, who claimed southern Greek origins, to be 'barbarians', savages ('Philistines') culturally speaking, and non-Greek ethnically speaking (they did indeed speak among themselves a dialect of Greek that was incomprehensible to outsiders). Yet this was the Pella that Euripides – in what was seen as a kind of betrayal – had freely chosen to migrate to, and seemingly for good. He was joined there by fellow-Athenian and fellow-tragedian Agathon – it is his victory celebration in 416 that serves as the artificial dramatic occasion of Plato's brilliant philosophical dialogue on love in all its forms, the *Symposium*.

Euripides had his revenge on the Athenians, if revenge was what he was after. He not only wrote a play at Pella called *Archelaus*, named for an ancestor of his host, but he also wrote a tragedy which, though set elsewhere (Thebes), was clearly informed and inspired in good measure by a local Macedonian kind of worship of Dionysus not to be found in Athens, a more ecstatic, a more untrammelled, above all a more female kind. And of course this play was not written for performance on the Athenian stage, either. The play was the *Bacchae* (see figure 8).

An alternative name for Dionysus was Bacchus, from which came the verb *bakcheuein*, to act/go bacchic. Bacchae (Latin form of the Greek *Bakchai*) were female bacchantes, devotees of the cult of Bacchus/Dionysus. Our adjective 'ecstatic' comes from Greek *ekstasis*, meaning the individual or group-psychological process of standing (*stasis*) outside (*ek*) oneself, while at the same time displaying enthusiasm or possession by a god (*en-* in, *-thousiasmos* from *theos*, god). The plot of Euripides's *Bacchae* purports to show what happened – as a fact of history – when Dionysus arrived, in disguise, in pre-Oedipus, pre-Laius Thebes, a Thebes then ruled by King Pentheus, son-in-law of Cadmus. And at the same time it purports to show what it suggests is all too liable to happen – as a fact of psychology – if one denies the elemental force of Bacchus/Dionysus. A Dionysus who is capable of inspiring both terrifyingly murderous violence and blissful ecstatic release.

As in Sophocles's *Oedipus Tyrannus*, a cardinal figure in the unravelling and unmasking of the plot is the wise, blind seer Teiresias. T. S. Eliot, in his pathbreaking 1922 poem *The Waste Land*, was greatly intrigued by him, or more specifically by his bi-gendered identity ('old man with wrinkled dugs'), but Greeks of the fifth century BCE would have been more amused or bemused by the fact that he had been at different times both a man and a woman – and had had sex, presumably hetero, in both capacities. Whereafter he was thought to be in a good position to opine, with perfect authority, that in the sexual act the woman experiences precisely nine times as much pleasure as the man. What a secret to let out. Zeus endowed him with the gifts of prophecy and longevity, but Hera his sister-wife, as so often at odds with her mate, struck him blind as a punishment.

It is to Teiresias that Euripides in the *Bacchae* gives a long speech of mythography, addressed to Pentheus. Here Teiresias (in Colin Teevan's translation) tells the tale of Dionysus's birth, of how he

> *Was incubated in his father's thigh,*
> *A tale you scoff at, I will tell you, sir:*
> *As Semele lay dying from the bolt,*
> *Hurled at her in jealousy by Hera,*
> *Zeus snatched the still live fetus from her womb*
> *And brought it to Olympus . . .*

Unhappily, especially for Pentheus (his name is derived from Greek *penthos*, grief), the Chorus of bacchantes are *mainades*, maenads, or 'madwomen'. Pentheus, stiff-necked and conventional, rejects the newly arrived and disturbing young god no less enthusiastically than the foreign bacchantes/maenads who, joined by local Theban women, including crucially Pentheus's own mother, Agave, rush out onto the mountainside to accept him, and to revel in and with him. In her ecstasy of delirium, Agave rends in pieces with her bare hands, and proceeds to devour raw, what she thinks is a wild animal but which, when she's sobered up, she perceives to be her late, very dead son. How would an Athenian audience have taken all that?

With great difficulty. For them, Dionysus was precisely the god of the theatre, and the democratic Athenians had a special relationship with theatre, a genre they had pioneered. It was OK to have a good-natured belly-laugh at him, as in Aristophanes's ultra-successful comedy *Frogs*, in which he is portrayed as a lily livered, workshy coward, and a theatrical ignoramus to boot. But how could it be good to contemplate the Dionysus/Bacchus of the *Bacchae* – except so as to thank heaven that good respectable Athenian women (citizen wives, daughters and sisters), and regular Athenian Dionysiac cult worship, were not at all like *that*.

Of the three great fifth-century Athenian tragedians, the one whose plays on Theban themes have had the most lasting impact is Sophocles. His so-called 'Theban trilogy' was no such thing, as already explained, and the *Antigone*, which is now the most often performed and the most cherished, is in fact the earliest (see figure 9). Most ancient Greek plays were named after their Chorus – the *Suppliant Women*, the *Bacchae* and so on. Occasionally, they might be named after the lead male character, as in the *Oedipus* plays, for example. But to name a play after its lead female character – as in the *Antigone*, or Aristophanes's victorious *Lysistrata* of 411, the first known such comedy – was by itself to be making a point. What then was Sophocles's point?

Critics differ, often quite violently. What's in a name? *Lysi-strata* ('she who dissolves the army') puns on the real-life Athenian high priestess Lysi-mache ('she who dissolves the battle'). Antigone can likewise be deconstructed to mean *anti* (against, instead of) *gonê* (generation, procreation). Partly from fate, partly from her own choice, the Theban Antigone of myth-theatre was denied the opportunity or even the right afforded to all free Greek citizen females almost by definition, namely that of transitioning from girl or virgin (*parthenos*) to lawfully wedded – and deflowered – wife (*gunê*) and mother. It was very revealing of the Greek (patriarchal male Greek) mentality that the same word *gunê* served for both '(adult) woman' and 'wife', as *femme* does in French.

It is Antigone's status as a *parthenos*, still under the full legal control of her 'lord and master' (*kurios*) uncle Creon (her original *kurios*, her father/half-brother Oedipus, being dead), that makes her behaviour – her precisely political, oppositionist stand – quite so extraordinary. (And, I would add, in strictly realistic, contemporary human political terms, extremely unlikely, if not implausible or even incredible.)

In historical Greece at any rate, it seems that it was normal for adolescent, pubescent and therefore nubile Greek citizen females to be married off, by their father or other male guardian, as soon as was decent and practicable after menarche (puberty), which seems typically to have occurred around the age of 14 or 15. The marriage was strictly an economic contract (*engyê*), concluded between the betrother and the father/guardian of the intended groom, in which the girl in question or at stake had no formal, let alone legal say. Antigone had indeed been so affianced, or engaged, by Oedipus, her legal as well as natural father, to her cousin Haemon, the son of her maternal uncle Creon. Such first-cousin marriages were perfectly normal and regular in historical Athens and presumably also in Thebes, as a way of maintaining economic continuity and emotional solidarity within families. So far, so familiar. But of course Antigone is not a normal, let alone a girl-next-door fifth-century BCE sort of Athenian or Theban girl. She is a princess born to a man who is both her father and her half-brother, in a dim and distant past time, in an alien place of lore and yore. Considerable suspension of disbelief was therefore required on the part of the audience, if they were to approach her behaviour in anything like realistic terms.

And so here we must make a huge allowance for artistic, creative licence on the part of the dramatist. That in itself would not have been utterly unprecedented: in 458 (seventeen or so years earlier) Aeschylus in the *Agamemnon* had significantly manipulated the myth of the murder of Agamemnon upon his return home from Troy, both by placing his palatial seat in Argos – not Homer's Mycenae – and by having him murdered by his adulterous Spartan wife Clytemnestra and not (as in Homer) by her adulterous lover Aegisthus. All the same, Antigone's behaviour in *Antigone* does seem to have stretched the norms of credulity even further than that – for anyone, let alone a *parthenos*, even a royal one.

The plot, in brief, is as follows. Oedipus's crimes against humanity and convention have been horribly exposed and expiated, and he has departed into exile (and died there). Oedipus's two sons, Eteocles and Polyneices, have taken over the helm of the ship of state but fallen out spectacularly on the bridge. Polyneices has also gone into exile, but has adopted the highly risky strategy of calling upon six comrades, champions from other Greek cities, to join him in a war upon Eteocles – and Thebes. Which was of course also therefore a civil war (*stasis* in Greek) – something that Herodotus was to abhor as being much worse than a united war of one unified city against foreign attackers, something for him as much worse indeed as war is itself worse than peace.

That it was a civil war is exemplified dramatically – both literally and in terms of its emotional impact – when Eteocles and Poyneices actually kill each other. Creon, brother of Oedipus's late mother/wife Jocasta, takes over the reins of power, and as self-styled legitimate ruler of Thebes issues a decree which he declares to be universally binding on all Thebans, including immediate family members: Eteocles may be given due burial, but Polyneices, since he died as a traitor, shall be denied proper ritual obsequies, the penalty for disobedience of this edict being an instant and indefeasible sentence of death.

Which is where Antigone comes in, with a vengeance. Failing to persuade her more timid – or from one point of view, law-abiding – sister Ismene (a good Theban name) to join with her, she unilaterally steals outside the walls of Thebes to perform the absolutely minimal form of ritual burial, the sprinkling of some dust on the bloodied, decomposing, dog-eaten corpse of Polyneices. That is where the action of the play starts, with the discovery and deliberately comic reportage by a very ordinary Theban guard of what appears to be the act of burial.

So, one aspect of one reading of the play's message – which can be usefully interpreted by way of a series of mutually exclusive, binary polar cultural oppositions (Greeks were fond of those) – is that what is at stake fundamentally is the opposition between the woman/female-centred family and the male-dominated, masculinist public organs of state. Another way of putting that is to see it in more philosophical terms, as an opposition of divinely approved and sanctioned custom or convention (one sense of *nomos*) to a formally sacrilegious human *diktat* (another sense of *nomos* as 'law').

Except that it's clearly important – to Sophocles – that Antigone is female, because the precise way in which Creon reacts against his niece Antigone, when he discovers that it is *she* who has so flagrantly broken *his* law, is to say how dare *she* take against *him*, a man? Moreover, after Creon automatically condemns Antigone to a horrible death – he doesn't actually have her murdered outright, not wishing to incur the divine pollution (*miasma*) and fury of the avenging Furies that would arise from the slaughter of a *parthenos*, especially of one related by blood (compare Iphigenia, butchered by her father Agamemnon in the Troy cycle) – he has her immured so as to starve her to death. Antigone, however, anticipates that horrible fate by literally taking her life in her own hands and killing herself, recovering agency at the last.

Sophocles's *Oedipus Tyrannus* was, it is usually thought, first performed in the Theatre of Dionysus in 430 or 429. What a moment: the Atheno-Peloponnesian War had broken out in 431, Athens had been under siege once or twice from Sparta, and then – to cap it all – Athens had been struck by the devastating plague which took the lives of a third of its citizen population, well over 10,000 souls in all. Athenian audiences were already, like all Greeks, very familiar with a virtual plague – the one that afflicted Homer's Greeks in the tenth year of their besieging Troy, as related right at the start of the *Iliad*. They will not therefore have found it startlingly novel to be told at the beginning of *Oedipus Tyrannus* that Thebes is suffering a plague inflicted by Hera through the medium of the monstrous bird-woman Sphinx.

But the plague afflicting the audience in real life will have given that literary-dramatic scenario a particular resonance and relevance, and it will – surely – also have prompted them to start drawing comparisons and analogies between the situation of Thebes in distant mythical times and the situation of their own Athens in the very present circumstances of 430/429. In particular, perhaps, between the situation of Oedipus and the situation of their leading statesman, Pericles, whose aristocratic family, the Alcmaeonids, already laboured under an inherited curse and so, to the most pious Greek eyes, could even be viewed as polluted. (The inordinately pious Spartans in 432/1 certainly thought it was worth urging the Athenians to expel the 'accursed' – meaning Pericles.) Like Oedipus, Pericles was highly intelligent – but was he perhaps too clever by half, too clever for his own and the Athenians' good?

Sophocles is often thought to be the least 'political' of the big three Athenian tragedians, at any rate in the sense that none of his plays lends itself straightforwardly to a specifically political, above all democratic reading, as for example the 458 BCE *Oresteia* trilogy of Aeschylus does. But of the three he was actually the most directly politically engaged, as an Athenian citizen. By 440 he had served as an elected imperial treasurer, meaning that he was quite wealthy, and almost thirty years later, when aged over eighty, he was again elected to high office, this time to serve on an Emergency Security Committee at a time of extreme anti-democratic, pro-oligarchic crisis. You couldn't accuse Sophocles of shirking his public duties, as you could – and many did – accuse the philosopher Socrates. On the other hand, you could, as his son was moved to do, accuse Sophocles in extreme old age of legal incompetence, of a form of dementia: to which Sophocles replied devastatingly by quoting from what would prove to be his last play, the *Oedipus at Colonus*.

But if Euripides's Athens in *Suppliant Women* had been a full-on radical democracy, Sophocles's Athens in the *Oedipus at Colonus* was far less loaded politically, at least in terms of regime definition and contrast. In respect of space both physical and mental it packed a considerable punch, as well as being subtly autobiographical. For Colonus was Sophocles's own real-life deme (ward, parish, village). It was located just outside the city walls, which is why in 411 the extreme firebrand oligarchic counter-revolutionaries led by wily master-rhetorician Antiphon had chosen it as the location for an irregular, extraordinary meeting of the Assembly from which, de facto, the majority of ordinary poor Athenian citizens had been excluded.

This packed Assembly had duly passed the one motion put to it – to suspend the democratic constitution. Shortly thereafter the '400' ultras, with the aid of targeted violence by a bunch of paid 'Hellenic' thugs, seized ultra-oligarchic power and for four months made a ruin of the past century or so of democratic, egalitarian and free political progress. Eventually, after enduring two more bouts of oligarchic rule, one far more intense than the other, as well as total defeat by the major foreign Greek power, the partial disintegration of its civic territory, and ultimately civil war, Athens reconciled itself with difficulty to living in some simulacrum of domestic harmony from 403 on.

Thus, by making Oedipus breathe his last at Colonus, guided by an endearingly dutiful and, by Greek male standards, much more typically feminine Antigone, and by having the Athenians establish here a hero-cult to honour Oedipus as a civic benefactor, Sophocles helped both to detoxify Colonus and to detoxify the memory of polluted, patricidal, incestuous Oedipus at a stroke of his stylus or quill. By introducing good king Theseus, moreover, in characteristic reconciliatory regal mode, Sophocles may also have hoped to contribute to the eventual reconciliation of Athens and Thebes, something which did actually happen within a couple of years of his death (he died in 406/5).

He could not of course have known that the play would be staged, by his son, in 401, but that turned out to be another stroke of political genius, since it was in that year that Eleusis (the deme of Aeschylus) was restored, after two years of oligarchic bloodletting and resistant occupation, to its status as a full component of the Athenian democratic state. Together with Eleusis there returned also the vital sanctuary and cult of Demeter and Kore (the location, as noted, of Euripides's *Suppliant Women*). Most Athenian citizens male and female were themselves initiated in the Eleusinian Mysteries, which explains why one of the two choruses of Aristophanes's hit comedy *Frogs* of 405 BCE (re-staged, uniquely, in 404) was composed of such (male) initiates. Indeed, the Mysteries attracted Greek speakers from all over Hellas, and the Athenian democratic *polis* went to great lengths to supervise and control the cult for the city's economic as well as spiritual benefit.

As we shall see, after Thebes the city had been physically as well as politically resurrected in 316 BCE, one of the revived Thebans' very first acts was to pay posthumous homage to one of their greatest sons, who had by then been dead for getting on for a century. We don't know exactly when Pronomus lived, but 'late or later fifth century' will not be far wrong, and there is one contemporary or near-contemporary artefact which almost certainly alludes to him – it is known as the Pronomus Vase. This vase is sufficiently important to the cultural and musical history of ancient Greece, and indeed western civilization as a whole, for it to have been made the subject of an entire collective volume published by a major university press.

Tragedy and satyr-drama in Athens were accompanied by music that was composed by the dramatist himself, and played by a professional on the reeded instrument called an *aulos*. The usual English translation of 'flute' is misleading, since it probably sounded more like an oboe – or rather double-oboe, since it was usually a double 'pipe'. The noun for an *aulos*-player was *aulêtês*, and that is what our Pronomus professionally was. His given name means 'for *nomos*', which could mean 'mode' in the musical sense (as used in the *Agamemnon* of Aeschylus) as well as meaning custom/convention and law.

The *aulos* had a fundamentally religious connotation, hence its use for the religiously inflected drama in Athens (though it was also used to help trireme oarsmen keep time). So much so that Thucydides, when in the context of the battle of Mantinea (418) he was describing how Spartan armies marched rhythmically and slowly into battle to the sound of *auloi* (what John Milton transcribed and transposed as 'flutes and soft recorders'), had to go out of his way to point out that this was not – unlike many other of the Spartans' practices in regard to warfare, of which they were, as Xenophon observed, the past masters – a matter of religion. It was simply and solely a matter of urgent military practicality, since it was designed to help the Spartans' phalanx to keep in step immediately before engaging and thus retain its maximum cohesiveness and concentrated force when it crashed into the opposing phalanx, as at the battle of Mantinea itself, which the Spartans triumphantly won.

Just as the Spartans were the greatest military stars of Greece at that time, so Pronomus was in his day the greatest musician of Hellenic antiquity, a Theban cultural icon. He came from a dynasty of musicians, both his father and his son Oeniadas being champion *auletai*. He was the first to be able to play the three harmonies or modes known ethnically as the Dorian, the Phrygian, and the Lydian on one and the same, enhanced (double) *aulos*; and in an epigram that his Theban compatriots joyfully resurrected at the end of the fourth century he was hailed as the hero in whose honour and name 'Greece [Hellas] awarded to Thebes the victory in *aulos*-playing', a magniloquent if metaphorical boast. Possibly in his lifetime or possibly just after, in *c.* 400 BCE, a craftsman potter-painter working in the Cerameicus district of Athens (the Potters' Quarter) produced a simply magnificent volute *krater* (a rare version of this type of wine-mixing bowl) in the red-figure technique and style. On it – among the huge number of other figures – is depicted an *aulos*-player labelled 'Pronomus'. This is the famous Pronomus Vase (see figure 10).

Like so many other intact Athenian pots or vases of this general period, the Pronomus Vase was not found in Athens. It was exported and buried in a grave in southern Italy, at Ruvo in Puglia, in Italy's heel, where it was unearthed in 1835; it now graces the Naples Archaeological Museum. Altogether, no fewer than thirty-one divine and human figures are painted in a continuous frieze around the vase's two sides: that is, Dionysus, patron of drama, and his Cretan partner, princess Ariadne (daughter of King Minos), rescued by him from the island of Naxos where Theseus the cad had dumped her, together with a female attendant (possibly representing Tragedy, the divinity of tragedy, herself); plus twenty-eight 'theatricals' of various sorts – the playwright called Demetrius, costumed actors, and the costumed chorus of the play(s) in question, together with perhaps its impresario (*choregos*) called Charinus (depicted holding a lyre).

The play or plays being performed were of the satyr-drama genre – of which we have extant just the one more or less complete example, the *Cyclops* ascribed to Euripides (named for the one-eyed monster giant whom 'No Man' Odysseus successfully confronted and blinded), and one substantial fragment preserved on an Egyptian papyrus, the *Trackers* (*Ichneutai*) of Sophocles – which English poet-dramatist Tony Harrison incorporated in his masterfully updated and transposed *The Trackers of Oxyrhynchus*. Most painters who chose to depict theatrical scenes elected to paint particular moments from well-known tragedies (or comedies): see figure 8. This vase, then, is really rather special.

Our painter, moreover, has decided to depict not a dramatic scene but a dramatic triumph, possibly at the very moment the jury's decision was announced to the assembled masses. (A random jury of ordinary citizens was selected on the day to vote the winners and rank-order the losers. Their decisions were not necessarily purely aesthetic, but might be seriously swayed by such extra-dramatic considerations as the generosity or otherwise of the impresario in his spending on costumes, scenery and other paraphernalia.) His vase should therefore not be taken to be and be read as (merely) a photographic snapshot of any one actual performance or victory, but as more of a generic reflection on and celebration of theatricality and theatrical representation as a whole. It is particularly pleasant to record that it is a highly cultured Theban (almost certainly) who takes central place in this unique representation and has given his name to a treasured ancient Greek artefact.

Another, rather earlier fifth-century Athenian artistic treasure with a specifically Theban connection is the Sphinx Vase attributed to the accomplished Athens-based vase-painter known as the Sotades Painter. He, together with (unless he is one and the same) the craftsman Sotades, who modelled the plastic vase in the shape of the Sphinx, between them created this minor masterpiece. It forms a key link in the chain of tradition and reception both ancient and modern of Thebes. Study of the history of ancient Greek vase painting and consideration of the peculiarly modern practices of classical archaeology and classical art-collection and curation coalesce here to throw an exceptionally bright light on the Thebes of Myth.

The Sphinx Vase (figure 20) was found in an extraordinarily lavish tomb at Capua in Campania, southern Italy, loaded as it was with imported Greek fineware that had clearly appealed to the occupant's educated tastes. It had been made in c. 470–450 BCE in Athens, no doubt in the Cerameicus, using the naturalistic red-figure technique, and then exported as a luxury good, eventually to enhance a non-Greek's funerary accoutrements. We are dealing here with 'the' Sphinx (capital 'S'), not 'a' sphinx, because this is the specifically Theban Sphinx celebrated contemporaneously in Athenian tragic drama: for example, Sophocles's *Oedipus Tyrannus* was performed some twenty years later (see above).

The Sotades Painter's activity belongs in the thirty or so years after the Graeco-Persian Wars, so this plastic vase comes at the end of his brilliantly original and experimental career. There are many ways of 'reading' Athenian painted pottery, one of which is to understand such an object as a work of 'art', not just as a purely functional grave-good, and to situate that artwork as a document of a whole culture or civilization. That approach seems especially productive here, since the scenes and images depicted around the neck of the vase (a *rhyton* for pouring wine) behind and above the Sphinx's head seem to be specifically, peculiarly Athenian in their mythology – and yet, *via* the Theban connections of the Sphinx's myth, have a wider both Theban and indeed Hellenic resonance.

The *rhyton* shape is the first clue to its social function both pre-
and during burial: it is the sort of vessel that would have been used
at an expensive banquet, whether a living banquet or a funerary
feast, of the type the Greeks called a *sumposion* or 'drinking together'.
The three *gorgoneia*, images of the petrifactory Gorgon Medusa,
confirm the connection with death and burial, but add a further
apotropaic dimension. That is, by invoking the power of the Gorgon,
the commissioner or purchaser of the vase, and/or his kindred buriers,
seek to 'turn away' forces of evil that might cause this death and
burial to generate pollution (*miasma*).

This function, together with a possible extra dimension of guard-
ianship or protection of the buried dead, explains the widespread
adoption of the sphinx in Athens and elsewhere as a funerary symbol
par excellence. Yet other dimensions may be and have been invoked
to account for the symbolic associations of the sphinx, for instance
those of boundary and taboo. Altogether, this is a quite exceptionally
rich and revelatory art-object, for which Thebes, mythical Thebes,
served as the fount and origin.

Another such is a fragmentary *askos* (imitation goatskin) terracotta vase very recently (2012) excavated in Thebes itself. It too was
made in Athens, in the mid-fourth century BCE, and has been attributed to the workshop of the Cleophon Painter (a modern name).
But it was found in the area of and in possible original association
with the temple of Apollo Ismenius. It shows not one but two
sphinxes, who are being confronted by two mortal men.

It has been quite plausibly suggested that behind this lies an
original Theban version of the myth of Oedipus and the (one) Sphinx,
according to which Oedipus didn't just solve her riddle but also
killed her. The further notion that the vase was a bespoke commission by a Theban customer is also formally unprovable but in the
best sense suggestive. It reminds us that for the Greeks, myths were
not set in stone but malleable and pliable traditional tales, almost
infinitely extensible and adaptable to suit taste and circumstance.

CHAPTER 8

The Peloponnesian and Corinthian Wars

The (Atheno-)Peloponnesian War (431–404 BCE) was for the ancient Greeks the equivalent of a world war. It lasted for a whole generation, caused untold destruction of both human lives and property, and left deep and lasting scars both physical and psychological. Some six centuries later, the Greek travel writer and pilgrim Pausanias, looking back from the vantage point of imperial (Roman) Greece, likened its effects to that of a severe earthquake that had shaken a previously stable world decisively off balance. But not everything about it was all bad: the war found its historian in its contemporary and – barely – survivor, Thucydides son of Olorus of Athens, whose 'possession for ever' creation is still a living presence (see also Chapter 1.)

It is largely due to him that the war is usually referred to as 'the Peloponnesian War', in other words as the war against the Peloponnesians as seen from an Athenian angle. But Thucydides himself called it 'the war of the Peloponnesians and the Athenians'. Even that title, however, is a little misleading, since his 'Peloponnesians' is shorthand for 'Sparta and its allies, both those of its Peloponnesian League and others'. Besides, to paraphrase Voltaire on the Holy Roman Empire, Sparta's Peloponnesian League alliance was not either (just) Peloponnesian or a League. It was not solely Peloponnesian in a geographical sense, since it included members from outside the Peloponnese, such as Aegina and Thebes. (Or rather 'the Boeotians', since Thebes joined, in or after 447, as the leading member of the Boeotian federal state.) And it was not a league in the complete sense, since Peloponnesian League members were not necessarily allied to each other, but rather each member state was allied individually to Sparta.

Sparta was the League's overall *hegemon* or 'leader'. To summarize, the alliance was technically a *summachia*, that is, a fully offensive and defensive alliance under the terms of which each ally swore a religious oath to have the 'same friends and enemies' as the Spartans, and to 'follow the Spartans whithersoever they might lead them', on condition that any joint League initiative had both to be proposed by Sparta (who could not be committed to an initiative it opposed) and to be ratified by a majority vote of allied delegates at a conference that only Sparta could convene (see also Chapter 5). The only recorded exception to that rule of following the Spartans' lead is when an ally might legitimately invoke a prior and conflicting religious obligation.

Unlike in the Athenians' mainly naval 'Delian League' alliance, there was no financial obligation on member-states, no money tribute for allies to pay annually. But if and when a joint campaign was agreed, then it was for the Spartans to decide what military contribution the individual allies were respectively to make (e.g., what percentage of their total available troops), for the Spartans to appoint Spartan officers to command the allied contingents, and for the Spartans to decide which of their two kings would serve as overall commander-in-chief. After the 505/4 debacle, the Spartans passed a law forbidding both of its kings to be simultaneously in joint command of one and the same army.

Of course, this chapter revisits the Atheno-Peloponnesian War from a specifically Theban angle rather than attempting a comprehensive and balanced overview of an exceptionally long, complicated and game-changing episode in ancient Greek history. But as it happens, the interventions by Thebes were made typically at major pressure-points, for example, at its very start. So a Theban perspective actually does often shed powerful light on the war overall.

The old problems of why the Atheno-Peloponnesian War – or wars – broke out, in 431 BCE, and of which side was really or chiefly responsible for the outbreak, have had a recent infusion of oxygen from Graham Allison's coinage of the phrase 'the Thucydides trap'. This notion, which postulates that an established power will be tempted, perhaps irresistibly, even 'inevitably', to go to war in an attempt to nip in the bud any rising power that threatens it (for example, the United States and China today and in the foreseeable future) has been applied or rather misapplied to relations between Sparta and Athens between the 470s and the 430s, and used – quite wrongly – to 'explain' the war's outbreak. But by 431 both those powers – each of them had substantial permanent alliances behind them, if of very different kinds – had definitively and long since 'risen'. Arguably, it was the older-established of the two alliances (the Spartan) that felt the more threatened by the other, and Sparta that started the war – that is, made the difference as to whether or not there would be a war at all (it did not in fact make the first attacking move). But the war was in no sense 'inevitable', and Thucydides does not say that it was.

I wrote 'arguably' above, meaning that those positions can be argued for – but also argued against. My own opinion, for what it is worth, is that Thucydides's repeated statements of his own view in different words are correctly to be interpreted as arguing for both those positions. Legally, in terms of the formal sworn treaty relations between the two sides before the outbreak of war, the framework was set by a lengthy accord – technically a truce (*spondai*) rather than a peace (*eirene*) – concluded between them in 446/5. Sparta's mainly land-based alliance swore to respect what Athens's mainly naval alliance 'had' or 'held', and the Athenians' alliance swore vice versa – provided that, if either side wished to submit matters of difference or grounds of complaint to neutral, third-party arbitration, they could do so (though the identity of any potential arbitrator was unfortunately not specified). This was, in short, a bipolar stitch-up of the eastern Mediterranean, Aegean Greek world, in which subordinate allies on either side in practice had very little say or room for manoeuvre.

The treaty, like all Greek treaties, was formally a religious instrument, sworn in the name of the gods, goddesses, heroes and heroines who would act as guarantors and punish any breaches appropriately as sacrilegious perjury. It was supposed to last for thirty years in the first instance – hence its usual name, the Thirty Years' Peace. But in fact it lasted for only about fourteen. For in 432/1 the Spartans, after first deciding their own view by a vote of their Assembly, and then calling a congress of the Peloponnesian League allies in Sparta to ratify their decision, also done by majority vote, declared to the Athenians that the treaty was null and void, since in their view the Athenians had breached it. After sending three ultimatums via envoys to the Athenians, all rejected outright, the Spartans further declared that they considered a state of war to exist.

Various Spartan allies, especially Corinth, Megara and Aegina, also had urgent grounds of complaint against Athens that they wished the Spartans to act upon. Thucydides, however, was surely right that it was not so much these relatively minor treaty breaches as the Spartans' strategic fear for the future solidarity of their alliance under Athenian pressure, and the consequences that might ensue should their alliance break up in terms of loss of control of its home base of Helots, that really determined their decision to go to war, on their own rather than their allies' account. The Spartans were careful to request the support of the divine authority of Apollo of Delphi, which was indeed forthcoming, but even they themselves acknowledged much later that formal legal right had not been entirely or unchallengeably on their side.

The war began in 431, though it was not the Spartans but their Boeotian allies led by Thebes who made the first aggressive move. It was an attack by Thebes upon the hated Plataea, ethnically Boeotian but an Athenian ally, that officially marked the outbreak of hostilities. Thucydides is very careful to date it in accordance with all the relevant Greek calendars. Only thereafter, in late spring/early summer

431, did the Spartans mount the first of several large overland expeditions against Attica and Athens, thereby implementing what they thought would be the strategy most likely to force the Athenians to capitulate soonest, in at most three campaigning seasons. The idea was that either the Athenians would forgo their grain harvest and so eventually starve, or they would feel compelled to come out and fight – and lose. Actually, as with the short 446/5 Peace, the Spartans' sense of timing in their strategic expectations in 431 was going to be falsified very badly indeed, as we shall see.

Thucydides, in describing this first campaigning season, is at his alert best, giving lots of graphic and memorable detail of the Thebans' assault on Plataea. He says that the attack party numbered some 300 or more men under the command of a federal Boeotarch called Pythangelus son of Phyleides and one other. Presumably both were Thebans. What sticks in the memory is how the attackers' feet stuck in the rain-sodden mud. Also that, as so often, it was betrayal from within by a pro-Theban faction in cahoots with one of the most powerful Thebans of the time, Eurymachus son of Leontiadas, rather than technical expertise or ingenuity in siegecraft, that rendered the Thebans' siege and assault initially successful.

However, an unexpected reversal ensued, something to Thucydides's general taste as he considered this to be a normal feature of wartime, and the Plataeans were able to turn the tables on the Theban attackers once they realized how few they were. Free, Athenian-allied Plataea thus lived to fight another day. In 427/6, however, the Thebans at long last achieved a cherished aim, with direct and powerful Spartan encouragement and facilitation. If they could not persuade the Plataeans, who were ethnic Boeotians, to abandon their alliance with Athens (concluded as long ago as 519, and lying behind the remarkable co-operation between those two cities at Marathon in 490 and later), then they must at least see to it that their city was destroyed.

But first they had to capture it, and this was to take the Spartans and Thebans two whole years and three whole campaigning seasons, from 429 to 427. At last, in summer 427, the Plataeans – on the verge of starvation – were compelled to surrender. Thucydides considered this Plataean episode of pivotal importance. Not only does he give an exceptionally detailed account of the mechanics of the siege, involving tunnelling and counter-tunnelling, and the invention of quite complicated flame-throwers and other mechanical devices, but, once the siege had been concluded successfully, he wrote up full-scale speeches for Plataean and Theban representatives to deliver and counter-deliver before a panel of Spartan 'judges', to which we shall shortly return. One reason for according the episode quite this degree of space and attention was that the Athenians seem to have prized their relationship with Plataea almost as much as the Plataeans did theirs with Athens. This was partly for pragmatic – strategic, geopolitical – reasons, but only partly. What lay behind it all was Plataea's simply huge symbolic significance, for all Greeks and for Hellenism as such, as the site of the decisive battle against the Persians in 479, and as one of the major sites, along with Delphi and Olympia, of commemoration of that victory – a commemoration annually repeated in a religious ritual.

To return to the debate and the Spartans' judgement, as presented most artfully by Thucydides (*History*, Book 3, chapters 53–68). He says that it was not originally intended by the Spartans to be a debate, only the Thebans chose to make it so. In accordance with his normal practice, Thucydides attributes the two speeches – that he himself of course wrote up – to 'the Plataeans' and to 'the Thebans' respectively. This is to convey the point that these are the official manifestos of the two contending cities, rather than random, individualistic takes on the matters at stake. However, whereas the Theban speaker(s) are cited only generically as such, he gives the names of the two men whom the Plataean survivors chose to speak for them: Astymachus ('battler for the city') son of Asopolaus ('Asopus – people') and Lacon son of Aeimnestus ('Ever-remembered'). But both men cannot both have spoken, at least not at once.

Thucydides was making a particular point in naming the latter, at least, since he adds that Lacon was the *proxenos*, the official diplomatic representative, of the Spartans in his native Plataea. What he did not feel he needed to spell out for his original Greek readership was that Lacon's father Aeimnestus had named his son literally 'Spartan'. Clearly, the Plataeans believed not unreasonably that Lacon was just the right person to present a convincing reply to the one, impossibly leading question that 'the Spartans' (it is not specified which Spartans precisely) put to the Plataeans: have you, in the course of the present conflict, done anything to benefit the Spartans and their allies?

'The Plataeans' in Thucydides begin forensically by saying they are surprised to find themselves effectively on trial rather than taking part in a more conventional post-battle procedure, and on trial moreover before prejudiced judges who have asked them a single, unfair question, on the answer to which hangs their life or death, an answer they already know. They also plead that they have no new evidence to adduce. They begin their 'defence' positively, therefore, with the more distant past, by rehearsing their good deeds in the great events of the Graeco-Persian Wars (though they tactfully do not go as far back as 490, when they assisted the Athenians at Marathon, in a victorious battle for which the Spartans turned up too late). In a dig at the Thebans, they state, 'We alone of the Boeotians joined the earlier struggle for the freedom of Hellas.' By contrast, as they later state, they had had their name inscribed on the official victory-monument – the so-called bronze Serpent Column set up by the Spartans themselves at Delphi (now in the ancient hippodrome at Constantinople, today's Istanbul, whither it was removed by Byzantine Emperor Constantine in the early fourth century CE).

This reference has a further, rather more subtle point too: in 480/479 the Plataeans had formed part of the 'Hellenic' alliance concluded in 481, within the framework of which Sparta had led the Greek resistance to Persia. That alliance had never formally been abrogated, although the Spartans in 477 had given up leading it in any positive, aggressive way, and had ceded that role to the quite separate, Athens-led Delian League alliance formed earlier that year. The Plataeans now claim that it was under the terms of that alliance that, in about 464, when the Spartans' Helots of Laconia and Messenia rose up in a great rebellion and the Spartans called on allies for aid in repressing it, they – like the Athenians – responded to the call with military aid. Indeed, they claim that they sent no less than one-third of their hoplite fighting men. (The Athenians sent 4,000 hoplites, which was roughly the same proportion.) And, they add, it was not they who had broken that anti-Persian 'peace'. (The Spartans had summarily dismissed Cimon and his troops, fearing, so Thucydides reports, that the Athenians were showing alarming sympathy for the Helots' liberationist cause.)

Then, more riskily and strictly irrelevantly, they track back even further in time, to the circumstances in which they broke with Thebes and the Boeotians in 519 and allied themselves with Athens, and so became Sparta's enemies. It was – of course – all the Spartans' fault. When the Plataeans had asked Sparta for an alliance to help them resist what they call the Thebans' 'violent oppression', it was the Spartans who'd advised them to ally with Athens, which they did. Why then had they not broken with the Athenians since? Because the Athenians had treated them with honour, and indeed granted them special (Athenian) citizenship privileges, so that to break off their alliance would have been dishonourable.

They then turn to the attack – against the Thebans. Many are the outrages the Thebans have committed against them, they say, the assault on their city in 431 and then the siege of 429–427 being merely the most recent. The Thebans, moreover, had attacked them in peacetime – arguably: this is a reference to the Thirty Years' Peace/ Truce of 446/5; and that in itself was a sacrilege, since that treaty had been sworn in the names of the gods. Besides, the Thebans had compounded their crime by attacking Plataea on a day that was itself holy, so that the Plataeans in resisting were carrying out an inexorable sacred duty.

This invocation of religion was calculated to appeal to the sensibilities and sensitivities of the pious Spartans. But their attack on the Thebans' misdeeds is, rather surprisingly, brief. Painfully aware that, in the end, what the Spartans will weigh up is the balance between their own immediate and future pragmatic, military-political interests on the one hand, and considerations of honour on the other, and apparently all too aware that the balance was most likely to tip in favour of the former, the Plataeans spend most of the rest of their 'speech' banging on about honour – about what they have done to deserve to be treated with honour, and what the Spartans should do if they are to act honourably and to decide the issue in such a way as to incur honour and a high reputation rather than shame.

They therefore return to the honour that they claim is their due for the role they played in 480/479. But they add a couple more arguments, both religious, and both in the service of the broadest claim of all. The first religious argument is that, as the anti-Persian alliance was concluded and conducted in the name of the gods, so for the gods' sake the Spartans should now support them against the Thebans – regardless of any considerations of mere self-interest or sense of obligation to their current allies. Second, and even more emotively, they point to – perhaps literally – the tombs and other memorials not only of their own ancestors but of the Spartans' ancestors too. These are the tombs and memorials which, they say, they still tend observantly and regularly as the Spartans' 'friends' (another allusion to the Hellenic alliance of 481).

Those two arguments are deployed to subserve what the Plataeans hope will be their 'killer' defence. If the Spartans decide to put the Plataeans to death as enemies, and 'make the land of Plataea a part of Thebes', they will be 'enslaving the land in which the Greeks won their freedom'. 'Freedom' was precisely the slogan under which the Spartans had declared in 432/1 that they would be warring against the Athenians, to liberate the Athenians' allies from Athenian imperial tyranny. How good would it look, how would it enhance the Spartans' honour and reputation, if they committed such a heinously contradictory act?

Finally, in their peroration, the Plataeans present themselves to the Spartans as suppliants, throwing themselves on the Spartans' mercy both in the name of universal justice and as 'the most devoted supporters of the Hellenic cause'. This was not the first time the Spartans had been so appealed to – the Samians had done the same in the 520s, with success. But that was then, and the circumstances of 427 were incommensurably different.

'The Thebans', according to Thucydides, were sufficiently alarmed by the potential persuasiveness of such emotional arguments to request from the Spartans a right of reply, which was duly granted, thereby turning the exchange formally into an antithetical debate – what the Greeks called an *antilogia* or *agon* ('contest'). They begin (in the Thucydidean version) captiously, with a sly allusion to the Spartans' eponymously 'laconic' mode of utterance: they not only state the obvious – the Plataeans have not answered the Spartans' question – but also complain about the length as well as the irrelevance of their opponents' self-defence.

They then open their counter-attack with a remarkable and highly questionable assertion. Whereas the Plataeans had traced the origins of their enmity with the Thebans no further back than 519 BCE, the Thebans claim that it had existed from the very foundation of Plataea as a city, a foundation for which they, the Thebans, were allegedly responsible. In other words, as in the dispute between Corinth and Corcyra in the mid- to late 430s, which Thucydides had also chosen to write up in the form of an agonistic antilogy (in Book 1), Thebes is presenting itself here as a *metropolis* (founding mother-city) being wronged by its daughter 'colony' (*apoikia*). (Actually, as we saw, being a founding mother-city was not something the Thebans had ever been.) The ongoing relationship between a *metropolis* and a colony was not normally political in any pragmatic sense, but sentimental and religious. The Thebans therefore allege that, by allying with Athens and separating themselves off from the other Boeotians, the Plataeans had not only rejected the Thebans' leadership of Boeotia but also breached the universal, customary Greek honour code of respect and duty. The Theban speakers do rather spoil the effect, though, by saying that in establishing their Boeotian leadership they had had to use force rather than persuasion, 'driving out various mixed populations'. Boeotia for the Boeotians.

They next seek to spike the Plataeans' guns over their anti-Persian role. It was not principled hostility to Persia or devotion to Hellenism that had motivated the Plataeans, they counter, but 'only' their devotion to the Athenians. But the Thebans sensibly spend very little time on this argument, and only very briefly and later on do they address the Plataeans' claims based on their ritual tendance and commemoration of Hellenic war-graves. Instead, they attempt to disclaim or at any rate minimize responsibility for the medism of their own city in 480/79, a medism which had been officially punished by the Spartans.

Their exculpatory argument is that the city was not then a 'normal' polity, governed legally either under a regime of democracy or what they call *isonomos* oligarchy. (By the latter they must mean something like a moderate oligarchy, in which, although power was in the hands of the *oligoi*, the rich few, equality under the laws was practised as a maxim of governance. By implication, that is the sort of oligarchy that Thebes itself was enjoying in 427.) In 480/479, they aver, Thebes had been in the hands of a *dunasteia*, a junta or small cabal, so that most 'ordinary' Thebans had had no say whatever in whether they fought for or against the Persians. That argument might have cut some ice with the Spartans, who themselves could be said to run an *isonomos* oligarchy at home, in 427. But, as Thucydides's original readers would have known, it would not have worked after 404/3, when the Spartans themselves imposed and propped up precisely a *dunasteia* in Athens, the regime of the so-called Thirty Tyrants, against which the Thebans actively campaigned.

Next, echoing the Spartans' own war propaganda, they accuse the Plataeans of guilt by association with the city – Athens – that, having helped to liberate Greece from the Persians, had since then turned to 'enslaving' it. This is a reference specifically to the way in which the Athenians had, after taking over from Sparta by consent the liberationist anti-Persian cause in the 470s, turned their attention from conducting more or less directly anti-Persian maritime activities to extending their 'empire' (*arche*) by land. The Thebans hyperbolically call this 'trying to bring under their control both the rest of Greece and our country', but it is 'our country', Boeotia, that they really have in mind, which the Athenians had indeed conquered and controlled between 457 and 447, and which the Thebans say they had 'liberated' at the battle of Coronea.

The Plataeans as Athens's devoted allies were clearly guilty by association in the eyes of the Thebans, but their guilt is represented as being more extensive. Turning the sworn Hellenic alliance argument back on the Plataeans, the Thebans argue that by being good allies of the Athenians in all their imperial ventures they had violated the Hellenic alliance oaths by helping the Athenians to 'enslave' the Aeginetans and other alliance members. This is a reference to the Athenians' conquest, depopulation and repopulation in 457 (the same year as the battle of Oenophyta) of the island-city of Aegina, which had kowtowed to Persia in the 490s but performed heroically against the Persian invaders at Salamis in 480. From the point of view of the Aeginetans, who were allies of Sparta within the Peloponnesian League alliance, that was indeed an act of 'enslavement', but whether the Plataeans had really had much actively to do with it is very doubtful.

The Thebans then turn to the more immediate circumstances, to their behaviour in and after 431. Interestingly, they had earlier admitted that a partial cause of the Athenians' successful occupation of Boeotia was the Boeotians' 'internal disputes', a veiled reference to the fact that in the 450s disagreements over governance within the cities had spilled over into disgreements over foreign policy, especially policy towards Athens. In 431, the Thebans are keen to point out, not all Plataeans had been pro-Athenian and anti-Theban. So far from attacking a uniformly hostile city, the Thebans had actually been invited in as 'friends' by 'good' Boeotians, that is, leading Plataeans of wealthy substance and aristocratic birth. They admit that the *demos*, the majority of citizens, had not invited them, but in terms of moral guilt, that in the Thebans' view was more than cancelled out by the Plataeans' outrageous murdering of Theban suppliants. (A sideswipe at the Plataeans' 'suppliants' argument.)

Responding to the Plataeans' claim that justice is on their own side, the Thebans wrap up with a litany of moralizing rhetoric, displaying envy, malevolence, hatefulness, hypocrisy and sophistry. In a nutshell, the burden of their counter-argument is that the Spartans are duty-bound to 'defend the law of the Greeks'.

Brutally, but with predictable laconic curtness, the Spartans – in Thucydides – merely repeat to the Plataeans their same original question. To which some few Plataeans apparently replied that they really were not anti-Spartan. But the majority, about 200 in all, admitted that they had indeed done nothing to benefit the Spartans and their allies in the present conflict, and so were put instantly to death. The Spartans also had killed twenty-five Athenians who had been caught up in the siege. The women survivors whom they had captured were not killed but sold abroad into slavery, a form of living death. To ram home the point about how important the alliance of the Plataeans with Athens was, Thucydides rounds off his account of the Thebes–Plataea episode thus: 'That was how events ended at Plataea, in the ninety-third year after they became allies of the Athenians.'

But that is not the end of this story, not by a long chalk. At first, the Spartans made over the site of Plataea to those (few) Plataean survivors who they agreed had indeed been pro-Spartan, together with some pro-Spartan exiles from Megara, another Peloponnesian League ally (with a special grievance against Athens). This situation continued for about a year, until in 426, at a time when the Spartans were intervening aggressively in Phocis and Thessaly to the north of Boeotia, they did to Plataea what the invading Persians had done to it in 480 – they razed the city to the ground. In some sort of attempt at religious compensation, they paid new honours to the goddess

Hera, constructing a new hostel beside her existing sanctuary, together with a new 100-foot-long stone temple.

The *chora*, the land of the *polis* of Plataea, they rented out to Theban tenants, which is a clue to the probable fact that this exceptionally brutal treatment of Plataea was meted out at the urgent insistence of the Thebans. At any rate, as Thucydides realistically and unsentimentally concluded, 'in almost every respect this Spartan hostility to the Plataeans was due to their desire to gratify the Thebans, since the Spartans believed that the Thebans might be useful to them at this juncture of the war'. Utility – not justice, not honour – was in the eyes of Thucydides the Spartans' overriding guiding principle of interstate policy.

Having achieved the physical elimination of Plataea, a couple of years later the Thebans inflicted a significant defeat upon Athens at Delium, although, as in 457, Athens had been the aggressor. This was a major pitched battle and as such needs to be put into the context of how the war had been waged on land in mainland Greece since 431.

Up until 425, the Spartans' chief war strategy had been to launch an invasion of Attica in early summer just before the main barley crop was ripe, knowing that, if the Athenians were to accept the challenge to come out and fight a full-scale battle in defence of their crops, the Spartans would surely win. Actually, that strategy was based on a grave miscalculation, since the Athenians relied on their navy and an unchallengeable control of the Aegean and the approaches to the Black Sea to ensure the regular importation of basic foodstuffs, especially bread wheat, from overseas. The longest invasion that the Spartans ever managed lasted for just forty days, almost six weeks. Nevertheless, even such an invasion did have an importantly negative impact on Athenian morale, and in 430 the Spartans were gifted an unexpected bonus in the form of the great plague (typhus?) that afflicted the city for several years and carried off perhaps as many as one-third of its citizens.

In exchange, however, the Athenians in 427 started to develop a new tactic of their own: the occupation of strategic positions either within the territory of a Spartan ally or, much more effectually, within Sparta's own *polis* territory. In 425, they struck a major such blow by occupying the islet of Sphacteria and the onshore settlement known alternatively as Pylus or Coryphasium on the south-west coast of Messenia. This was a *polis* in its own right, one of the fifty or so dependent Perioecic *poleis* of Laconia and Messenia, citizens of which were free Lacedaemonians within the Spartan *polis* but without any political rights or powers of decision in Sparta itself.

Sparta naturally had sent a taskforce to try to fend off the Athenian attack, but a garrison of 420 Lacedaemonians on Sphacteria made up jointly of Spartans and Perioeci had felt compelled to surrender to the Athenians under Cleon and Demosthenes rather than fight to the death – to the consternation of the Spartan authorities, and to the shock of many non-Spartans too. The Athenians thus, from 425 BCE onwards, had in their possession, imprisoned in the centre of Athens, 292 hostages (Thucydides is very precise), 120 of them Spartans, including some particularly eminent and prominent. That was the strategic background to the battle of Delium of 424.

The immediate circumstances of the battle illustrate a feature of the war that Thucydides says had become ever more prevalent since 427, namely, the ideological conflict in cities outside Athens and Sparta between pro-Athenian democrats and pro-Spartan oligarchs. For, according to Thucydides, it was an exiled pro-Athenian democrat from Thespiae called Ptoeodorus (gift of [Apollo] Ptoios) and some other like-minded Boeotians who had got into touch with the Athenians and invited them to invade – much as it allegedly had been pro-Theban Plataeans who had begun the Plataean affair of 431. From the point of view of loyalist, oligarchic Thespians, Ptoeodorus was guilty of 'atticism' (*attikismos*), being pro-Athenian, an ideologically loaded word formed along the same lines as 'medism' (being pro-Persian) and 'laconism' (being pro-Spartan).

Thucydides spells out that what Ptoeodorus and co. desired was not merely independence from Thebes but regime change at home:

'they wanted to change the form of government and turn it into a democracy *such as the Athenians had*' (my emphasis). As ideology, that was probably the right way to appeal to the Athenians for their military support, but as practical politics it was a nonsense. In 424, the Athenians had already been through at least one major political transformation, in the late 460s and 450s, that made their existing democracy even more democratic than it already was. The Thespians conceivably had enjoyed some form of democracy between 457 and 447, but that was by now a distant memory, and it would not have been feasible to introduce Athenian-style democracy lock, stock and smoking barrel in 424.

Delium was named for Apollo of the sacred isle of Delos (his birthplace); it possessed a celebrated sanctuary of that divinity, who was widely worshipped in Boeotia (Chapter 4). Delium lay on Boeotia's east coast, within the territory of Tanagra and about 1.5 km from the contested border region of Oropus. The aim of the Athenians' campaign, their major breakout effort by land since the war began, was at least to inflict a major set-piece defeat on one of Sparta's major allies, and possibly even to re-occupy all Boeotia, as they had done between 457 and 447, and thereby gain some revenge for their severe defeat at Coronea. We happen to know that the future major Athenian politician Alcibiades, now in his mid-twenties, was a combatant at Delium: his father had been killed at Coronea, and he had been brought up in the celebrity household of Pericles and his partner Aspasia.

Delium proved to be the biggest hoplite battle of the war so far, and is mainly significant for a number of tactical innovations that presage military developments of the post-war fourth century. The Athenians intended a co-ordinated pincer operation involving two of that year's board of ten generals: Demosthenes (who had been chiefly responsible for the Pylus success of the previous year) and Hippocrates (his name – a compound of *hippos*, horse, and *kratos*, power – suggests aristocratic origins). Demosthenes's force unfortunately arrived too late, and Hippocrates found himself compelled to face the Boeotian forces under their Theban general Pagondas alone. (Pagondas, probably a substantial landowner, has recently turned up on a legal document dealing with a property adjudication.)

As was conventional, the best troops on each side were stationed on the right wings of their respective lines, the Thebans thus forming the Boeotian right. In the Boeotians' centre were men from Haliartus, Coronea and Copae, and on their left troops from Thespiae, Tanagra and Orchomenus. The second most distinguished position in a Greek hoplite line was the extreme left, since the troops stationed there would be confronting the enemy's best fighters. It is estimated that Hippocrates had under him some 15,000 troops as opposed to Pagondas's 18,500, the largest number of whom were light-armed, the rest being some 7,000 hoplites and 1,000 of the cavalrymen for which Thebes and Boeotia were renowned. In numbers of hoplites and cavalry, therefore, the two sides were fairly evenly matched. But in skill, in tactics and in morale the Boeotians probably had the upper hand from the outset.

They were fighting on and for their home territory, to resist and beat off foreign invaders. Hippocrates's planned partner Demosthenes and his troops had not succeeded in co-ordinating the Athenian attack. The Boeotian cavalry was also superior for sure, but what was most strikingly original was the depth of hoplite line that Pagondas elected to deploy. In a hoplite battle there was always a trade-off between width of front (to counter the possibility of being outflanked) and depth of files (to provide muscle and weight in the grand push). The figure that turns up quite regularly in the sources for the latter is eight: it seems that Greek hoplite forces were regularly deployed eight files or ranks deep. Pagondas, however, arrayed his Theban hoplites three times that deep, in twenty-five files or ranks. In consequence his battle line was narrower than that of the Athenians, and his left flank was at risk of being outflanked by the Athenians stationed opposite the men of Thespiae, Tanagra and Orchomenus. And so it turned out. Although the Boeotians took the initiative in charging the

Athenian lines, the Athenian right surrounded the Boeotian left, forcing the Tanagrans and Orchomenians to retreat.

It seems, however, that some confusion then unfortunately afflicted the victorious Athenians, who started killing each other rather than the enemy. In a hoplite battle hearing and vision were very limited, once the phalanx's tight initial formation had been disrupted, and equipment on both sides would have looked outwardly very similar. It was apparently not yet standard practice to display 'national' symbols such as a distinguishing letter of the alphabet on one's shield (e.g., lamda for 'Lacedaemonians', sigma for 'Sicyonians'). At this point Pagondas sent in his cavalry to support his left wing and turn the tables on the Athenians. He, as was normal for the commanding general, had stationed himself on the right wing, with his Theban troops, who had already won their contest against the Athenians' left. The two victorious Boeotian wings thus commanded the field and won the day. It is estimated that about 500 men were killed on the Boeotian side, about double that on the Athenian side. Delium was not only the first full-blown hoplite battle of the whole war, but also one of the bloodiest.

Normally, that would have been that: the Athenians would have conceded victory by suing for a truce and for the return of their dead so as to be able to to perform the sacred rituals of burial. But this was not a normal battle either in its evolution or in its aftermath, and it reflected all too well the growing bitterness and brutality and indeed abandonment of customary norms of behaviour that characterized the war as a whole, as it dragged on year after year. For a start, the Boeotians continued to hunt down and kill any Athenians they could get their hands on until nightfall. Some of the Athenian survivors managed to get away by ship, but a significant number found themselves holed up and trapped in the fortification they had constructed at Delium, where the Boeotians besieged them.

The Athenians did then request that the corpses of their people be handed over to them; but in a vehement diplomatic exchange, involving a Boeotian delegation going all the way to Athens to make a formal representation, the Boeotians alleged that the Athenians had violated sacred space at Delium and so refused to hand back the corpses until the Athenians had evacuated the site. The Athenians retorted that they had done no such thing and, perhaps seeing the Delium fort as a kind of parallel to Pylus – which they had fortified in 425 and continued to occupy within the Spartans' territory – refused to depart. The result was that the siege was prolonged for over two weeks after the battle, and was ended only when the Boeotians deployed some kind of flame-thrower that Thucydides enjoyed describing in considerable detail. The condition of the Athenian corpses by that time beggars the imagination. Perhaps this was one reason why Thucydides wrote up this unhappy affair as a paradigmatic instance of the moral and religious decadence brought on by the war, warfare in general being a 'harsh teacher', as he put it elsewhere.

We happen to know by name two of the Athenian combatants who survived, one a cavalryman, the other a hoplite: respectively, the already mentioned Alcibiades (then aged about twenty-five) and his mentor Socrates (forty-five). Plato, Socrates's devoted intellectual disciple, was keen to emphasize – in light of Socrates's later conviction for impiety in 399 – just what a solid and brave citizen Socrates had been at this moment of crisis. Hippocrates, on the other hand, did not survive, as even victorious commanding generals often did not in ancient Greece.

Several Boeotian victims of Delium are also known by name thanks to an officially published casualty list (now on display in the Thebes Museum). One of them was a certain Saugenes. It cannot be proven, but it is a very tempting hypothesis, that this inscribed Saugenes is identical with the Saugenes whose handsome funerary stele was found at Tanagra (see figure 11). The painting on the stele in both its subject matter and its manner shows considerable panache and originality, using polychromy to achieve a skiagraphic (impressionistic) effect. It has therefore been suggested that its creator might be identified with a known painter called Aristides of Thebes. As for the scene itself, Pindar sings about the afterlife but never about a banquet taking place there. The earliest references to such are in the Athenian comic poet Aristophanes (active from 427 to 385). However, banquet scenes are frequently depicted in the Cabeiran pot scenes we have looked at in detail in Chapter 4, so familiarity with those could have been a further facilitating factor. As it is, this is the earliest known portrayal of a banquet on a funerary monument.

In the pediment zone are depicted both a man and a woman. If she is correctly identified as Saugenes's wife – rather than a *hetaira* (courtesan) or a dancer – and if this afterlife monument is depicting a real-life conjugal scene, then to me one of the most striking things of all about this scene is how – deliberately? – un- or anti-Athenian it is. In Athens there were of course public banquets; indeed, it was a form of indirect taxation to require the richest citizens to pay for a slap-up banquet for their fellow tribe-members at major public religious festivals (the requirement was called *hestiasis*). But the private banquet known as the *sumposion* or symposium (a 'drinking-together'), which took place usually in the *andreion* ('men's room') of an expensive mansion, was strictly an affair for male citizens and sometimes male resident aliens (metics) together with female non-citizens to provide the extra – typically sexual – entertainment. The latter participants might be legally free, indeed highly cultured, or they might be slave dancers and sex workers; but none of them would be a lawfully wedded wife. Wives – respectable Athenian wives – were kept strictly compartmentalized, away from unrelated males as far as possible, and certainly in any scenario involving the consumption of alcohol and sexual intercourse.

What also distinguishes the accoutrements of Saugenes's funerary stele is the depiction of a set of craftsmen's tools. They have been identified as the tools of a bronzesmith, and more especially those of a bronze armourer – such as the Pistias in Athens whom Xenophon celebrates as engaging in an imaginary conversation with his philosophical Socrates. But are they tools wielded actually by Saugenes himself, or was he the owner of a workshop whose possibly slave employees made armour? We know from their expensive dedications on the Acropolis that in Athens such workshop owners could do very well and have themselves commemorated lavishly in death. But in Thebes and, one infers, in Tanagra too, there was a dominant attitude to manual labour that was much more negative than in Athens, so it's somewhat surprising to find craftsmanship celebrated and commemorated in this funerary way – unless of course Saugenes was somewhat Athens-leaning. As Plato's Protagoras (a visiting intellectual at Athens who originated in Abdera in northern Greece) is made to say in a context of the 430s BCE, Athens was the *prutaneion tes sophias*, or 'city hall of Wisdom', and exerted a strong cultural fascination – even over the 'swine' of Boeotia.

Our secondary narrative source for the Atheno-Peloponnesian War, Diodorus of Sicily, at this point adds a valuable detail. So important did the Thebans consider this victory that they used it to establish a new religious festival, which – naturally – they called the Delia, in honour of Apollo Delius. However, that just happened – or rather did not just happen – to already be the name of one of the festivals dearest to the Athenians' hearts. This Athenian Delia was celebrated annually on the eponymous sacred Aegean islet of Delos, which was a common sanctuary for all Greeks of Ionian heritage. Moreover, the Thebans made a great song and dance of their spoils of war. Before returning the putrid Athenian corpses for burial, they had stripped them of their bronze defensive armour (helmets, breastplates, arm-guards, stomach-guards, greaves). Some of this they sold and from the proceeds built a great stone portico (a *stoa*) in their civic centre (*agora*). The rest, especially the helmets, they nailed up as trophies. No wonder the Athenians regarded the defeat at Delium as a great disaster.

Quite soon after, the Thebans capitalized on their renewed domination of Boeotia by destroying the city walls of Thespiae, home city of traitor Ptoeodorus, precisely on the grounds of 'atticism'. The Spartans too made significant inroads into the Athenians' sphere up north in Thracian Chalcidice, where in 424 they managed even to secure the defection of Amphipolis, a strategically vital city that the Athenians had themselves founded a mere dozen years before. Partly out of mutual exhaustion, in 423 the two sides made a temporary truce; but when this broke down and the Athenians in 422 suffered another significant defeat trying to regain Amphipolis, proper peace negotations were set in motion in order to end the war definitively.

In 421, the first, ten-year phase of the Atheno-Peloponnesian War was at last concluded with two sworn treaties: first, an open-ended peace agreement involving Athens and its allies on one side together with Sparta and its allies on the other; then, a separate, bilateral treaty of alliance, for fifty years, was concluded between just Athens and Sparta individually. The former treaty is usually referred to as the Peace of Nicias, after the name of its principal Athenian negotiator, who had inflicted considerable damage on Sparta earlier in the war by occupying the Spartans' offshore island of Cythera in 424. But it could and should no less justly be referred to as the Peace of Pleistoanax, after Spartan king Pleistoanax, who led the negotiations on the Spartan side. Unlike his co-king Agis II, he seems to have believed on principle in the 'dual hegemony' thesis, promoted earlier by the pro-Spartan Athenian Cimon, whereby the Athenians should be the leaders of the Greeks by sea and the Spartans by land, and the two great powers should coexist peacefully rather than war against each other for overall supremacy.

But it was the treaty of bilateral alliance to which some of Sparta's most important allies objected: to the point indeed of considering their treaties of alliance with Sparta to have been broken unilaterally by Sparta and so to be void, and of being willing even to enter into alliances with Sparta's sworn enemy Argos – and later also with Athens. However, the Thebes-led Boeotians conspicuously did not go down that oppositional route. They did indeed send ambassadors to Sparta to remonstrate, and these envoys did return to Thebes bearing news of an approach that had been made to them by Argos. Matters went so far that the elected chief executive officers of the Boeotian federal state, the Boeotarchs, were prepared to meet with delegates from Corinth and Megara, both Peloponnesian League members, and even from Chalcidice to discuss the possible terms of an anti-Spartan alliance.

But when the Boeotarchs put such proposals to the four federal Boeotian councils, they could not secure support even for alliance with Corinth alone – which though anti-Spartan at this time was nevertheless still oligarchic – let alone with democratic Argos. Feeling threatened by the democratic, 'atticizing' pull that several Boeotian cities were still experiencing, the Boeotians collectively stuck doggedly with Sparta, precisely because Sparta favoured their oligarchic mode of self-government and was likely to be willing to fight to help defend it. Not that this prevented the Boeotians from being prepared to risk Spartan anger in other ways, as we shall soon see.

Between 421 and 414, there thus ensued a kind of 'phoney' peace. Technically, that is, the war had been ended or at least suspended by the Peace of Nicias (and Pleistoanax); but actually a good deal of fighting still continued for several years, partly because key conditions of the Peace had not been fulfilled by both sides. For instance, the Boeotians not only did not hand back the Athenian frontier-fort of Panactum but actually destroyed it, whereas the Athenians did not evacuate Pylus (and didn't do so until 409). In 419, the Boeotians again made a seemingly anti-Spartan move when they acted to dismiss the Spartan governor of a military colony that the Spartans had established in 425 in the region of Trachis and had named Heraclea after their founder-hero Heracles. But in 418, to demonstrate their pro-Spartan loyalty, they did send troops into the Peloponnese in response to the formation of a new alliance concluded between Athens and Argos and two ex-Peloponnesian League members, Mantinea and Elis. This at least democratic-leaning alliance constituted a major threat to Sparta's hegemony in its own backyard and eventuated in a major pitched battle, but by then the Boeotian troops had returned home.

The battle took place in 418, within the territory of the Arcadian *polis* of Mantinea. It took place there because Mantinea was one of those few Peloponnesian allies which in 421, together with Elis and briefly Corinth, had so objected to the Athens–Sparta separate alliance that they had broken off relations with Sparta and formed an alliance with Athens. Arcadia had always been a crucial territory for the Spartans to control, both to enable their egress from Laconia towards and beyond the Isthmus of Corinth and, with special reference to their perennial enemy Argos, to prevent ingress by a hostile power.

One potent way of ensuring at least a good foothold in Arcadia was for the Spartans to subjugate or at least indirectly control Tegea, the nearest *polis* of any size to the north of the Laconian frontier. They had tried, twice, to subjugate it in the mid-sixth century – only to end up humiliated and wearing the fetters they had brought with them to enslave the Tegeans. (Those same fetters were allegedly still on display in the Tegeans' temple of Athena Alea some seven centuries later, when traveller-pilgrim Pausanias passed by and saw what he was told were they.) Instead, the Spartans decided to conclude a one-sided treaty of alliance, thus making the alliance with Tegea the germ and model of the alliances that a half-century or so later would form the basis of their new Peloponnesian League.

There was one, not incidental benefit for the Spartans of coming to an amicable agreement with Tegea. It was likely to ensure that the Arcadians, who like the Boeotians had a strong 'ethnic' identity, would be less able or willing to combine effectively into a single power-unit. For the other major *polis* of Arcadia, Mantinea, which was located at the other, north-eastern end of the region, was very jealous of Tegea and resented its Spartan affinity. There is a direct parallel – but also a contrast – with the situation of Boeotia in the second half of the sixth century. There Thebes and Orchomenus were the two rivals for regional-ethnic hegemony, but Thebes somehow managed not just to exert its political dominance over Orchomenus but also to persuade, cajole or coerce Orchomenus into joining a pan-Boeotian federation. The Arcadians did from time to time show signs of incipient political unification, for example in the early years of the fifth century; but it was not until the 360s – that is, only after Sparta had been trounced by Thebes and only with Theban direct intervention – that they formed a full-blown politico-military federal state (Chapter 9).

In 418, however, Athens was able to exploit Mantinea's hostility to Sparta (and Tegea) and its own alliance with a resurgent Argos. Elis, which was then in the middle of a bitter territorial dispute with Sparta, and had used its presidency of the Olympic Games to exclude all Spartan competitors in 420, was also prepared to secede from the Peloponnesian League and join in alliance with those three. It was probably no coincidence that both Mantinea and Argos were then under democratic regimes of governance.

Thucydides is, as ever, our main source for the 418 battle of Mantinea, which is sometimes called 'First' Mantinea to distinguish it from the second major inter-Hellenic battle fought there, in 362. By 418, he had been in exile from Athens for six years (for having failed to prevent Amphipolis from falling into Spartan hands). In a second preface to his work, he claims that this exile of his was no bad thing historiographically speaking, since it enabled him more easily to garner information from both sides of the conflict. That claim to credibility is rather seriously compromised if not undermined, as regards his account of the Mantinea battle, by what he very honestly but also rather alarmingly calls 'the secrecy of the *politeia*' of the Spartans.

Politeia, as noted earlier, can mean 'constitution' or the arrangements in place for a city's civic-political governance; but it can also mean 'way of life' or overall character, and there was a principled secretive streak to the Spartans' whole cultural as well as political demeanour and lifestyle. For example, they were said periodically to expel from Sparta all *xenoi* – strangers, foreigners, non-Spartans, whether Greek or non-Greek – of set purpose, and not only in wartime. And it was secretly too that they murdered Helots, under cover of a general, pseudo-legal declaration that they were all enemies of state. Thucydides records one particularly notorious instance in which no fewer than 2,000 were callously and mendaciously murdered – 'and no one knew how each of them was killed'. This was a classic state-terroristic means of reasserting and reinforcing their control of the Helots and of emphasizing, despite or rather because of the Helots' being Greeks, their servitude.

Thucydides's usage of *politeia* here seems to be a combination of the two senses. What in particular prompted his irritated remark about the Spartans' secrecy was the refusal to disclose to him or his sources their battle casualties and losses at Mantinea: their own, Lacedaemonian losses, that is, not their allies'. Already, as we have seen, Thucydides had shown a special interest in Lacedaemonian numbers in his account of Pylus in 425, where he had revealed that a 'Spartan' contingent actually contained side by side both full Spartiates and Lacedaemonian Perioeci. Such was the case also with the 'Spartan' regiments deployed at Mantinea in 418, and many scholars believe – as I do – that the Spartans' 'secrecy' was so successful that not only did it prevent Thucydides's discovering the Spartans' casualty figures but it also fooled him into getting the overall 'Lacedaemonian' numbers fighting there wrong – very wrong indeed, since he may actually have halved the true figure.

This error, if it was such, is of huge historical significance. The Spartans had probably already begun to suffer from *oliganthropia*, a shortage of full-citizen military manpower, as a consequence of losses due to the great earthquake of 464. (Diodorus says it killed as many as 20,000.) Their reaction to the Pylus disaster of 425 confirms that that negative process was still ongoing forty years later. The brigading of Spartans and Perioeci together at Mantinea in 418 and the use from 424 of both unliberated Helots and liberated, ex-Helot soldiers as frontline hoplite troops are further clear signs. Almost a century later, Aristotle in the *Politics* was to write that *oliganthropia* was the single main cause of Sparta's downfall – at the hands of the Thebans. But that is another story (Chapter 9). For, by decisively winning the battle of Mantinea, Sparta restored its reputation and the self-confidence it had lost since 425.

However, the Mantinea battle had not resolved the underlying tensions between Athens and Sparta that had led to the outbreak of the war in 431. In 415, the Athenians sought to open a new front and entered into yet another phase of restless expansion such as had powered the resilient generation of the 450s and 440s. The main theatre of their fresh enterprise was far away from home – in what proved to be a reckless as well as fruitless attempt to defeat Sparta's ally Syracuse, the most powerful *polis* on the island of Sicily, and perhaps capture the island. That venture occupied them for three whole campaigning seasons, two whole years, and ended in utter catastrophe with major political repercussions at home as well as military repercussions abroad.

Some Boeotian soldiers served on the Syracusans' side between 415 and 413, but it was the Syracusans' own resistance efforts and ingenuity, bolstered by the arrival of the Spartan general Gylippus in 414, that saved the day. The culminating act of the Athenians' Sicilian campaign was a terrific naval battle in the Great Harbour of Syracuse; many thousands of Athenian lives were lost there, and many more in the immediate aftermath, including those of the two Athenian admiral-generals, Nicias and Demosthenes. Yet more Athenians were taken captive and incarcerated in the open-air stone quarries of Syracuse, there to perish from starvation, thirst and exposure. Out of so many, so few returned to Athens, lamented Thucydides, who retrospectively saw the Sicilian disaster as one of the main contributory causes of Athens's eventual defeat in the war as a whole.

Yet even while the Sicilian campaign was in full flow, in 414, the Athenians had also seen fit to launch another naval expedition – against the Peloponnese and more particularly against Sparta's own home *polis* territory of Laconia, thereby indisputably breaking the Peace of 421 and their consequent alliance with Sparta too. The Spartans rightly felt far more justified in 413 than they had in 432/1 in declaring treaty relations with Athens to be at an end and launching a full-scale, allied invasion of their own, into Attica. The final phase of the Atheno-Peloponnesian War, 413–404, had begun.

This was alternatively known either as the Ionian War, because much of it was fought at sea off that part of what is now western Turkey that the Greeks knew as Ionia, and the overall result was finally decided in the north-east Aegean, around the Hellespont strait (modern Dardanelles); or as the Decelean War, since the Spartans from 413 on permanently occupied the Athenian deme of Decelea, roughly midway beween the city of Athens itself and the Boeotian frontier. The idea had reportedly been suggested to the Spartans the year before, by the Athenian Alcibiades who, summoned back from Sicily on a major religious charge of impiety, turned traitor and defected to Sparta.

It is the Decelean designation that holds most meaning and resonance for us. For during this final phase of the Atheno-Peloponnesian War in mainland Greece it was the Thebans who benefited the most, economically speaking, from the Decelea occupation, whether through pilfering Athenian country houses under the protection of that Spartan garrison, or by buying up cheap the literally thousands of slave runaways who escaped from the certainty of an early death working in the Athenians' silver mines. It was this access to economic prosperity which in its turn emboldened the Thebans to put pressure on their Spartan allies to conclude and enforce a peace with Athens that would be to their, the Thebans', differential benefit. That, however, was not how things turned out.

Thucydides reports on how the Spartans' occupation of Decelea, something they considered so important that they placed King Agis in personal charge of the garrison town, impacted upon the Athenians' economy and so war-making potential in two ways. First, it made it much more difficult if not impossible for the Athenians to extract silver ore from the mines of south-east Attica. This was the resource from which they coined currency, and which they used as bullion for purposes of making payments (political as well as commercial) – effecting the exchange of necessary imported goods such as papyrus and flax, and timber for their warships, or wheat for ordinary Athenians to buy at sub-market prices.

Second, as alluded to above, the occupation facilitated and indeed encouraged the flight of huge numbers of the Athenians' servile labour-force. A few of the slaves in Athens, almost all of whom were non-Greeks bought in slave markets, were publicly owned and relatively privileged; they acted as a kind of civil service. But the vast majority of the perhaps 80,000 to 100,000 slaves in Athens and Attica were privately owned, and many or most of them were used – either directly or as hired labour – to work in the silver mines. Thucydides estimated – or guesstimated – that, as he expressed it, 'more than two times 10,000 slaves' ran away out of Attica between 413 and 404, the largest part of that figure being constituted by skilled manual workers.

How did he arrive at even that approximate global figure, which I interpret to mean 'between 20,000 and 30,000'? It is a huge figure, roughly half the size of the Athenian adult male citizen population, and several times the size of the modal citizen population of an average Greek *polis*. There are two possible routes for us to consider. A runaway slave's first port of asylum, assuming that he ran away overland, would have been the Spartans' garrison at Decelea. But a successful escape from an Athenian master or mistress followed by refuge at Decelea did not automatically mean freedom, since the Spartans then sold the slaves on – to new, Boeotian masters, at a price that the Spartans were probably more able to determine than the buyers.

We know that the Spartans had an official office of 'booty-sellers' (*laphuropolai*), who presumably kept some record of the sums of booty gained: presumably, because at the end of the war in 404, in accordance with their normal pious practice, they dedicated to Apollo at Delphi (where in 479 they'd set up the Hellenic victory-monument) a tithe of all booty garnered at Decelea. If 'tithe' meant anything like its literal meaning of 'tenth', Thucydides (or whoever) might have done a rough calculation as to how many slaves the total sum of booty represented. Alternatively, the figure of '20,000 to 30,000' could have been just an arbitrary percentage – say 25–30 per cent

– of what people reckoned the total servile workforce employed in the mines in 413 might have been. Either way, it was Boeotians and especially Thebans who received the profits from this servile windfall.

One of Thucydides's successor historians, the anonymous Athenian usually known as the 'Oxyrhynchus Historian', is exceptionally informative on other ways in which the Thebans profited during the Atheno-Peloponnesian War as a whole. Looking back from a vantage point of the mid-390s, he distinguishes between what we might call the Ten Years' War (431–421) and the Decelean War (413–404). As for the former, he notes that Athenian attacks had redounded to the economic and political benefit of Thebes, by making the inhabitants of such unwalled towns as Erythrae, Scaphae, Scolus, Aulis, Schoenus, Potniae and 'many others' relocate for security to the shelter of Thebes and double it in size. As for the latter, Decelean War, his text is worth quoting in full:

> With the Spartans, they fortified Decelea against the Athenians. They purchased the slaves and other spoils of war for a low price, and, living as they did nearby, they transported home what Attica had to offer by way of material equipment, beginning with the worked timber and the clay tiles off the houses.

As regards the more immediate aftermath of the Spartans' occupation of Decelea in 413, Thucydides reports two incidents involving Boeotians. The first, of 413, concerned Thebes only indirectly. Blocked from attempting to repeat their invasion of 424, the Athenians sought to do damage to Boeotia by proxy. They had earlier recruited a mercenary force of non-Greek Thracians – ancient Thrace is roughly modern Bulgaria – but this had arrived too late to join a taskforce of reinforcements being sent to Sicily, and the Athenians were allegedly hard put to pay the 1300 mercenaries their agreed daily wage. However, instead of just sending them back where they had come from, the Athenians appointed an Athenian called Diitrephes (who later worked in the service of the counter-revolutionary oligarchic regime of the 400) to command them and escort them up north by ship, stopping off en route to plunder Boeotian territory. That way the Thracians would not return empty-handed, and the Athenians would both inflict material damage on important enemies and gain some mental compensation for the humiliation of the Decelea occupation. But it all turned out quite horribly.

Diitrephes landed his party on the Boeotian east coast and led them to the outskirts of the small Boeotian town of Mycalessus, where they spent the night, before attacking the town itself the following morning. What followed was indiscriminate slaughter. Respecting neither age nor gender, the Thracians massacred every living creature they could get their murderous hands on, not excluding working and domestic animals. Thucydides singles out for mention as especially deserving of sympathy the boys who were slaughtered in their school. There may well be a hidden agenda here. Thucydides was himself part-Thracian, on his father's side: his father's very name, Olorus, was not Athenian Greek but Thracian – though he had been named of course after a noble if not royal Thracian, not just any old Thracian commoner.

News of what was going on at Mycalessus was brought to the Thebans, who took it so seriously as to dispatch at once a mixed force of hoplites and cavalry under Boeotarch Scirphondas. This moved so fast that it caught up with the Thracians before they could get back to their ships and killed around 250 out of the original 1,300. But the Thracians fought back violently enough to kill about twenty of the Thebans, both cavalrymen and hoplites, including Scirphondas. Thucydides's Thracian family background on his mother's side gives especial point and force to his classically ethnocentric comment that 'the Thracian people – like most non-Greeks – is at its most homicidal when it has its boldness aroused'. Or as we might say, when its blood is up. It might also help to explain Thucydides's otherwise rather surprising judgement that 'This catastrophe that befell the whole town was unsurpassed in its terrible unexpectedness' and his parting shot, that Mycalessus 'in relation to its size suffered a disaster as grievous as any in the war' (by which he presumably meant the whole Atheno-Peloponnesian War, in which there had been many such calamities).

The other post-Decelea incident concerned the island of Lesbos, the inhabitants of which were in a sense 'related' to the Boeotians and also spoke the Aeolic dialect of Greek. Fourteen years earlier, in 427, and with strong Spartan encouragement, four of Lesbos's five *poleis* had revolted from their Athenian *hegemon* under the leadership of oligarchic Mytilene; the fifth city, which did not join the revolt, was Methymna, a democracy. The Athenians' repression of the revolt and their punishment of the rebels had been severe, including not just the killing of known rebels and the sale into slavery of many women and children but also confiscation of much land to the economic benefit of several thousand new Athenian landlords. In winter 413/12 'the Lesbians' (as Thucydides rather unhelpfully puts it) applied to Agis at Decelea with a view to their revolting from Athens, again, in the following summer of 412. 'The Boeotians' (presumably including if not meaning specifically the Thebans) supported the Lesbians in this, and Agis acceded to the Lesbians' request.

In summer 412, thanks to the Athenians' Sicilian disaster and access to Persian funds, a Spartan navy under the overall command of Astyochus was operating in the northern Aegean. The Boeotians had promised and presumably duly sent as many as ten triremes, some 2,000 men in all, in support. Lesbos was seen by the Spartans as a stepping stone en route to the strategically vital Hellespont, so their aim was to get Lesbos to revolt again and to use the island as a forward base. To begin with, they had success: first Methymna (a turnaround from 427), then Mytilene and then Eresus came out for the Spartans. But then Astyochus proved here, as elsewhere on his watch, to be an incompetent commander and lost the initiative, and an Athenian fleet seems to have had little difficulty in reconquering Mytilene and Methymna.

Over the next year, and into the summer of 411, some presumably wealthy and oligarchic exiles from Methymna gathered together a small mercenary troop from the Asiatic mainland opposite Lesbos. It was placed under the command of a Theban called Anaxandrus, whom Thucydides pointedly describes as a 'kinsman', with a view to retaking Methymna from the Athenians. But the mission failed. Eresus, however, remained in revolt – and was still apparently so when Thucydides's narrative abruptly comes to a dead stop in mid-sentence, in midsummer 411, just a few chapters later.

Thereafter, Thebes had very little to do with Athens's eventual total defeat. Our main extant narrative source for the years 411–404 is the *Hellenica* of the Athenian Xenophon (see Chapter 1), who was one of at least four writers to begin his account more or less where Thucydides had perforce left his off. Xenophon, however, despite a personal Theban connection, shared the anti-Theban prejudices of his Spartan patron, King Agesilaus II, and certainly never went out of his way to mention the deeds of Thebes or Thebans except when he had to – and not always even then (as we shall see). It was thus left to Diodorus in his *Library of History* to supply a quite fascinating detail omitted by Xenophon from his account of what was probably the single most important naval battle that occurred between the two major Athenian naval defeats of the war, that fought in the Great Harbour of Syracuse (413) and that in the Hellespont at Aegospotami (405).

This, the naval battle of the White Islands, Arginusae, took place to the east of nearby Lesbos in 406. The Athenians went to extraordinary lengths in an extra-special effort to win it, because the Spartan fleet under Callicratidas had stormed Methymna and was blockading their main fleet under Conon at Mytilene. In extremis, golden statues representing Nike the goddess of victory that had been piously dedicated on the Athenian Acropolis were melted down to fund the construction and equipment of new warships. Resident aliens were recruited to swell the numbers of crews. Freedom and even a form of citizenship were promised to any slaves who would serve as sailors and survived the battle. Eight of the Athenians' ten elected generals (who acted also as admirals) of that year were appointed to the command of a fleet that eventually numbered about 150 trireme warships or some 30,000 men.

Callicratidas, funded as Sparta had been since 412/11 by Persian money, had almost the same number of warships potentially at his disposal, but chose not to bring them all to the Arginusae battleground. As a result, he was outflanked on his right by the Athenians' left wing. That was not his only mistake: he also divided his fleet, rendering both sections even more vulnerable. On his left, however, his ships put up a better show and resisted for longer – those ships, Diodorus tells us, were commanded by a Theban called Thrasondas.

The Athenians thus won the battle of Arginusae comprehensively, but alas, for them, they proceeded to lose its aftermath in an equally big way. Suffice it to say that six of the eight Arginusae generals, the six that had – foolishly as it turned out – attended a heated session of the Assembly on Pnyx hill, were illegally condemned to death for dereliction of duty and executed; one of those six, rather tragically, was the younger Pericles, son of the great Pericles and his Milesian partner Aspasia, and a near-coeval of Pericles's controversial ward Alcibiades. Huge internal recriminations ensued, not yet overcome before the war's endgame, which came towards the end of the next year, thanks largely to a unique Persian–Spartan personal combination.

The war was won, as Athens's rebellious Mytilenaean allies had predicted as early as 428, in the north-east Aegean and the approaches to the Black Sea, the source of Athens's basic imported supply of grain that came ultimately from the northern shores of the Black Sea (Ukraine and southern Russia today). Since 412, Sparta had made dirty deals to secure huge inflows of cash from Athens's perennial enemy Persia. That tainted income stream flowed with especial speed and force once Great King Darius II's younger son Cyrus was given a huge overall command in the west and fell into cahoots with the hyper-efficient Spartan admiral Lysander, first in 407 and again in 405. In late 405, Lysander finally secured the decisive Spartan victory over Athens at sea, at Aegospotami in the Hellespont strait, a victory he capitalized upon by executing or maiming large numbers of captive Athenian citizen sailors and then blockading the port of Piraeus over the winter of 405/4. At last, in March/April 404, Athens capitulated in unconditional surrender to Sparta. The Atheno-Spartan or Peloponnesian War was over.

Sparta's price for this hard-won and ill-gotten victory was predictably high indeed. Athens's central fortification walls, and the so-called 'Long Walls' (about eight kilometres in length) that linked the central city of Athens to its port of Piraeus and so made of Athens a kind of island, were all pulled down – a savage revenge for the trick Themistocles had played on Sparta when he had contrived to get Athens re-fortified in 479/8 after the Persians' destructions in 480 and 479. Xenophon rather mischievously says that those involved in the walls' dismantling 'believed that day to be the start of freedom for all Hellas'. History proved otherwise.

The Athenian navy, what was left of it after Aegospotami, was further decimated on the Spartans' orders, leaving Athens with a mockery of a 'fleet' of just twelve ships. Worse, Athens's very identity as a democratic city was brutally terminated. True, that had happened twice before within the previous decade (both times in 411) due to civil war, but even a 'narrow' oligarchic regime of 400 was large in comparison with the junta (*dunasteia*) of a mere thirty that Spartan commander Lysander was now able to impose. For Lysander preferred to exercise his own and Sparta's imperial rule in the Aegean through local groups of just ten fanatical pro-Spartans, decarchies as they were known; and the Thirty at Athens were indeed assisted by a board of ten, who governed the crucial port of Piraeus. Plato had relatives in both ultra-oligarchic governing groups (which did not help his mentor Socrates's defence against an accusation of irreligion and treachery in 399).

Quite soon, the Thirty felt the need for a further prop to their widely unpopular regime, and Sparta duly supplied a garrison of liberated ex-Helots under a Spartan commander – housed on the

Acropolis. The Thirty, on top of scrapping all democratic institutions and safeguards, also reduced the number of full Athenian citizens from something of the order of 25,000 to just 3,000 (of whom Socrates was one), a classic extreme-oligarchic political ploy.

That was a high price for Athens to have to pay for defeat. But it was still not high enough for two of Sparta's major allies: Corinth – and Thebes. These two cities wanted to have done to Athens in 404 what the Spartans had done to Plataea in 426 (and the Persians before them in 480). Total urbicide. The Spartans demurred, giving as their reason that it would not be right so to treat a city which had performed such signal services to Hellenism in the past. They were referring of course to what the Athenians had done in 480 and 479, years in which, as just mentioned, their city had been violently destroyed twice over. But was the Spartans' motive as pure and honourable as all that? They themselves had not scrupled to ally even with Persia in order to defeat Athens. In 404, moreover, it might well have seemed to them that a tamed and occupied Athens could serve as a restraint on the alarmingly expanding wealth, power and influence of the Thebans in central Greece at a time when their own imperial ambitions extended far to the north of Boeotia.

However, by declining to destroy Athens the Spartans played into the hands of a faction of anti-Spartan politicos that was contending for domestic power within Thebes against a pro-Spartan faction. The Oxyrhynchus Historian, who will be a crucial source for Theban and Boeotian history over the next decade, is unusually well informed on these factional struggles within Thebes. We shall return to them and some of the major players later. In the short run, Thebes, the former unswerving ally of Sparta, was to play a key role in helping rid Athens both of Spartan direct rule and of an oppressive native oligarchy. In the longer run, the next fifty or so years of mainland Greek history can be seen as playing out within the frame of the fateful Thebes–Athens–Sparta triangle.

There was often a counter-current, if not quite an opposition, to the dominant political strata in Thebes. Consider that at

Thermopylae in 480 several hundred Theban volunteers, Hellenic patriots presumably, had fought shoulder to shoulder with Leonidas. During the Athenian occupation of Boeotia between 457 and 447, there was a strong pro-Athenian democratic faction in a number of cities, such as Thespiae. And at the very end of and immediately after the Atheno-Peloponnesian War, even oligarchic Thebes grew increasingly disaffected with Spartan imperial high-handedness. This disaffection manifested itself first in 404/3.

At Athens the Thirty Tyrants junta at first turned on its ideologically motivated democrat opponents, killing many, forcing others into exile. But soon it turned on anyone who was not enthusiastically favourable towards it, especially if they happened to be very rich. Rich resident aliens, such as the family of Cephalus – originally from Syracuse – that owned many slaves who made shields, were an obvious target, and they were duly targeted. It's estimated that between 1200 and 1500 Athenians and Athenian residents were killed by the Thirty and their henchmen during their year-long reign of terror.

But it's the exiles who interest us as much as the slain, since many of them, including devoted democrats, chose to flee north across the border into Boeotia, and there, remarkably, they found a welcome and shelter even in oligarchic, Spartan-allied Thebes. And not only shelter but active encouragement and support when they bid to return by force to their home city, a project which would involve successfully confronting militarily not only the Thirty and their Athenian citizen troops but also the Spartan garrison.

In deep midwinter 404/3, a very small force of Athenian exiles led by Thrasybulus seized the Boeotia–Attica frontier fort of Phyle; this was the start of a successful mission not only to recover Athens from the clutches of the Thirty but also to restore a *demokratia* as close as possible to the one forcibly terminated by Sparta in the previous spring. Thrasybulus had excellent credentials: he had been elected General several times and had served with distinction in the last phase of the Atheno-Peloponnesian War. For example, he had been a trierarch – captain and chief funder of a trireme warship – at the battle of Arginusae. Above all, perhaps, his record was impeccably democratic at a time when many elite Athenians had succumbed to the temptation either (like Sophocles) not actively to oppose or even (like Pisander) to join in with politicians of an oligarchic or ultra-oligarchic mindset (such as Antiphon and later Plato's relative Critias, leader of the Thirty).

Other exiles flocked to enlist under his liberationist banner, and these thoroughly democratic anti-Tyrants managed to make their way into the city within a city, the Piraeus, the heartland of the resistance. Most residents of Piraeus were in some way implicated in the business of the port's three naval and commercial harbours, and most citizens of the deme of Piraeus were both poor and fervently democratic. Few or none of them therefore were wealthy enough to count any longer as Athenian citizens under the new ultra-oligarchic dispensation. So sharp indeed was the division of the former united citizenry that Athens could now be spoken of as two cities: the 'Men of the [upper] City' (around the Acropolis and Agora), seat of the Thirty, on one side, and the 'Men of Piraeus' on the other.

A military showdown was only a matter of time in coming, and the battle of Piraeus, in which the Thirty's leader Critias was killed, was won conclusively by the democrats. Other oligarchs leaped to fill the breach and applied for assistance to Sparta which, thanks mainly to Lysander, was instantly forthcoming. But then something quite unexpected occurred, partly because of Thebes's role in supporting the Athenian resistance. Not one but two Spartan forces turned up in Athens, one led by Lysander, a resolute supporter of 'his' brutal settlement of 404, the other led by King Pausanias, who had succeeded his late, peace-making father Pleistoanax in 408. It was forbidden by law, as already noted, for both Spartan kings to be involved together in the same campaign in charge of the same force, and that law had been duly observed; but the other king, Agis, we may be sure, supported Lysander's hard line. The Spartans called on all their allies to join them in restoring and shoring up a narrow oligarchy in Athens, but the Thebans and the Corinthians, at the Thebans' urging, refused. In what followed Pausanias came out on top, and it was his settlement and his view of the correct way to conduct relations vis-à-vis Athens – and Thebes's Boeotia – that prevailed.

To be brief, Athens continued to be deprived of its autonomy, its independence from foreign influence or control, but – subject to overall Spartan authority and indeed suzerainty – was permitted to regain most of its old democratic framework of self-governance. A general amnesty sponsored by Pausanias was declared and observed for all except the most extreme oligarchs of 404/3. Ceremonies of reconciliation were performed. On the other hand, a part of the *polis* – Eleusis – was formally separated off as an exclave under the control of the oligarchic ultras and under the protection of Sparta. The question of who exactly should count as an Athenian citizen after 403 also proved extremely knotty. By 401, however, the Eleusis statelet had been dissolved and Eleusis reintegrated in the Athenian *polis*; this was also the year that Sophocles's Thebes-related *Oedipus at Colonus* was performed, posthumously (see Chapter 7).

But despite the amnesty, there remained simmering personal animosities and tensions in Athens, which from time to time bubbled over in the form of major criminal trials. One of the most notorious of these was the trial of Socrates for alleged impiety compounded by treachery as late as 399. Much is unclear about the motivation and timing of this prosecution, the main evidence for which is both disparate – the imaginative reconstructions of the accused's *Apologia* or defence speech by his very dissimilar Athenian followers Plato and Xenophon are very different – and very one-sided. What is not as widely known as perhaps it should be is that Socrates's disciples had included two Thebans: Simmias and Cebes. Both of them are featured as characters in Plato's dialogue *Phaedo*, which is set movingly in the Athenian state prison on the eve of Socrates's death by self-administered hemlock poison; and both of them composed philosophical dialogues in their own right. This is yet more evidence to counter the 'Boeotian pigs' canard.

In 403, King Pausanias was put on trial for his life back at Sparta for being, in effect, soft on democracy. He was acquitted by Sparta's supreme court, but his fellow king Agis voted against him. The following year Agis vengefully embarked on a major Peloponnesian League expedition against an ally that had shown far too much recalcitrance and far too little respect to Sparta during the past war. That ally was Elis, and the outcome as described by Xenophon was both regime change at Elis (Agis ensured that government was transferred to buddies of his) and an economic windfall for those allies that participated. One ally which conspicuously did not follow where the Spartans led against Elis was the Boeotian federal state. It was probably around this time too that the Thebans made another show of their independence from Sparta by appropriating a portion of the booty collected by the Spartans at Decelea. The hand of the leading Theban anti-Spartan campaigner Hismenias can be detected.

The Spartans' Elis campaign was wrapped up in 400, the year that Agis died and was succeeded controversially, thanks to Lysander, by his congenitally lame half-brother Agesilaus (II). By then, the Spartans' attention had shifted from mainland Greece to western Asia, that is to the Persian sphere. For as well as the Athenians' Aegean Empire, in 404 the Spartans had inherited their anti-Persian liberationist project. This was despite their having kowtowed to the Persians in 412/411 by ceding to them control of all Asia, including the Greek cities therein, in return for cash to fight Athens. Now, at last, they could at least try to make good on their promise to 'liberate' the East Greeks. But they did so only indirectly at first, by supporting the young Persian prince Cyrus: having helped Sparta immeasurably between 407 and 405, he now wished to supplant his older full brother who had succeeded their father Darius II as Artaxerxes II in 404. There was, however, little reason to suppose that, had Cyrus succeeded, he would have been any more keen to relinquish control of the Greeks in his empire.

In 402, the Spartans permitted the fearsome Spartan Clearchus to serve as Cyrus's gangmaster and chief recruiting sergeant in gathering together a huge Greek mercenary force. This body is conventionally referred to as the Ten Thousand, but actually more like 13,000 were recruited to start with – among them Xenophon of Athens (our principal source) and his Theban buddy (*xenos*) Proxenus. From Sardis in Lydia they marched to Cunaxa near Babylon, where Cyrus's death in a major battle in 401 rendered their further services redundant. Soon after, Artaxerxes's chief agent, the Persian viceroy Tissaphernes, captured the leaders of the Ten Thousand by a trick and and had them summarily executed, including Clearchus.

The Spartans' Persian project was thus still there for the taking, and in 399 they launched a campaign which was to occupy the next six campaigning seasons. In 396, the stakes were greatly raised when, for the first time ever, a Spartan king was appointed expressly to lead a military expedition in Asia (unless one counts the role of King Latychidas II as joint leader of the Hellenic forces at the battle of Mycale in 479). That king was Agesilaus II, by then aged about fifty. Never backward in putting himself forward, he promoted the expedition as nothing less than a new Trojan War with himself in the role of Agamemnon. Agamemnon's '1,000' ships had been launched – not altogether auspiciously (Agamemnon felt he had no choice but to execute sacrificially his own daughter) – from Aulis, and Aulis just happened to be in Boeotian and so Theban territory.

Agesilaus, whose father-in-law served as the Boeotians' diplomatic representative in Sparta, was under the illusion that the Boeotians would be only too delighted to repeat their eminent Trojan War role (see Chapter 3). But not only did they reject with contumely Sparta's call to contribute troops to the expedition, they also authorized the federal Boeotarchs to send men to wreck – physically and very inauspiciously – Agesilaus's attempted pre-launch sacrifice at Aulis. These wreckers even overturned the very altars on which propitiatory and votive animals had been sacrificed to all the relevant gods.

Agesilaus, so his biographer and confidant Xenophon relates, was a man of hyper-observant piety and never forgave Thebes for this calculated personal insult. It was added to the growing list of examples of *hubris*, outrageous insolence, perpetrated since 404 by the Thebans against the Spartans, and for which the Thebans must in due time be made to pay.

Agesilaus's Asiatic campaign was not an unmitigated disaster but nor was it an unqualified success. To counteract it, the Persians employed precisely the successful tactic they had employed against Athens in and after 412. They supplied their enemy's enemies with large amounts of cash in hard currency. Indeed, by this effective bribery they helped to bring about in 395 a major anti-Spartan coalition of Greek mainlanders. This Quadruple Alliance included, of course, the Boeotians led by Thebes, together with the likewise disaffected Peloponnesian League ally Corinth, as well as the resolutely anti-Spartan Argos and, naturally, Athens.

The Oxyrhynchus Historian pregnantly offered his account of the Boeotian federal state (Chapter 1) to mark the point in 395 just before the defection of Orchomenus (below), which of course increased even further Thebes's politico-military preponderance and control (see figure 12). To recap, the Boeotians had been a federal unit since 447, and annually elected eleven Boeotarchs and 660 federal councillors; they could call upon some 10,000 light-armed troops drawn from the poorer social classes, 11,000 hoplites of middling socioeconomic status, and 1,000 elite cavalrymen. A fourth-century BCE bronze muzzle from Thebes now in a Berlin public collection is a mute testimony to this key arm of the Thebans' fighting machine.

The war that ensued is conventionally labelled the 'Corinthian War', since most of the fighting on land, including the major pitched battle of the Nemea River (394), took place around the Isthmus of Corinth. Xenophon says optimistically that the Spartans relished this chance to requite the Thebans (he never speaks of them as 'the Boeotians') for their *hubris*, but actually the Corinthian War was by no means comfortable either for the Spartans at home or for Agesilaus, who had to be summoned back peremptorily from Asia in 394 to meet the growing threat to Sparta's hegemony. Nor was this war, any more than the Atheno-Peloponnesian War, won by the Spartans solely or even mainly by exploiting their superiority in conventional hoplite fighting.

As was the case of the Atheno-Peloponnesian War, it was actually the Thebans who started the Corinthian War, this time by invading neighbouring Phocis. The silver coinage bearing the legend SYN ('Together', short for SYNMAKHIA, 'Alliance') and the image of Heracles strangling a snake with his bare – infant – hands ('Heracliscus drakonopnigon') was issued by the Boeotians partly for practical, commercial purposes, and partly for symbolic, propagandistic reasons.

The Spartans, under the overall command of their other king, Pausanias, responded with an invasion of Boeotia. In presumably unconscious imitation of the Athenians in 424, they launched a two-pronged attack, the two prongs of which likewise failed to coincide and co-ordinate. The results were the death of Lysander in battle at Haliartus, the failure of the expedition, and the re-trial and this time the condemnation and exile of Pausanias. However, the Spartans did score one big gain, the Thebans one big loss: Lysander had persuaded Orchomenus to defect from the Boeotian confederacy, hence its pro-Spartan role at Haliartus in 395 and again at Coronea in 394; indeed, Orchomenus remained outside the federal structure for over a quarter of a century. Pericles's remark about the Boeotians being their own mutual executioners again comes to mind.

The battle of the Nemea River in summer 394 was a signal Spartan success, with extremely few Spartan casualties. Xenophon says that the Boeotians supplied as many as 5,000 (almost half) of their available hoplites, and 800 (four-fifths) of their cavalry. But he also takes the opportunity to impugn, not for the last time, their fighting spirit. He claims that they were most reluctant to be drawn up on the left wing, where they would have had to face the Spartans, but were quite content to be placed on the right, where they had to fight against only the men from the neighbouring north Peloponnesian region of Achaea. Far more likely, however, the Boeotians waited their turn to command the Alliance army, and when their turn came, they positioned themselves conventionally on the right, the place of honour.

Xenophon also can't resist a dig at the fact that the Boeotians drifted off further to the right, claiming this to be a sign of their disregard for their allies, when actually, as Thucydides had observed in relation to the battle of Mantinea, this was a universal tendency in all Greek hoplite armies. One other feature of the Boeotians' comportment at the Nemea River battle was consistent with the Delium battle precedent: they lined up many ranks deep, in this case well over sixteen. All to no avail, of course.

The other major pitched battle of the Corinthian War took place within Boeotian territory, at Coronea, in the same year. The Spartans' side was this time commanded by Agesilaus, by then recalled from Asia at the urgent command of the home authorities. Under him served Xenophon, by then the commander of the remnant of the 'Ten Thousand' mercenaries, so that uniquely the accounts we have from him of this important encounter are those of not just an eyewitness but a participant.

Besides his main report in the *Hellenica*, Xenophon also included a version in his posthumous encomium of his former patron the Spartan king (Agesilaus died in 360/59, aged eighty-four). What Xenophon emphasized, apart from Agesilaus's courage and leadership, was the odd nature of the way the Coronea battle evolved. It was a sort of double battle. First time round, the two right wings – as usual formed by the best troops (Spartans and Thebans) – defeated their respective opposite numbers on the left: the Argives and the – defected – Orchomenians. But just as some of the Spartans' allies were celebrating their victory, prematurely, the Thebans attacked and threatened Agesilaus's baggage train and his vast Asiatic booty, necessitating a second round, Spartans versus Thebans: this the Spartans decisively won.

Even the Spartans' two big victories of 394 did not, however, settle the Corinthian War in their favour. Hostilities dragged on and off for another seven long years, especially vigorous and vicious in the Isthmus area (where Boeotian troops were sent to garrison Lechaeum, one of Corinth's two harbours, alongside numerous mercenaries). In 390, the Spartans suffered a major 'disaster' (*pathos*) at Lechaeum, as even Xenophon could not disguise. But the outcome of the war was decided not by Spartan prowess (or lack of it) in battle on land but by yet another Spartan diplomatic *volte-face* and a decisive success at sea.

Convinced that they could not win by military means alone, the Spartans sent Persian-expert Antalcidas more than once as special envoy to the court of Artaxerxes II. In 388/7 he secured not only new funds, so as to be able to defeat the Athenians at sea (as in 405 in the choke-point of the Hellespont), but also nothing less than a new kind of 'global' diplomatic instrument, what came to be known as a 'Common Peace' (*koine eirene*). Agesilaus had no direct hand in negotiating this, but he saw more clearly than anyone how it could be exploited to (what he took to be) Sparta's best advantage. When accused as a result of having betrayed Hellas and having (like the Thebans in 480) committed medism, he is said to have retorted that it was not the case that the Spartans had medized but rather the other way around: the Persians had 'laconized'.

The peace of 386 had alternative names: the Peace of the (Persian) King, or the Peace of Antalcidas. The former more accurately conveyed its source and direction: it was 'sent down' from the Persians' imperial capital of Susa by Artaxerxes, and the Greeks had no choice but to accept it. The Spartans nevertheless preferred the latter title, and certainly exploited their victory of 386 in an extreme, both narrow-minded and vengeful, fashion. In essence, the peace drew a diplomatic dividing line between east and west, between the Persians' sphere ('Asia') and that of the Greeks to its west. Within the Persians' sphere, the Great King's writ was to be absolute and unchallengeable.

In other words, as in 412/411, the Spartans, in order to persuade the Persians to abandon the Quadruple Alliance and support them instead, had been prepared to abandon any pretensions to securing the freedom of the Greeks of Asia, who, as before 480, were once again to be Persian subjects. As for the mainland and Aegean island Greek cities that lay outside that Persian zone and within the purview of the Greek cities most immediately involved in the prior fighting, all alike, 'both great and small', were to be 'autonomous' – a source of enduring contention with eventually momentous consequences.

The word could in principle mean having and being able independently to enforce one's own (*auto-*) laws and customs (*nomoi*). (Sophocles's character Antigone controversially used the word in that sense – of herself.) But it could also be taken to mean independent *from*, in the sense of not having one's independence as a sovereign political entity in any way diminished or compromised or shared. That was the sense in which Sparta under Agesilaus interpreted and enforced the peace's autonomy clause, with Persia's tacit backing.

Of the members of the former anti-Spartan Quadruple Alliance, Athens suffered the least, because in 386 it had the least to lose. But the progressive – democratic – political union effected between Argos and Corinth in 392, which the Boeotians though not themselves democratic had supported, was instantly dissolved. However, it was the Thebans and Boeotians who lost the most by far. The peculiar animus of Agesilaus towards Thebes soon became apparent. As we shall see, the swearing of religious oaths that was the normal way to render any peace treaty valid was to have important consequences in this particular instance. But in its way no less consequential was the issue raised now by the Thebans of who precisely would do the swearing: that is, as members of which political entity. The Thebans wished to swear as 'the Boeotians', as they always had done before. But hardline Agesilaus, invoking the 'autonomy' clause of the peace, threatened another Spartan invasion of Boeotia if the Thebans refused to swear as 'Thebans', and the Thebans had no option but to back down.

Agesilaus thus ensured that the moderately oligarchic Boeotian federal state that had existed since 447 was forcibly disaggregated, and reduced again to its constituent cities and even villages. The Thebans swore perforce to the Peace of 386 as (only) 'the Thebans'. Fifteen years later, however, as we shall see, the oath-swearing tables were to be turned on Agesilaus and Sparta in a quite original and quietly devastating way.

In 385, Sparta's attention was directed nearer to home, to dealing with democratic Mantinea, where Pausanias was being harboured as a refugee. After a short siege, not only was regime change enforced on Mantinea and the city's walls dismantled (Sparta itself had no defensive walls and hated other cities having them – compare its treatment of Athens in 404), but the synoecized (unified) *polis* of the Mantineans was also de-synoecized, dismantled, in an act of disaggregation called *dioikismos*. The town of Sparta itself was and always had been settled 'by villages' (*kata komas*), five of them; from 385, now oligarchic Mantinea too was to be settled and inhabited in the same, Spartan way. That amounted to an act of depoliticization. Xenophon reports the Spartans' – Agesilaus's – dishonest and disingenuous ideological spin: the Mantinean wealthy were reportedly delighted to be able once again to live as country gentlemen on or nearer their landed estates. But he does not disguise the outcome of this reactionary, anti-political manoeuvre. It was an omen of even worse to come for Thebes.

Athens, as mentioned, suffered least from the peace of 386. Two years later, the Athenians even felt bold enough to begin the process of reconstituting a replacement for the imperial naval alliance of which they had been forcibly deprived in 404. The Spartans meanwhile, having settled the Peloponnese, pursued their wider ambition of reducing all mainland Greece as far north as Macedonia to the status of Sparta's subjects. It was within that framework that in 382 a Spartan army under the command of Teleutias (a half-brother of Agesilaus) and the brothers Eudamidas and Phoebidas was sent north against Olynthus, the main city of the Chalcidian federation.

Reaching Boeotia, however, a party under Phoebidas made a diversion to Thebes, which it occupied and then permanently garrisoned. Regime change resulted in the creation of a Thirty Tyrants-style *dunasteia*. This action was of course in flagrant breach of the autonomy clause of the King's Peace, though the Spartans claimed, as had the Thebans in regard to Plataea in 431, that they had been invited in – by Leontiadas (ominous name), one of the polemarchs (leading officials) of that year. By no coincidence, he was the leader of the extreme oligarchic faction in Thebes. His father Eurymachus had been one of the most powerful men of Thebes in 431, instrumental in starting the Atheno-Peloponnesian War. The name of Eurymachus's father was Leontiadas, after whom his own grandson had been named.

Until 382, the Leontiadas-led, pro-Spartan faction had not had things all their own way. Another of the polemarchs of 382 was Hismenias (or Ismenias), who had championed the Theban opposition to Sparta since 404, and with Androcleidas had been instrumental in provoking and promoting the Corinthian War. He was now subjected to a show trial before a kangaroo court. As at Plataea in 427, the Spartans acted as judges, sending out three of their own citizens together with one from each of their allies. The capital charge formally brought against Hismenias was, breathtakingly, medism. Talk of the pot calling the kettle black. He was of course found 'guilty' and summarily executed, along with Androcleidas, to the delight at any rate of Xenophon, who blamed the pair for being 'responsible for all the disorder in Hellas' – that is, to put it rather differently, for doing the most to upset the good, Spartan-imposed order that he, like Agesilaus, cherished.

Yet even the pro-Agesilaus, anti-Theban Xenophon condemned the military occupation of Thebes in 382. But he did so not on a political but on a religious ground, that of sacrilege, since the Spartans had broken the oaths they had sworn in 386 in the name of the gods to leave the cities 'autonomous'. Xenophon being Xenophon cites this as only the most conspicuous illustration and demonstration of the fact (as he saw it) that the gods do intervene to make human history happen in certain ways, since it was thanks to their enforcement of their religious will to exact punishment on oath-breakers that the Spartans – eventually, over a decade later – paid the price for their sacrilegiousness. The Spartans, mind, not Agesilaus: Xenophon is careful not to name him specifically in this highly damaging context. Phoebidas was put on trial at Sparta, but clearly it was Agesilaus who got him off, as it was surely he who had put Phoebidas up to his Theban misadventure in the first place.

The Spartans also imposed garrisons on a number of other key Boeotian cities, such as Thespiae, and helped impose *dunasteiai*, collective tyrannies like the Thirty in Athens, elsewhere in Boeotia as well as in Thebes. The Spartan commanders of such garrisoned towns and cities were called *harmostai* or 'fixers'. That office had been invented by the Spartans during the Atheno-Peloponnesian War and massively increased in numbers and weight after 404 as a key element of their new-found overseas imperialism. It was a persistent source of grievance and cause of opposition from those genuinely freedom-loving Greeks who resented Spartan domination. Thebes, being especially important strategically, politically, and ideologically, received in 382 three joint harmosts.

Following the occupation, a number of influential Thebans escaped into exile, and as many as 300 or so in all fled the city. They fled to Athens above all, where they received honourable asylum, the Athenians thereby repaying the Thebans' favour to them of 404/3. As we shall see Philip of Macedon doing in the 360s, after being held hostage in Thebes for three years (Chapter 9), the three years these Theban exiles spent in Athens between 382 and the end of 379 will surely have taught them a thing or two that they could put to profitable use when restored to a position of power.

None profited more in this way than Pelopidas (his name means literally 'descendant of Pelops', the eponym of the Peloponnese), as we shall soon see in some detail. One of those prominent Thebans who did not leave, however, was Epaminondas, about whom Plutarch says – in his *Life* of Pelopidas – that during the occupation he encouraged young Thebans to take on members of the Spartan garrison in wrestling matches. Wrestling in the ancient Greek world was an Olympic sport, particularly indulged in by members of the social elite, for whom prowess in the wrestling-ground (*palaestra*) was a sure mark of outstanding masculine virtuosity (*andragathia*).

As it happens, no Theban won a victory in the wrestling at a panhellenic games for Pindar to celebrate in an ode, but he was commissioned to hymn the Olympic wrestling victory of one Epharmostus of Op(o)us, and he did so in fine style in over 100 verses (in his ninth *Olympian Ode*). He concluded thus ringingly: 'this man by the benison of the gods was born with deftness of hand and litheness of limb, and with valour before his eyes'. Epaminondas no doubt had it in mind that any individual Theban winning a wrestling bout against a Spartan would do something to dent the occupiers' self-image and bolster the Thebans' self-confidence, all to work towards eventual liberation from the Spartan yoke of what he reportedly described as 'slavery'.

That liberation finally came in the winter of 379/8, when, with crucial Athenian help, a band of these Theban exiles not only liberated Thebes from Sparta but straight away placed it on an entirely new footing by introducing a democratic constitution at home and then re-founding the Boeotian federal state on the same, moderately democratic basis.

The story – or a version of it – of how exactly Pelopidas and his mates achieved the overthrow of Leontiadas and his pro-Spartan gang, despite the Spartan garrison, is told with relish though not approval by Xenophon in the fifth book of his *Hellenica*, and with approval by Plutarch in his biography of its main architect. It is also told, more surprisingly, in a work of a quite different genre, Plutarch's essay on Socrates's *daimonion*, or the small interior warning voice of Socrates. The tale involved trickery and disguise, including cross-dressing, but also bravery and considerable political acumen.

In brief: the inevitably pro-Sparta board of polemarchs for 379 were collectively marking the end of their year in office by conducting a festival in honour of Aphrodite. Ominously for them. For they were unaware that their secretary, one Phillidas, was in cahoots with exile Pelopidas's resistance band, and when in their cups (this is the city of Dionysus . . .) they were fooled into receiving what they took to be female prostitutes and entertainers. Throwing off their disguise, the exiles murdered first the polemarchs, who presumably were all what the exiles would have regarded as collaborators, and then Leontiadas, in his own home in front of his wife. They also released from their imprisonment some presumably openly resistant political prisoners and armed them with weapons taken from public buildings. They then issued a proclamation to all Theban heavy-infantrymen and cavalrymen to join them in storming the 1500-strong Spartan garrison on the Cadmea, as well as providing arms and armour (presumably supplied with the help of the Athenians) to any sub-hoplites who wished to join in the resistance.

What followed the next morning had, for the Spartans, uncomfortable echoes of their experience in 425 at Pylus: the heavily outnumbered garrison and their harmosts meekly surrendered on condition of being granted safe passage. This the Thebans duly guaranteed under oath. Xenophon, anti-Theban as always, reports that the oath was not in fact completely honoured. Whenever a Spartan was recognized as an individual personal enemy, the Thebans not only killed him but also cut the throats of his children. The three harmosts did, however, escape, only to be tried and found guilty of dereliction. One of them was executed, at Corinth, the other two were heavily fined and exiled by the Spartans.

The Spartans next, presumably with the formal consent of the Peloponnesian League, declared war on Thebes, and the 'Boeotian War' was to occupy most of the rest of the 370s. It was a sure sign of crisis-thinking in Sparta that fighting was embarked upon early in 378, well before the end of winter. The war began well enough, with a Spartan force cutting to pieces a garrison made up of 150 of those recently released Theban political prisoners, which had been planted to guard a pass over Mount Cithaeron. From there they proceeded *via* Plataea (restored after four decades in either 386 or 382) to Thespiae, where they reinforced the already garrisoned town. But the war was to end badly for Sparta, very badly indeed.

CHAPTER 9

Theban Heyday:
City of Epaminondas
and Pelopidas

Under the remarkable and often joint leadership of Epaminondas and Pelopidas, Thebes achieved an extraordinary flowering in the 370s and 360s, making it temporarily the leading power in all mainland Greece. Indeed, the period of Greek history from 371 to 362, framed between two major battles both won by the Thebans, is often referred to as the 'Theban hegemony'. Some prefer the more qualified term 'Theban ascendancy'. Of course, Thebes did not then preside over or dominate anything like the whole of the ancient Greek world, but only much of mainland Greece and some of the Aegean area. 'Hegemony', moreover, is used rather than 'Empire' to indicate that Thebes's supremacy was exercised in significantly different ways from the preceding 'empires' of Athens or Sparta. All the same, in terms of political, military and diplomatic impact, this was Thebes's most important and surely proudest historical decade.

If we were to list just some of the high spots, they would have to include: two major victories in pitched battles, the first announcing to a stunned world the demise of Spartan invincibility, the second betraying a secret of empire – that none of the previous holders of the title was any longer capable of exercising it; a great leap forward in federalism, prefiguring the primary role that would be played by federal states in Hellenistic, pre-Roman conquest Greece (and ultimately influencing thereby even the federal United States of America); the foundation of the original Megalopolis (so named) – as a federal capital; the liberation and enfranchisement of a long-enslaved mass of Greek humanity, and the construction of a walled city for those emancipated, the remains of which still excite the admiration of posterity; and the career of an individual deemed by an acute English judge to be 'the worthiest man that ever was bred in that nation of Greece'.

Even the greatest of 'great men' cannot make history happen just like that, however. But heroes such as the Thebans Epaminondas and Pelopidas do mark their societies and epochs in powerful ways. Besides his extraordinary military, political and diplomatic talents, Epaminondas was also an intellectual, indeed something of a philosopher of a broadly Pythagorean persuasion.

This was a combination that appealed strongly to Sir Walter Raleigh, languishing in the Tower of London under the dictates of first Elizabeth I and then James I. It was he who, in the third volume of his posthumous *History of the World*, pronounced Epaminondas the 'worthiest' of all the ancient Greeks. Among his qualities of the very highest distinction, Raleigh discerned in Epaminondas justice, sincerity, temperance, wisdom, and magnanimity, allied with graces including eloquence, and of course those virtues that were required to make him 'an heroic general'. In sum, he was hardly to be matched in any age or country; for he 'equalled all others in the *several* virtues which in each of them were *singular*' (emphasis in the original).

It's a verdict I'm inclined to share. But ancient anti-intellectuals preferred to sneer at him. In the words of Aelian (second century CE), a magpie compiler of all sorts of supposedly funny stories, 'Epaminondas possessed just the one, rough cloak – and it too [*sc.* like Epaminondas] was dirty. Whenever he had it sent to be cleaned, he would stay at home – because he lacked another' (*Varia Historia* 5.5). The word I have translated as 'rough cloak' (*tribon*) was peculiarly associated, from the time of Socrates, with the garb of a sartorially challenged philosopher. It is a great shame we know so little about Epaminondas's life as a whole, especially his early life before he bursts onto the scene in the late 370s, by when he was in his forties.

One major reason for our ignorance is that the *Life* Plutarch (*c.* CE 46–120) composed of him is one of the very few of his biographies not to have survived. We may be sure, though, that in this as in his other *Lives*, Plutarch, who was himself a Boeotian from Chaeronea, would have done due diligence and not only consulted but also cited by name a host of sources otherwise lost or even unknown to us, starting with the few available contemporary writers and historians. The extant brief life in Latin penned in the first century BCE by Cornelius Nepos is no substitute. He says Epaminondas's father was called Polymnis, but even this detail has been queried in modern scholarship by one of today's greatest ancient Boeotia experts, Denis Knoepfler.

We know far more about Pelopidas. For happily, as we have already had good cause to note, Plutarch's parallel *Life* of Pelopidas – paired honorifically with that of the Republican Roman M. Claudius Marcellus (*c.* 268–208) – does survive. Our other main source of continuous, year-by-year description for the lifetimes of Epaminondas and Pelopidas is the *Library of History* by Diodorus of Sicily, written up some three centuries later. The sources that he used rightly put Theban affairs front and centre and occasionally add something significant.

One of the contemporary sources available to Plutarch and still available to us is Xenophon's *Hellenica*, but sadly such was his hostility to Pelopidas and to Epaminondas, as well as to their anti-Spartan project, that he could not even bring himself to mention either of them by name until well after the damage – to Sparta – had been done.

Early in 378, Thebes – and 'the Boeotians' – were thus re-established as independent political entities. What kind of entities they were, however, is harder to determine. In 447, Thebes had taken a political lead in devising an original and effective form of federal constitution that more or less harmoniously married the single, superordinate *polis* of Thebes with the other sixteen constituent political entities of the Boeotian federal *polis*. That constitution may be described as timocratic (political power distributed according to wealth) but moderately oligarchic. It had been dismantled, by former ally Sparta, in 386. The re-established Boeotian federal state of 378 and following was, arguably, democratic.

True, it cannot be proven that there was democracy in Boeotia – or Boeotian democracy – after 379/8. No ancient text unambiguously describes the new Boeotian state as democratic, and there is no clear evidence that the revived Boeotia was considered democratic at the time. But the probabilities seem to me to be cumulatively overwhelming that democracy did then come, internally generated not externally imposed, to all Boeotia and above all to Thebes. Would it not have been rather extraordinary if, after Thebes's experience with Sparta and Athens between 404 and 379/8, Thebes itself – and therefore Boeotia (the revived federal state) as a whole – had *not* been democratic?

Consider the following: in 403 Thebes – moderately oligarchic Thebes – had helped Athens become a democracy again, partly if not mainly because it felt very let down by its Atheno-Peloponnesian War *hegemon*, oligarchic and pro-oligarchic Sparta. In 395 (still) oligarchic Thebes led 'the Boeotians' in revolt from Sparta and remained at war with Sparta for eight to nine years – until in 386 Sparta, as president of the new Common Peace, adopted the harshest measures against its traitorous former ally. Sparta compelled the break-up of the Boeotian federal state as a condition of Thebes's being included within the Sparta-friendly framework of the King's Peace (or Peace of Antalcidas).

Four years later, Sparta compounded that felony and actually broke the terms of the King's Peace – and so committed a form of sacrilege – by infringing Thebes's *autonomia*. It then propped up a *dunasteia*, a very narrow oligarchy of diehards, by imposing a Spartan garrison located on the symbolically charged Cadmea. This was, in other words, a repeat of the 404/3 situation at Sparta-dominated Athens, against which even moderately oligarchic Thebes had reacted. Even the Thebophobic Xenophon, as we saw, condemned the Spartan intervention and occupation of Thebes in 382 outright. Indeed, he regarded it as the ultimate cause of Sparta's downfall over a decade later.

Further considerations lead in the same direction. Where did Pelopidas and other future Theban liberators who fled into exile in 382 seek and receive political asylum and refuge? Democratic Athens. In winter 379/8 it was they who – with help from that same Athens – actually effected that liberation, and shortly thereafter brought Thebes into alliance with Athens. On the face of it, this was surely a mésalliance, since the Athenians were thereby making landlocked and navy-less Thebes one of the six founder members of a new alliance, the Second Athenian Sea-League. But presumably the nature of the new Theban *politeia* was at least part of the reason for the Athenians' confidence in their new, first-time-ever ally.

Since Thebes simultaneously also somehow refounded the Boeotian federal state, it is an economy of hypothesis to suppose that, as with the oligarchic dispensation between 447 and 386, so from 378 onwards the Boeotian federal state would have had the same kind of *politeia* as Thebes. As stated above, there is no proof that it was democratic, but the inference that it was seems to follow easily from the circumstances both immediate and longer-term of the triangular relationship between Thebes, Sparta and Athens. Indeed, it seems to be almost unavoidable.

One might even speculate further and regard Pelopidas returning to Thebes as liberator in 379 as somewhat similar to Lenin arriving at the Finland Station of St Petersburg in October/November 1917. What he had learned above all from his three years of exile in Athens was that the best way to resuscitate post-occupation, liberated Thebes and Boeotia was by going democratic. It is therefore important to remember that democracy in fourth-century BCE Greece was no one simple or single thing. That is one of the chief lessons that master-analyst Aristotle has to teach us in his disquisition on *politika*, matters relating to the *polis*.

Most *poleis* of his day (the 330s and 320s), so his and his students' researches taught him, governed themselves under either a form of *oligarchia* or a form of *demokratia*; but as discussed in Chapter 5, each of those two genera could be subdivided into four main species, depending on the extent to which the power wielded by either the *oligoi* (the rich minority of citizens) or the *demos* (the poor majority) was more or less (un)fettered. Aristotle's own ideal-pragmatic preference was for some mixture of oligarchy and democracy. He does not happen to cite Thebes as an example of such. But post-378 Thebes – and Boeotia – were surely moderately democratic: for example, I imagine that all citizens could stand for most offices and had to deliver the final sign-off vote in matters of legislation and foreign policy decision-making, but that for some offices, most obviously those of Boeotarch (now seven per annum instead of the previous eleven), polemarch and chief treasurers, only members of the wealthy elite were eligible, and that jurisdiction, unlike at radically democratic Athens, was not conducted by publicly paid judge-jurors selected by the random mechanism of the lottery but by elected officials.

There is one further possible argument for a post-378 democratic Thebes. In acting in the way proposed above, the Thebans would for once have been marching with the times, for the first half of the fourth century BCE, and especially its second quarter (*c.* 375–350), was the great age of democracy in the Greek world as a whole; that was not – as might have been supposed – the second half of the fifth, when democratic Athens and its empire had ruled supreme.

Further confirmation of this more widespread democratic evolution in Greece of the earlier fourth century has recently emerged from the city of Argos, where a few years ago a cache of over 130 inscribed bronze tablets documenting transactions of public finance was uncovered. However, a peculiarly vicious bout of civil war at democratic Argos in the late 370s, known graphically as the 'Clubbing' (in a far from convivial-entertainment sense: some 1,000–1,500 oligarchs were clubbed to death by democrats), reminds us of the tenseness and fragility of political governance in these hothouse and all too face-to-face communities. A more moderate and balanced form of democracy would therefore have had its obvious attractions, especially to a fledgling democracy such as I imagine Thebes then to have been.

Nor, by any means, were the liberated Thebans' innovations confined to the political sphere. The Boeotian military too flourished as never before, thanks to its federalist character, its liberationist spirit and its creative structure. A quite remarkable military innovation of this new Thebes was its 'Sacred Band' (*hieros lochos*). This was not the first elite, specialist troop to be raised in Greek history. Argos, for example, had anticipated Thebes in the late fifth century, and there is perhaps even a slight anticipatory hint in Herodotus, in the Theban '300' he referred to in the context of the battle of Plataea (*Histories*, 9.67). Even for Thebes, however, the Sacred Band was an unusual, and for Greece an unprecedented, social formation.

The city was especially renowned – or, according to taste, excoriated – for its alleged (in myth) 'invention' of the partly pedagogic, partly social-bonding, partly sexual-emotional, social practice of pederasty (*paiderastia*), and for its actual, historical practice of male–male homosexuality. *Paiderastia* must be sharply distinguished from our 'pederasty'. It denoted and connoted the sexual desire (*eros*) of an adult male, typically in his twenties, not for a very young child of either sex, but for an adolescent (*hebon*) boy or youth (*pais*), aged about 14 and up. Its origins are lost in the mists of time, though an Archaic stone relief from Thebes depicting an older and a younger man may take its existence here back at least to the sixth century, when the dedicated exercise ground known as the *gumnasion* (our 'gymnasium'), with its associated homosocial culture, was becoming a very widespread feature of many Greek cities. The *gumnasion* was so named because participants took their exercise, often wrestling, stark naked (*gumnos*).

At all events, the practice was sufficiently embedded and normative in Theban society and culture that in 378 it was possible to create a crack infantry force of 300 composed of 150 pairs of male 'lovers'. But with this ingenious twist: that both parties to the publicly sanctioned relationship were adult, full-citizen warriors. The force's creator, according to Plato, was the otherwise unknown Gorgidas, who thus takes his place alongside Epaminondas and Pelopidas in the trinity of great Theban military innovators of the 370s BCE and indirect founders of the Theban hegemony that followed.

Oddly enough, in a way, this new creation was complete anathema to Sparta. Not just because it was anti-Spartan in terms of Thebes's foreign relations but because, although institutionalized pederasty of a heavily ritualized and pedagogic kind was widely practised in Sparta too, the Spartans had not sought to integrate it into their adult army arrangements. We know much more about how the Spartans' pederastic system worked than we do about same-sexuality in Thebes. We know, for example, how the Spartans had made pederasty, that is homosexual relations between an adult male and an adolescent boy, an integral part of their uniquely comprehensive and compulsory state educational system (later known as the *agoge* or upbringing). The Thebans, like all other Greeks, had no such centralized educational system, and it may be that adult–adolescent (*erastes–eromenos*) sexuality was not institutionalized in the same way. Evidence that we shall come to regarding Epaminondas, however, suggests that it was at least as prevalent – and acceptable – as in Athens, at any rate among the social elite.

Unlike in a Spartan pederastic relationship, such as that between Lysander and Agesilaus half a century earlier, both partners to the 150 pairing relationships that constituted the 300-strong Sacred Band of Thebes were, as noted, adult citizens; though it may be that there was a hierarchy of seniority within each and every pair – if for example the older of the couple was married and the younger was not. The number of 300, on the other hand, may have been calqued from the number of the Spartan kings' regular royal bodyguard, known as the Hippeis or 'Cavalrymen'. We know a little about how that body was recruited, annually, among those eligible aged between twenty and twenty-nine; and how fierce was the competition for admission. We know too that in 480, when King Leonidas was deputed to lead the Hellenic forces at Thermopylae, he did not take his regular royal bodyguard with him to the pass, but instead a taskforce specially chosen by him, also numbering 300, but consisting of men who not only were married but already had sired at least one living son. Spartan males typically married in their late twenties, meaning that many, perhaps most of a typical royal Spartan body-guard of 300 would have consisted of unmarried men. Probably Theban males did likewise, since a generation of twenty-five/thirty years would have eased succession to inherited property, and an age-gap of a decade or more between a Theban and his wife would have accorded both with hierarchical Greek gender norms and with the imperious necessity for a wife to be fruitful and multiply, and so beyond menarche at her marriage.

Possibly the Theban Sacred Band was likewise a mixture of married men and bachelors, both within and between the 150 couples. At any rate, the number of 300 is in itself explicable, in terms not only of Spartan and possibly also Theban precedent but also of the military-psychological dynamics of small-group solidarity. On the other hand, we are still not sure why the band was given its name of 'Sacred Band' (*hieros lochos*), unless this was another borrowing from Sparta, where the smallest unit (thirty/thirty-five persons) in a regiment was called an *enomotia* or 'sworn unit', in other words, one tied together by the bond of an oath taken in the name of the gods.

It would have taken some time for Gorgidas to instil the neces-sary co-ordination and esprit de corps into the Band. At any rate, its first recorded major success came in 375, at Tegyra on the north shore of Lake Copais, over a Spartan force. Before then the Spartans had been invading Boeotia annually for three campaigning seasons running. Agesilaus's co-king Cleombrotus took the lead early in 378, but not only did he fail to retake Thebes but it was probably his unhappy idea that an attack should be made that year on Piraeus by Sphodrias, the Spartan harmost of Boeotian Thespiae.

This proved to be both a military and a diplomatic fiasco, rescued (as per Phoebidas) at great diplomatic cost by Agesilaus, who nevertheless saw to it that Sphodrias was acquitted by Sparta's supreme court (and probably also that he died, fighting under Cleombrotus in Boeotia seven years later). The anti-Spartan alliance between Thebes and Athens was greatly solidified as a result. Sphodrias was replaced at Thespiae by Phoebidas, but he was soon killed by the Thebans. Panthoidas, harmost of Tanagra, was perhaps killed around the same time. Likewise – and this is another remarkable epigraphic instance – probably also one Hippocles.

The Spartans had a peculiar (in both senses) rule, designed to encourage the others, as it were: namely, that the only male Spartans who were entitled to receive a named tombstone were those who achieved the ultimate honour and posthumous glory of dying 'in war', that is, when fighting for Sparta. Over thirty such inscribed stone tombstones – usually with just a name followed by 'in war' – have been identified so far, most of course from Sparta and its home territory of Lacedaemon. But from Boeotian Thespiae comes a singular outlier – the tombstone, named but without 'in war', of the Spartan Hippocles. That he was a Spartan is in one sense certain from the form of the lettering: it belongs to the very last decades of the use of the local, Laconian script (*c.* 380–360). That he was a full Spartan citizen, a Spartiate, and not a Perioecus seems to be guaranteed by his aristocratic given name, which means literally 'famed for [ownership of] horses'. Spartan cavalry was, as noted, lousy – but, also as noted, the elite royal bodyguard of 300 were called honorifically Hippeis or 'Cavalrymen'.

Nor does that exhaust the interest of Hippocles's tombstone. For it was actually a re-used local Boeotian tombstone, that had first been used some seventy to eighty years earlier for a Thespian nobleman bearing the equally aristocratic name of Aristocrates ('best for power'). Needs must: in a crisis, necessity dictated that an available local tombstone belonging to a suitably elite Thespian be commandeered quickly in order to mark the last resting place of Spartiate Hippocles. The Spartans back home would have applauded.

What Aristocrates's descendants, if there were any, thought of this appropriation is another matter – unless of course they took pride in this funereal Spartan association and had voluntarily offered the tombstone of their ancestor for honorific re-use.

In 377, it was the turn of senior king Agesilaus (by then aged almost seventy) to lead the Spartans and allies against Thebes, but he too achieved little and sustained a crippling injury to his good leg on his return home, which meant that in 376 it was again Cleombrotus who led the Peloponnesian League attack on Boeotia and Thebes. Although all attempts had so far failed to recapture or subdue Thebes, ravaging Theban land two grain-harvests running did threaten the Thebans with starvation. This was alleviated by the purchase of grain grown in the breadbasket of Thessaly.

In 375, however, no Peloponnesian invasion was initially forthcoming, and the Thebans seized the moment to re-establish their control over all Boeotia, excepting only Orchomenus, Plataea and Thespiae. It was against the Spartans' permanent garrison based at Orchomenus that the Sacred Band in this year won the signal victory at Tegyra mentioned above. Thus emboldened, the Thebans reverted to their policy of 395, by attacking their old enemies the Phocians. To which Sparta and the Peloponnesian League responded in force, and a stalemate ensued.

So matters stood in autumn 375, when a diplomatic message arrived in Greece from Persian king Artaxerxes II, reminding the combatants of their oaths of 386 and demanding a renewal of that Common Peace, since he wished to recruit Greek mercenary hoplites for purposes of fighting his own domestic wars (especially to recover Egypt, lost to the Persian Empire since 404). The three main Greek parties concerned – Sparta, Athens and Thebes – all had their own reasons for agreeing to a cessation of hostilities; the Spartans and the Athenians mainly because Thebes's post-378 resurgence had been alarmingly too swift and too complete. Sometime between 378 and 373, for example, Thebes had grabbed back from Athens the perennially disputed borderland of Oropus.

Peace was thus sworn in 375 on the same 'autonomy' principle as before – but had much less practical effect than in 386, especially as regards Thebes. Formally, the city should have relinquished any control over other Boeotian cities, and above all should have disbanded the revived Boeotian federation, especially as the Spartans agreed to withdraw all their remaining garrisons from Boeotia. Not only did Thebes not do so, however, but in 373 it destroyed the fortifications of Thespiae and, following the precedent of 426, annihilated the resurrected Plataea.

The conservative Athenian pamphleteer and educator Isocrates (born 436 BCE), who had been advocating for a rapprochement between Athens and Sparta since about 380, now composed a 'Plataean oration' to reinforce that desired effect. His words fell on willing ears, Athenian as well as Spartan, especially as the Thebans in 371 once again launched hostilities against Phocis. Artaxerxes too, further pressured now by the revolt of Egypt, again had his begging bowl out for yet more Greeks to press into service as mercenaries. Once more, unto the breach, once more: the Spartans in 371, this time with Agesilaus very much in the van, summoned Greek delegates to a peace conference at Sparta. Thebes – or, as Epaminondas preferred, 'the Boeotians' – was represented there by him, for the first time unambiguously leading if not determining Theban foreign policy.

The peace terms on offer from Persia and Sparta in 371 were as before, in 386 and 375, so there was no room for unclarity or wrangling in that regard. But when it came to the swearing of the oaths, above all the oath to respect the 'autonomy' of all Greek cities great and small, the issue again arose as in 386 of in whose name – 'Thebans' or 'Boeotians' – the Thebans should swear. But this time the Thebans did not back down. Instead, Epaminondas squared up to Agesilaus like a boxer, but employing all the ringcraft of a champion wrestler. When Agesilaus demanded that Thebes swear as 'the Thebans', since to swear as 'the Boeotians' would be to infringe the autonomy of the other Boeotian cities, Epaminondas retorted that the Spartans swearing – as they habitually did – as 'the Lacedaemonians' (not to mention on behalf of their Peloponnesian League allies) infringed the autonomy of the other 'Lacedaemonian' *poleis* not a jot less. Thus it was formally in defence of the 'autonomy' of the Laconian and Messenian Perioecic cities, their freedom from Sparta's iron grip, that Epaminondas refused – in the name of 'the Boeotians' – the demand by Spartan king Agesilaus that the Boeotian cities swear separately and individually to a further renewal of the Common Peace of 386.

Hence the irretrievable breakdown of the negotiations of 371, of which the more or less immediate consequence was war between Sparta and Thebes. Hence the battle of Leuctra, one of those watershed battles in human history that divide off very sharply a Before and an After. Before Leuctra, Sparta was still, in ancient Greek terms, a great power. Its military reputation, despite the setback of Tegyra, was more or less still intact. Its hypertrophied *polis* comprising some two-fifths of the Peloponnese in extent was still intact. Its Peloponnesian League alliance, despite the defection of Thebes and most of the Boeotians, was mostly still intact. After Leuctra – and as a direct consequence – came the deluge.

Diodorus says Sparta did send an embassy to Thebes to demand a change of mind, but this is more reminiscent of the virtue-signalling and high-ground-claiming embassies that Sparta had sent to Athens in 432 than it was a serious effort to avert all-out war. At the time of the failed conference in Sparta, Cleombrotus was already present in Phocis, adjoining Boeotia, with an army. Three weeks or so later, despite some rather muffled internal opposition at home, he received the order from Sparta, clearly inspired by Agesilaus, to invade Boeotia. By a roundabout route he fetched up at Leuctra, within the territory of Sparta-friendly Thespiae, and not far north-west of Plataea. And battle soon commenced.

The Spartans and their Peloponnesian League allies mustered some 10,000 hoplites and 1,000 cavalry, 11,000 all told. But only a few hundred of them were Spartan hoplites (700 out of a total adult male Spartiate citizen population of little over 1,000), and the cavalrymen that the Spartans supplied were poorly trained and motivated. The Thebans, who had no other allies but Boeotians, were clearly outnumbered, perhaps almost two to one. That no doubt was one reason for some disagreement among the Boeotians' high command over the advisability of trying conclusions with the Spartans. But they more than compensated for numerical inferiority by their superior skill, morale and above all leadership.

Xenophon suggests that Cleombrotus was more than a little tipsy by the time battle was joined, but this may simply reflect Agesilaus's post-battle propaganda, shifting the onus of defeat onto his now dead fellow king's shoulders. Epaminondas's tactics, clearly long-meditated, were both brilliantly original and devastatingly effective. He mustered his Theban troops to a depth of no fewer than fifty ranks, and alongside them placed the crack Sacred Band that was commanded by Pelopidas. What is more, these elite Theban troops were all deployed on the left of the line, that is, directly opposite Cleombrotus and his Spartans, and not as would have been conventional on the right. The idea was to crush the head of the snake – Sparta – and preserve the tail – the Spartans' allies – intact as far as possible.

The battle began with a confrontation between the two cavalry forces, which the Thebans easily won, pushing the Peloponnesians' cavalry back into their own hoplite line, thereby disrupting it. Epaminondas directed his hoplite line to advance obliquely rather than head-on, causing further disruption and confusion to the Spartan side. The outcome was a total victory for Thebes, with very low loss of life (a late source claims under fifty dead), whereas the Spartans alone lost 400 citizen soldiers, perhaps more than a third of their entire citizen body at one stroke.

King Cleombrotus was among the dead, the first Spartan king to be killed in battle since Leonidas at Thermopylae over a century earlier. So too were Sphodrias, the disgraced harmost of Thespiae and a supporter of Cleombrotus, and his son (the former beloved of Agesilaus's son Archidamus). Of the Spartan survivors, some at least seem to have fought with less than the customary Spartan vim and vigour; so badly in fact that in happier times they would all have been reduced to less than full citizen status as a punishment for what the Spartans euphemistically called 'trembling'. But so short of manpower had Sparta become by 371 that Agesilaus sophistically allowed the rigour of the laws to 'sleep' for that one day of the battle.

Moreover, not all the Peloponnesian League allies had given their unswerving commitment; indeed, Xenophon claims that some of them were actually quite pleased with the outcome. I imagine these were citizens of allied states in which the Spartans, prompted and led by Agesilaus, had intervened politically to enforce extreme oligarchy – for example, at Phlius ten years earlier. The Phliasians had a citizen body of about 5,000, most of whom were not pleased to be ordered by Agesilaus after a lengthy siege to receive back just a few of their ultra-oligarchic exiles and subject themselves to their *dunasteia*. So much for the vaunted 'autonomy' allegedly guaranteed by Sparta.

The defeat at Leuctra was, in Aristotle's privileged retrospective view, the 'single blow' that destroyed Sparta as a great power. That was a little reductive perhaps, but essentially correct. The Thebans later – possibly as much as over fifty years later (see Chapter 12) – erected a suitably impressive victory-monument on the battlefield, a circular stone *tropaion* (trophy) decorated with a frieze of hoplite shields that has been pieced together in modern times; it stands sentinel to this day (see figure 13). This was one of the first such, if not the first, permanent, commemorative trophies to be raised in Greece; normally – as in the actual example preserved today in a Munich museum – a battlefield trophy consisted of a tree trunk or wooden stump adorned with the arms and armour stripped from the dead defeated enemy.

The Sacred Band had performed exceptionally well at Leuctra, and it is tempting to suppose that at least some of its members made a pilgrimage thereafter to Thespiae. For (as noted in Chapter 4) Thespiae, now firmly back in the Theban fold, housed a celebrated cult of Eros, god of sexual attraction and physical love. As for Epaminondas, who is said to have referred to Boeotia as the 'dancing-floor' (*orchestra*) of the war god Ares, he will doubtless have danced for joy at the outcome of this Boeotian battle. But such was the rivalry if not jealousy among the Theban political elite that it is not clear whether his joy was shared equally by them all.

At any rate, a stone grave stele – a funerary marker – now in the Thebes Museum has a tale to tell too (see figure 14). In big bold letters at the top, disposed in three lines, are inscribed the names of Xenocrates, then Theopompus, then Mnasilaus. They were three of the seven Boeotarchs of 371, representing an almost 50 per cent casualty rate of the top command. But how (well) had they died at Leuctra – or how did their relatives and perhaps also the Theban authorities wish their deaths to be viewed and construed?

The inscribed epigram that follows is ambiguous: 'we did not run second to Epaminondas'. The metaphor of a competitive race, an *agon*, was thoroughly Greek in spirit, but it is not clear whether the race in question here was the race of life as a whole, or the specific race of the battle of Leuctra. If we were to take the more optimistic view, the late Boeotarchs are being made to claim that they were just as brave and resourceful and patriotic etc. as their unquestioned leader and inspiration Epaminondas. But if we were to adopt the more pessimistic interpretation, what the epigram might be saying is that in the view of its composers Epaminondas should not receive any degree of honour superior to that to which the named honorands, by the manner of their deaths, were entitled. If that latter interpretation is right, it is a broad hint of the rather vicious internal politicking from which Epaminondas was to suffer throughout the rest of his life (just under a decade).

Soon after Leuctra, a third renewal of the King's Peace was finally concluded, but the conference was held in Athens, not Sparta. Athens as *hegemon* of the Second Athenian League, of which Thebes was a founder member, might still reasonably take the lead in negotiations involving Persia. But the limitations of Athenian power and ambition were to be fully exposed in 370, at any rate so far as the Peloponnese was concerned. In that year two big events occurred, and both redounded to the discredit and diminishment of Sparta: first, the foundation of an Arcadian federation, then the liberation of Messenia and its Helots. In both, the determining hand was that of Epaminondas.

The Arcadians, like the Athenians, considered themselves to be 'autochthonous', literally '[born] of the land itself': that is, for as long as memory stretched, they and their ancestors had – so they believed – always occupied the same tract of land in the central Peloponnese, sharing a common (if fictitious) eponymous ancestor Arcas, and speaking the Arcadian sub-dialect of Greek (one that had most in common with the sub-dialect spoken by Greeks on the island of Cyprus, where the Greeks certainly were immigrants). The Spartans had exerted their domination and control over most of the Arcadians by the middle of the sixth century, but that hegemony had come at a cost – a growing sense of Arcadian ethno-political unity, fuelled no doubt by the contemporary movement towards political unification undertaken by another Greek *ethnos*, that of the Boeotians.

The Spartans famously refused to coin money until centuries after the Greeks of Asia Minor had been the first Greeks to do so, in the late seventh century. So one way of signalling one's difference from and to some extent one's independence from Sparta was to coin money. This the Arcadians did round about 500 BCE, marking it with the superscription ARKADIKON, meaning belonging to the *koinon*, commonwealth, of the Arcadians. Much of Arcadia, however, was poor in economic, that is mainly agrarian, terms, and this meant that there were always many poor Arcadians. As early as the Graeco-Persian Wars of the early fifth century, we hear of impoverished Arcadians seeking to better their lot by signing up as mercenaries for foreign states, both Greek and non-Greek. When the Persian pretender prince Cyrus raised a vast mercenary troop in 402/1 (the 'Ten Thousand'), several thousands of his recruits flocked to his standard from Arcadia. One of them, Aeneas from the town of Stymphalus, actually wrote an account of his experiences (disliked by Xenophon, since he felt it didn't give him his due meed of glory), then went on to write a textbook treatise on military matters – of which the section on siegecraft alone survives. The Spartans were notoriously disesteemed as besiegers.

Arcadia's two principal cities were Tegea in the south-east and Mantinea in the north-east. Tegea typically was Sparta's good and faithful servant; for one thing, it was far easier for the Spartans to get at it, being not all that far from the northern border of Laconia. But as early as the Graeco-Persian Wars there are hints of disaffection at Mantinea, and in the 460s the Spartans were obliged to fight a couple of battles in Arcadia to reassert and re-emphasize their domination and control. In the Atheno-Peloponnesian War, Mantinea again was a cause of bother to Sparta and, as discussed, the site of a major pitched battle in 418. But it was in the aftermath of that war, during the ensuing Corinthian War, that Mantinea really aroused the wrath of Sparta, not so much by any overt anti-Spartan action as by what the Spartans perceived to be their less than total dedication to the Spartan cause. So, in 385, the very first year after the conclusion of the King's Peace, the Spartans' first target under that treaty's 'autonomy' clause was, as noted, Mantinea.

Hardly unexpectedly, following Sparta's disaster at Leuctra, this was the golden occasion for anti-Spartans in Mantinea – and elsewhere in Arcadia – to raise the banner of Arcadian federation. Mantinea itself was first reunified as a single *polis* and its city walls rebuilt. Then was the moment to call upon the victor of Leuctra, the most flourishing federal state in Greece of the day, that is Boeotia under the leadership of Epaminondas and Pelopidas, to lend its weight to the creation of 'the Arcadians' as a new political entity. The new state needed a new capital, which like Rome could not be created in a day and was not in fact completed until 368. Since it 'housed together' no fewer than forty existing Arcadian communities, it was given the name 'The Great *Polis*' (*he megale polis*) or, in one word, Megalopolis. Epaminondas, as we shall soon see, claimed the credit for being its founder, its *oikistes*. Its location, in a big plain in south-west Arcadia, blocked the Spartans' easiest route of military access to Messenia and its liberated ex-Helots, which says it all.

A new federation required redefinition of military as well as political functions and offices: new officials, a new army, a new command structure, new buildings and spaces to hold meetings, and, not least, a new definition of citizenship, federal as well as local. None of that will have been easy, and despite all Epaminondas's best diplomatic efforts, within a very few years Arcadians were every bit as divided politically as Boeotians, but lacking the Boeotians' long experience of coping with such division. As we shall see, it was the fissile nature of the Arcadian federation that indirectly occasioned the demise of the Thebans' hegemony just half a dozen years after the foundation of Megalopolis.

Far happier was Epaminondas's intervention in Sparta's own backyard, within the bounds of the Spartans' own massive *polis* territory. Towards the end of 370 an appeal was made to Athens for action against Sparta by the now politically united Arcadians led by re-synoecized Mantinea, together with Elis and Argos. Memories of the 390s were reawakened, perhaps, but the appeal was rejected. Thebes's Boeotia, however, accepted it with gusto. Epaminondas led altogether four invasions of the Peloponnese between 370 and 362. Far and away the most dynamic and effectual was the first, conducted, unusually, in deep midwinter 370/69. Our main sources of evidence are as usual Xenophon and Diodorus; it would be nice, to put it mildly, if there were a Theban – or Spartan – source available. Instead, we have a terrific outpouring of the invention of tradition, the creation of an entire pseudo-history, on the part of or on behalf of the liberated Messenian ex-Helots.

Epaminondas, together with Pelopidas, amassed a huge army, numbering perhaps as many as 60–70,000. The core was his Boeotian alliance, which by late 370 included Phocis, Euboea, Locris, Acarnania, ex-Spartan Heracleia in Trachis, and Malis. Collaborating with them were Argos, Elis, and the Arcadians. Epaminondas's forces invaded Laconia by four separate routes, the first time that Sparta's home territory had been penetrated by any hostile land force for centuries. The Perioeci of northern Laconia made things easier for the invaders, as Thebes had done for the Persians in 480, by defecting. Epaminondas did not, however, attack or even stop at the town of Sparta itself, although Xenophon and later Aristotle made a meal of the panic-stricken reaction of the Spartan women huddled inside the wall-less settlement. Instead, with the troops under his immediate command, he passed on down the Eurotas valley to the Spartans' port and dockyards of Gytheum, which he did put to the torch. He then retraced his steps back up the Eurotas valley and, rounding the northern end of the lofty (2404 m) Taygetus mountain range, passed on *via* southern Arcadia, firmly anti-Spartan, and into northern Messenia.

Whereupon, if not sooner, the Messenian Helots revolted again, en masse, as they had done last in 464. Sparta's Helot system had long been controversial. The Atheno-Peloponnesian War, especially the Pylus affair, had exposed its fault lines. Recruitment by Sparta of large numbers of Helots and specially liberated Helots for military and imperial policing purposes from 424 had served only to expose its own growing shortage of citizen military manpower. An abortive internal revolution led by a certain declassed Spartan called Cinadon in about 399 laid bare just how fragile at its base was Sparta's seemingly impregnable hegemony. Some fourth-century Greek intellectuals criticized Sparta's Helot system on purely utilitarian, management grounds. It was a mistake, they said, to hold in slavery so many people of the same – not to mention, Hellenic – ethnicity. The philosopher Alcidamas, however, criticized the very slave basis of it, on ethical grounds, writing in 373 that 'God has made no man a slave'; that was as close to abolitionist talk as a fourth-century BCE Greek was likely to get. But it took a star like Epaminondas to translate pious talk into concrete deeds.

The post-invasion Spartans were helpless. Messenians – people of Messenian ethnicity – flocked back from what they saw as exile, not only from elsewhere in mainland Greece but even from as far afield as Greek north Africa. There was never any question as to where the new city would be constructed. Both symbolically and strategically, Mount Ithome was the Messenians' equivalent of the Theban Cadmea or the Athenian Acropolis. But the new city on its western flank needed to be fortified, and quickly. It comes as no surprise that anti-Spartan Argos vigorously assisted in the foundation of Messene, and made a huge song and dance about it at Delphi.

However, in terms of numbers of walls and the amount of walling erected within a short timespan, it would be hard to beat the Theban and Boeotian murifacturing boom of 370–62 presided over by Epaminondas. The first of his enceintes was that of Messene, made of massive cut-stone blocks, 9 kilometres in length all told. Other wall constructions soon followed at Boeotian Siphae, Creusis, Chorsiae, and the Gyphtokastro fort. As happens all too often, a pervasive Athenian perspective in fortification scholarship has obscured the specifically Theban contribution.

One partly symbolic point of this massive walling was to show just how un- or rather anti-Spartan this new settlement of Messene, probably originally called Ithome, really was. Famously, the Spartans themselves dispensed with walls around their own central settlement in the Eurotas valley, boasting in a sexist way that only women would (need to) fortify their cities and that the 'walls' of Sparta were its fighting men. Actually, the topography and location of Laconia deep in the Peloponnese and the *cordon sanitaire* provided by Sparta's northern and coastal Laconian Perioecic towns had rather more to do with their absence, together with the physical separation of Amyclae from the other four villages that made up the town and central place of Sparta.

Besides, that old boast started to look a little hollow from the early 360s onwards. The Spartans, in fact, never reconciled themselves either to the economic and psychological loss of Messenia (and its Helots), which cost them half of their home territory, including its most fertile areas, or to the emergence of their liberated ex-slaves as forming the new *polis* of 'the Messenians'. This reactionary Spartan irredentism was to generate a whole series of major geopolitical ructions and boundary disputes for centuries. Much more importantly, it seriously hobbled, if not crippled, the Spartans' engagement in wider Hellenic affairs thereafter. The citizens of New Messene, for their part, were keen to rub salt in the Spartans' wounds, and they did so in several ways both material and symbolic.

In the sphere which the Spartans prided themselves on and valued above all others – relations with the gods, or religion – it is very noticeable how prominently the Messenians worshipped Artemis Orthia, for example, the goddess who presided over the now discredited Spartan youth educational system. Epaminondas did all he could to encourage such religious provocation, while giving it a specifically Theban accent. He had the new city's sacred inauguration in 369 marked with a huge animal blood-sacrifice and with prayers to Theban Dionysus and Apollo Ismenius along with other Arcadian, Argive and, of course, Messenian divinities.

Back within Boeotia itself, however, something like a political civil war seems to have been raging in Thebes throughout its 360s heyday. Nothing new there, although the context and the stakes were unprecedented. In 369, for example, both Epaminondas and Pelopidas were brought to trial, and not for the last time. It was a sad reflection that their principal opponent was one Meneclidas, who had been among Pelopidas's band of liberators of 379/8. One of the issues raised against them was their alleged overstepping of the legally fixed chronological limits of office-tenure. It was a cardinal Greek republican principle that persons elected or otherwise selected for office should 'rule' (the Greek for 'office' was *arche*) 'turn and turn about', in other words, by rotation and not necessarily in successive civil years. As early as the 590s, Athens had experienced an unruly moment when its chief elected civil official had refused to step down after his year of office. Such a refusal might be construed as the equivalent of a bid for tyranny – an unconstitutional personal sole rule based on force, not legality. Allegation of a desire for excess personal power was a handy weapon to hurl at a rival, especially when, as in Thebes in the 360s, the stakes – and potential rewards – for success were so high.

Epaminondas and Pelopidas were never convicted of whatever high crimes and misdemeanours they were accused of, but it's very noticeable, as we shall see, that both did spend an awful lot of time away from Thebes on campaign. Epaminondas led a second invasion of the Peloponnese in July 369, his Boeotian contingent amounting to 7,000 hoplites and 600 cavalrymen, which detached Sicyon and Achaean Pellene from Sparta's Peloponnesian League. Another intriguing consequence was the brief career of a seemingly pro-democratic tyrant of Sicyon called Euphron, whose anti-democratic opponents pursued him to Thebes, where they murdered him, actually on the Cadmea.

In the spring/early summer of 366, Epaminondas mounted a third Peloponnesian expedition, which won for Thebes more ex-Spartan allies, namely the other cities of the region of Achaea on top of Pellene. Xenophon's account is, for once, particularly informative. In return for promising to respect the Achaeans' existing, oligarchic constitution and not to send into exile the existing leaders, Epaminondas, on behalf of the Thebans (and Boeotians), received a pledge from the Achaeans that they would 'follow wherever the Thebans led', the exact same formula as sworn by Peloponnesian League allies to their now failed *hegemon* Sparta.

Pelopidas's attention was directed more northwards. In 369 he helped reorganize the Thessalian confederacy and intervened in Macedon for the first time, concluding an alliance with King Alexander II. The following year, however, he was captured by another Alexander, the tyrant of Thessalian Pherae, who was an ally of Athens (which, taking fright, had also allied rather pathetically with Sparta). Pelopidas had to be rescued, in 367, by Epaminondas, meaning that it was Pammenes not Epaminondas who led that year's expedition into the Peloponnese, where the Arcadian federation and its new capital Megalopolis demanded Theban attention. (It was in the house of Pammenes, as we shall see, that the young prince Philip was just then being held hostage for the kingdom of Macedon's good behaviour.)

In between Epaminondas's second and third Peloponnesian forays, Thebes stepped up to the plate as Hellenic champion in attempting to negotiate yet another renewal of the King's Peace. Like the first attempt in 371, however, this too proved a failure, but eventually in 365, at a conference held in Thebes, a further renewal was indeed concluded. Sparta, as before, excluded itself, although by then Sparta was a shadow of its former self. The peace agreement did, it seems, directly or indirectly have two rather extraordinary consequences for Thebes. First, in autumn 366 or spring 365, Corinth, once the leading Peloponnesian League ally of Sparta, opened negotations to conclude a separate peace treaty with Thebes. Other Peloponnesian League cities followed suit, and peace was concluded between them and Thebes. That marked the effective end of Sparta's Peloponnesian League alliance altogether, after nearly a century and a half.

Second, in 365 or 364, Epaminondas raised a Boeotian fleet, as if, in belated acknowledgement of Thebes's (now broken) pseudo-naval alliance of 378 with Athens, he felt that it behoved the would-be *hegemon* of Aegean Greece to be a naval as well as a land power. Diodorus has him standing up addressing the Theban Assembly and demanding that they should strive for 'the supremacy of the sea'. The audience was persuaded, but it takes time and money to build trireme warships, let alone to recruit and train crews. The Athenians needed two to three years in the late 480s to raise a war fleet of up to 200 ships. Diodorus implausibly passes off the construction of Epaminondas's hundred-strong fleet as a mere bagatelle.

Its funding possibly came from Persia, ever alert to cause trouble for the Athenians. Epaminondas cruised with it in the northern

Aegean (where Athens was solely preoccupied with trying to regain Amphipolis, lost to them as long ago as 424) and even up as far as the Bosporus strait between the Propontis and the Black Sea. Byzantium on the Bosporus, another of the Athenian Second League's founder members, did defect to Thebes, as did the Cycladic island-city of Naxos and the cities of the island of Ceos. A recently discovered inscription from Cnidus in south-west Anatolia grants Epaminondas free entrance to and exit from the Cnidians' city, which suggests an Asiatic ambition. But Thebes's future did not lie in naval imperialism, or even on the sea.

In summer 364, Pelopidas was again deputed to go to Thessaly with an army. He was probably only too glad to be away from Thebes, where there seems to have been brewing an attempt at a reactionary coup designed to install or reinstall what the source calls 'aristocracy'. The object of the Thessalian campaign was to dethrone Alexander, the irritating tyrant of Pherae, but on 13 July there was a solar eclipse, which deterred many of the 7,000 soldiers originally called up from setting out as planned, and disheartened the remainder. (Eclipses of either sun or moon, especially if full, were often taken as negative military omens; a famous instance had occurred at Syracuse in 413, when the 'too superstitious' Athenian commander Nicias had fatally deferred to the advice of the soothsayers and delayed withdrawal.)

Instead, therefore, Pelopidas took with him 300 volunteer cavalry-men and a band of mercenaries, and recruited most of his troops from local Thessalians. The decisive battle took place at Cynoscephalae ('Heads of the Dog') in the heart of Thessaly (not to be confused with the homonymous alleged birthplace of Pindar in Boeotia). There Pelopidas was defeated and perished, but – as was only fitting – was buried with signal honours.

It was probably no accident, either, that it was in 364 that Orchomenus was annihilated by Thebes, while both Epaminondas and Pelopidas were quite far away from home. Since mythical times Orchomenus had been Thebes's only rival for domination of 'the

Boeotians'. In the late sixth century it had not committed fully to Boeotian unification. But in the 390s Orchomenus was guilty of the cardinal sin of defecting from the Boeotian federation altogether, for an alliance with Sparta, and had apparently never rejoined. So, in 364, Thebes seized the opportunity to carry out what it had threatened more than once before – the physical destruction of the ancient city of Orchomenus.

The motive or excuse offered was revenge, a dish proverbially best served cold. And Theban memories were long, as Plataea – destroyed by Sparta in 426 and again by Thebes in 373 – could bitterly attest. But probably it was merely a power-play, to rid Thebes of its one rival for hegemony at home. Nevertheless, Orchomenus was to rise again, and take its own revenge on Thebes, as we shall see.

With Pelopidas dead, and the Thebans acting in ways that he almost certainly would not have approved of, the star of Epaminondas too was temporarily on the wane. But the Athenians and the Spartans could be counted on to render his services once more indispensable, and once again he rose magnificently to the occasion. Probably somewhere between 364 and 362, a currency of silver coinage was struck by Thebes, of which a stater (two drachmas) coin weighing just under 12 grams was recently sold on the market for US$895; it depicts on the obverse a 'Boeotian'-style shield, and on the reverse an amphora with a miniature Boeotian shield above, flanked by the capital letters delta-alpha (DA) and mu-omicron (MO), standing for Damo-Æschylus had famously called Ares the money-changer of human souls. The god was back in business in a big way in 362 BCE (see figure 12).

In early summer that year, Epaminondas passed southwards through the Isthmus of Corinth at the head of an army for the fourth time, but for the first time without fear of opposition from any garrison posted by Corinth. Such were the temporary power and forcefield of Thebes's reach in the 360s that, as mentioned, democratic Athens and oligarchic Sparta had even felt obliged to ally with each other once more (they had last done so in 421) to meet this anticipated mutual Theban threat; but to no military avail. For once again, on the battlefield of Mantinea in Arcadia in 362, it was the Theban alliance led brilliantly by Epaminondas that won the day – though the great general, the Wellington of his epoch, himself lost his life.

What occasioned this Peloponnesian intervention was dissension within the Arcadian federation, divided between Mantinea and Tegea, but also between pro-Theban democrats and pro-Spartan oligarchs. Mantinea, now oligarchic, broke away to ally with Sparta – shades of Orchomenus in 395. In accordance with the hard line they had taken two years before against Orchomenus, the Thebans had even installed at Tegea a garrison of 300 Boeotian troops under a Theban military governor. The Thebans were also incensed that the Arcadian federation had made a peace with their (and ex-Spartan) ally Elis without consulting them. The Thebans therefore felt constrained to intervene militarily, together with their allies on both sides of the Isthmus.

Against them were arrayed Agesilaus's Sparta (though Agesilaus himself did not command) and Athens and other allies. The designated battleground was ultimately again, as in 418, Mantinea, for the obvious reason that its defection had caused the latest round of upheaval. But there was a curious preliminary: Epaminondas, it seems, had the idea of making a surprise assault on Sparta with a view possibly even to capturing it (as he had not attempted to do in 370/69). He was successfully forestalled by Agesilaus.

It is estimated that Epaminondas had under his command at Second Mantinea some 30,000 foot and 3,000 horse, as against his opponents' combined 20,000 foot and 2,000 horse. A reversal of the numerical situation at Leuctra. As at that battle, Epaminondas arrayed his Thebans in great depth on his left wing, placing in front of them his cavalry, with light infantry mixed in among them. Opposite him on the enemy right in the place of honour were not the Spartans – they were by then very few and demoralized by both military and diplomatic failures – but the Mantineans. It seems that

Epaminondas resorted to some initial trickery, fooling the enemy into thinking that he was not about to attack. When he in fact did, as at Leuctra, he again advanced his line obliquely.

The outcome was apparently decided on Epaminondas's left, with the defeat of the Mantineans. But the battle was a near-run thing, by no means a pushover, and both sides formally claimed victory by setting up a battlefield trophy. In fact, the Theban side had won, as even Xenophon was prepared to concede, at last lavishing praise above all on Epaminondas's 'second to none' preparation and boldness. Xenophon himself, as a former commanding officer, prized discipline and order above all else, and he commended particularly the 'willingness to obey' of Epaminondas's troops, even in the most demanding and difficult circumstances.

However, and it is a very big 'however', among the casualties was Epaminondas himself, killed at the age of perhaps fifty-six or so. He was buried some six kilometres from the centre of Mantinea, on the road leading to Pallantium. There, as traveller Pausanias recorded half a millennium later, presumably on the basis of autopsy, he was honoured with a tomb above which rose a funerary stele. Carved upon it were a shield (he does not say whether it was of the peculiarly local 'Boeotian' shape, as on the coin mentioned above) and on the shield a serpent – which Pausanias was probably fooled by a local guide into supposing to be an allusion to Epaminondas's native 'dragon's-teeth-sown' Thebes. Actually, serpents or snakes on grave stelae in Archaic and Classical Greece symbolized death – and renewal: Greeks believed that after death mortals or some portion of them somehow descended into the earth, the natural habitat of snakes, and the snake's periodic sloughing off of an old skin in exchange for a new one promised, by metaphorical analogy, a renewed afterlife of some sort. Hence too the 'Serpent' Column Greek victory-monument erected at Delphi in 479.

Pausanias adds a remarkable footnote, stating that two inscriptions were also carved into the stone stele, one of them in the by his day long defunct epichoric (local) Boeotian dialect, the other, assuredly, in the current *koine* (common) Greek of the second century CE. The latter was allegedly composed by none other than Roman Emperor Hadrian (reigned 117–138) and dedicated by him in person. Hadrian was of Italian-Spanish origin, like his immediate predecessor Trajan, and so a native Latin speaker. But he was a Hellene by cultural self-adoption, the first ruler of the Middle East to sport a (philosopher-style) beard since Alexander of Macedon had set the fashion for regal and imperial shaving. It therefore sort of followed that Hadrian should have acquired and developed a *grande passion* of a homoerotic kind, in imitation of and homage to the ancients, though it could hardly have been predicted that he would officially turn his prematurely deceased and hugely lamented *eromenos* (beloved) Antinous into a full-blown god, to be universally worshipped as such.

What Pausanias therefore missed out was what probably most attracted the largely unwarlike Hadrian to visit and venerate Epaminondas's tomb in the first place, namely the fact that – as Plutarch had written in his treatise *On Love* some four or five decades earlier – Epaminondas had been buried together with his own then *eromenos*, or beloved: Caphisodorus, who had also fallen at the battle of Mantinea. That does not necessarily mean that Epaminondas was a preferred or exclusive homosexual (see above), but it probably is significant that we are never told that he had a wife, and that the 'daughters' he chose to celebrate in his self-penned epitaph were not human beings but the two cities (feminine gender in Greek) of Messene and Megalopolis that he had founded:

> *This has come from my counsel:*
> *Sparta has cut the hair of her glory:*
> *Messene takes her children in:*
> *a wreath of the spears of Thebe*
> *has crowned Megalopolis.*

That epitaph is also preserved by Pausanias, describing, however, not the burial site in Arcadia but a memorial statue of Epaminondas erected in Thebes. According to this historically minded, eminently pious travel writer, Epaminondas 'found the Thebans in poor heart and used to taking second place, but in a short space he rendered them supreme'. True, but not for all that long, as we shall see in the next chapter. More resonant are the words of the epitaph's last line, which are a direct rebuke and challenge not only to Sparta but also to Epaminondas's own Theban ancestors and descendants:

Greece is free.

It was symptomatic of Thebes's hegemonic reach – not the same as grasp – after its crushing victory at Leuctra that between 368 and 365 Prince Philip of Macedon, son of King Amyntas III, was held hostage for his kingdom's good behaviour and placed under house arrest in Thebes in the dwelling of the otherwise too-little-known Pammenes. This unsought foreign tour taught the teenage Philip (born 382 BCE) a lot about diplomatic, fiscal and military affairs, before he unexpectedly became king of Macedon on the death in battle of an elder brother in 359.

Macedon hitherto had been an outlier of mainstream Greek culture both geographically and politically, except during the reign of Archelaus (413–400), who had hosted Euripides and other Greek intellectuals at his new court capital of Pella. Indeed, down to Philip's reign (359–336) Macedon had for long stretches been little more than a geographical expression, being politically neither advanced (it was resolutely non-*polis* and non-urban, agricultural and pastoral rather than commercial) nor unified (the upland west was almost a separate entity from the lowland east region). Philip will have learned from his stay among the Boeotians the value of regional unification, though federalism was something that he was to permit only in neighbouring Thessaly but not in Macedon – or greater Macedon – itself. The destruction of Orchomenus by Thebes in 364 was, alas, not merely emulated but far exceeded by Philip, first in the Chalcidice in 348 and then in Phocis in 346. It wouldn't be outlandish to suggest that Philip's lengthy incarceration in Thebes had also left a lasting scar of humiliation.

Earlier, I was careful to emphasize Boeotian prowess in wall construction and city building. Such emphasis is in order, but not necessarily also celebration, since as well as constructing a city the Thebans also destroyed more than one, belonging to their fellow Boeotians. Moreover, this rash of military construction indirectly bears unhappy witness to the at least partial accuracy of the conservative Athenian historian and thinker Xenophon's closing remark in the *Hellenica*: that the outcome of the battle of Second Mantinea in 362 was even greater Greece-wide confusion, upheaval and disturbance (*tarache*) than had existed before.

That was indeed partly accurate, but it was also partial in the partisan sense. Xenophon's word should not be taken entirely on trust. He despised Epaminondas's – democratic – Thebes, and Epaminondas himself for his role in resurrecting Messene and creating Megalopolis. As a loyal client and partisan of Agesilaus, Xenophon was one of those who yearned for the good old Sparta-dominated oligarchic international order, when 'those who had the best interests of the Peloponnese at heart' ruled the roost. Anything other than that was liable to be dismissed by him and his like-minded friends as mere 'confusion'.

That old Spartan order could never, however, be reinstated, as the Common Peace of 362 confirmed. The Spartans again refused to sign up to it, since that would have meant their formally acknowledging the 'autonomy', not to mention the existence, of Messene. What an irony, after their championing of the original Common Peace of 386 precisely on that ground. Moreover, as the career of Philip of Macedon was soon cruelly to demonstrate, the 'peace' was to be anything but 'common'. Indeed, the very notion of the *polis*, not just the existence of any particular individual *polis* such as Thebes, in its capacity as an independent power-unit was soon to be put in jeopardy.

PART IV

DOWNFALL

CHAPTER 10

Battle of Chaeronea, 338

The ancient Greek word *peripeteia* signifies a major downfall, a fall from grace and favour, of either an individual or a community. Herodotus had begun his *Histories* by musing on this cyclical fact, noting that cities that had once been great were now small, whereas those that were now great would, inevitably, in the fullness of time become small again. We have already considered one *peripeteia*, that of Sparta between 379 (or even 404) and, say, 365. Between 362 and 335, it was the turn of Thebes to suffer one even greater.

Major military and political reforms had led, as we saw, to Thebes's becoming powerful enough not only to take on and beat hitherto invincible Sparta in a major, decisive battle but also to establish what's conventionally referred to as the 'Theban Hegemony' between 371 and 362. In the longer perspective, however, this was but a brief, pregnant interlude between the Spartan–Athenian contested hegemony on one hand, and the Macedonian supremacy, of old, mainland Greece, on the other.

The latter was effected by Philip II during his exceptionally long (by Macedonian standards) reign from 359 to 336 BCE. Under Philip, the greatest man that Europe had yet produced, according to an admiring contemporary historian from the island-state of Chios, Macedon both consolidated the unification of its home territory that had been first accomplished under Archelaus (reigned 413–400), and then began to expand outside its borders in all directions of the compass.

Finally, though this was not his ultimate goal, Philip achieved control of all mainland Greece south of Macedonia, neutralizing Sparta along the way and triumphantly defeating the coalition of Athens and Thebes in 338 at the battle of Chaeronea in Boeotia, another of those landmark, turning-point battles in human history. A new common peace, a new alliance, a new political dispensation all followed, with momentous consequences, not least for the Thebans.

After Second Mantinea, the Thebans focused between 361 and 357 on preserving whatever they could of the gains of 370 to 362, both inside and outside Boeotia. In 361, yet another army was dispatched by them to the Peloponnese, this time to protect the legacy of Epaminondas in Arcadia against any Spartan attempt to reverse it, and to forestall the always threatened break-up of the still fledgling federation. That achieved, Theban thoughts turned to matters closer to home. In 357, using their leverage within the Delphic Amphictyony – the mainly central and northern Greek council that managed the affairs of the premier shrine of Apollo – they sought to have the Phocians, along with the Spartans, punished for failing to pay debts owed to Apollo for past infringements of religious propriety. A new source comes on stream for us here, Aeschines of Athens, an ex-actor and persistent rival of Demosthenes for domination of the democratic Assembly's geopolitical agenda.

The Phocians responded, with the tacit support of the Spartans, by committing an even greater sacrilege, that is, seizing control of the site and shrine of Delphi by main force in 356. Not only that, but they did not scruple to thesaurize the vast treasures in precious metals that the sanctuary had accumulated over many centuries. With the cash thus realized, they bought many thousands of free-booting mercenary soldiers and provided themselves with the wherewithal to carry on a war for as long as a decade. Sparta's former Peloponnesian League allies in Corinth and Achaea pitched in on their side, as did the Athenians, under the overall generalship of Phocian Philomelus.

Against them, the Amphictyony led by Thebes and their fellow federalists of Thessaly (who commanded the most votes on the council) declared a Sacred War (*hieros polemos*). It wasn't a holy war in any religious, let alone doctrinal sense; the religion of the ancient Greeks was in no way a matter of dogma or doctrine, and it lacked a vocational priesthood, let alone a foundational sacred book or books. Delphi, however, was considered the single holiest shrine in the entire Greek world, and it was precisely panhellenic, a shrine for all Hellenes; so seizing it under arms as the Phocians had was no trivial act. True, the idea of turning its treasures into hard cash for military purposes was not a new one – it had been mooted in the earliest days of the Atheno-Peloponnesian War – but religious scruple had prevented any state or alliance from actually taking that step. Until now.

In 355, the Thebans and Boeotians took up arms against a sea of Phocian troubles. On their western border, at Neon north-east of Delphi, a major battle was fought, which they with their 13,000 or so troops won against the Phocian side's 11,000. So decisive was his defeat that Philomelus threw himself off a cliff in despair. At about the same time, the Thebans sent Philip of Macedon's former host Pammenes off to Asia Minor, to support one of the several satraps who had come out in revolt against Artaxerxes III (he had succeeded his father Artaxerxes II on the Persian throne in 359). In this, Pammenes was following the lead of Spartan king Agesilaus, who had been active in a similar way in Egypt in the late 360s; probably Pammenes too, like Agesilaus, was chiefly out to raise substantial funds, the better to prosecute the war against the Phocians at home.

At any rate, the Boeotians certainly were keen to raise external funds where they could, and a lengthy document in Boeotian dialect was erected in Thebes listing contributions made over three years (354–352?) towards the (unnamed) 'war that the Boeotians were waging' concerning the sanctuary (*hiaron*) at Delphi. Contributions came in from far and wide: from Alyzea and Anactorium in Acarnania on the west coast of mainland Greece; from Byzantium; and from the north-east Aegean island of Tenedos. Some were official, state contributions; others, such as that of Athenodorus, the *proxenos* of the Boeotians on Tenedos, a mixture of public and private. The contributions from Byzantium were brought by individuals labelled *sunedroi*, that is, official delegates of an allied council, which suggests that the Thebans had followed the Athenians in organizing their alliance into some sort of permanent league. Other sums of money listed in minas (a mina was worth one hundred drachmas) and drachmas are unattributed to any named source and were presumably donated by Thebans and other Boeotians.

The document is incomplete, but, even had it been complete, it might not have listed the simply huge donation from Artaxerxes III (who had either forgotten or forgiven the recent Boeotian help to a revolted satrap of his) of 300 silver talents. (It's estimated that a private fortune of three talents would have qualified one as the equivalent of a drachma millionaire.) This may not have come in before about 350. What Artaxerxes urgently wanted in return was yet more Greek mercenary soldiers, to regain the province of Egypt lost to his empire through revolt since as long ago as 405/4. Thebes did actually send a commander, Lacrates, together with 1,000 troops to Egypt, but that was probably after the Sacred War was ended in 346. Artaxerxes did eventually recover Egypt in the later 340s (only for a successor to lose it – and a great deal more – to Alexander of Macedon a mere dozen years later).

Philip of Macedon, king de facto since 359, entered the Sacred War on the side of the Amphictyony. To begin with, he had had to stabilize his kingdom and his hold on it before introducing major military reforms. By 356, the year in which he became the father of Alexander with his Epirote Greek wife Olympias, he had not only beaten off a succession of rivals, but also occupied the strategically crucial site of Amphipolis and gained access to the gold and silver mines of the Mount Pangaeum district behind Amphipolis. Crenides there was renamed 'Philippi', Philipville. Philip's annual income from this source was said to amount to as much as 1,000 talents, the equivalent of the fifth-century Athenian Empire's income at its height.

Philip used the Sacred War as his entrée into the politics and eventually his route to the domination of central Greece. His war did not begin brilliantly, however. Indeed, in 353 he suffered what were pretty well the only two defeats of his entire regal career, against the Phocians under Onomarchus. But in 352, at the battle of the Crocus Field on the east coast of Thessaly, he more than avenged himself. The forces were evenly matched in terms of overall numbers, about 20,000 on either side. But Philip was already by then master of Thessaly to his immediate south (compare and contrast the Thebes-dominated Thessaly of the 360s . . .), and so had 3,000 crack Thessalian cavalrymen to call upon, as opposed to the Phocians' mere 500. Possibly as many as 30 per cent of all the Phocians present were killed in the fighting, and a further 3,000 of them were taken prisoner. Yet rather than either selling the captives into slavery or ransoming them, as would have been more usual, Philip brutally had them drowned in the sea. This atrocity he compounded by having Onomarchus crucified, a mode of execution normally reserved for slaves. But Philip had his justification ready too: technically, the Phocians were collectively temple-robbers, and everywhere in Greece temple-robbery (hierosulia) was treated domestically and individually as among the most heinous of capital crimes.

The rest of 352 and the year 351 involved mutual invasions and counter-invasions, mostly border clashes, between Boeotia and Phocis. These did not prevent the Boeotians in 351 from sending into the Peloponnese yet another army – 4,000 infantry, 500 cavalry – under the Theban Cephision. This expedition, like that of 361, was intended to shore up the Arcadian federation against encroachment by Sparta, for whom the establishment of Megalopolis was a running sore, and it had the desired effect. Sparta, now mainly dominated by Agesilaus's son Archidamus III, felt compelled to swear a truce.

It seems that the Sacred War went into abeyance during the next three to four years. In the interim Philip turned his attention to his east, aiming chiefly at the elimination of Olynthus and the Chalcidian federal state that it dominated – a potential locus of opposition to the extension of Macedonian power in the north. So effective was his devastation of the Chalcidice in 348 that the site of Olynthus and its port of Mecyberna were never reoccupied, which has enabled some remarkable archaeological discoveries, including recovery of full suites of domestic artefacts. Also caught up in that catastrophe was the Chalcidian *polis* of Stagirus or Stageira, the home *polis* of Aristotle (384–322), the Greek world's greatest intellectual of his day. From 348, Aristotle was thus a stateless displaced person, *apolis* as the Greeks put it, which perhaps partly explains the passion and thoroughness with which he later, from his Athens base, sought to classify, analyse and above all preserve that uniquely Greek institution, the *polis* itself (see beginning of Chapter 5).

In the democratic *polis* of Athens, the orator-politician Demosthenes, born in the same year as Aristotle, railed against the rise of Philip, whom he saw as a tyrant, the very opposite of a democrat, and in particular against his destruction of Olynthus. His three *Olynthiac Orations* of 349 are a rhetorical classic, a masterclass. In 346, however, he was to become much more directly embroiled with attempting to resist Philip, as we shall see. By that year, the Sacred War had taken a turn for the worse so far as Thebes was concerned. The Phocians had made such inroads as to be actually occupying eastern Boeotia, including the towns of (partially resurrected) Orchomenus, Coronea (site of the major battle of 447), and Chorsiae. In desperation, the Thebans turned again to Philip, who agreed to help them out, on his own terms: reportedly he was keen to humble the Thebans' still strong pride over their great Leuctra victory, and probably he was still smarting from his humiliating incarceration as a hostage in Thebes a score of years earlier.

First on his agenda, however, was not Thebes but Athens, which thanks to Philip's snatching and occupation of Athens's foundation of Amphipolis in 357 had been a strong supporter of the Phocians in the Sacred War, and a strong – if ineffectual – opponent of his northern policy more generally; this was because Philip's extension of Macedonian power through Thrace as far east as the Black Sea again potentially (as actually in 404 and 387) jeopardized the Athenians' literally vital annual grain supply. Negotiations, involving both Aeschines and Demosthenes among others on the Athenian side, were prolonged and tortuous. They culminated in the highly contentious Peace of Philocrates (named for the chief Athenian negotiator), which was very heavily weighted in favour of Philip and his global interests.

Philip's route south of Thessaly through the Thermopylae pass was now clear, and with a large army, including both Boeotians and Thessalians, he brought the Sacred War to an end militarily with a swingeing defeat of the Phocians. But Philip, as he himself said, normally preferred to fight his battles and wars *via* diplomacy, and the case of his 346 settlement was no exception. Having ousted the Phocians from their seats on the Amphictyonic council and taken them over for himself, he had little difficulty persuading the council to vote to fine the Phocians the huge sum of sixty talents per annum in compensation and reparations. But he also forced them to relinquish their occupation of eastern Boeotia and then inflicted upon them a kind of scorched-earth policy: for the future, Phocian settlements were to be decentralized and unfortified. In a way, this was a combination of lessons drawn from both Theban (destruction of Plataea and Orchomenus) and Spartan (de-synoecism and depoliticization of Mantinea) history.

All that accomplished, and a renewed peace formally sworn, Philip's icing on the cake was to preside over the 346 celebration of the quadrennial Pythian Games held at Delphi: part-athletic, part-hippic, but also high-cultural, involving competitions in music and poetry, and all and only Greek. Echoes of Pindar will have been heard, alongside strains of Homer. Philip, in other words, was doing absolutely everything he possibly could to block out any reminders of the anti-Hellenic role Macedon had played in the Graeco-Persian Wars of 480/479. Little though most Greeks knew it, or indeed had any inkling, he was thus preparing the ground ideologically for an even bigger adventure to come, or rather for one that was to be foisted upon a generally unenthusiastic Greek public.

The members of the Athenian negotiating teams that had plied back and forth between Athens and Pella earlier in 346, getting ever more irate with each other (Demosthenes and Aeschines had never been best friends) as well as exasperated by Philip's cunning machinations, were very soon at each other's throats in public back home, arguing both for and against repudiation or at least serious modification of the terms of the Peace of Philocrates. Aeschines, who was for retention, and Demosthenes, vehemently for repudiation, attacked each other both directly head-on and indirectly *via* proxies. In 343, Aeschines won a great victory in the Athenian popular jury-courts by successfully prosecuting one of Demosthenes's associates for committing a form of high treason. But that was to be his last such victory, and thereafter it was Demosthenes who occupied the high political ground, able as he was to point to a succession of incidents in which Philip intervened in the internal affairs of a Greek city in favour of either oligarchy or even tyranny, but always at the expense of democracy.

The issue between Philip and Athens was always likely to focalize geopolitically on the approaches to the Black Sea. In 341 the Athenians, almost but not quite breaking the Peace of 346, sent one of their ten elected generals of the year to ravage the territory of Cardia, an ally of Philip, in the Hellespont. In 340, Philip sought contrariwise to extend his control into the approaches to the Black Sea from the south: through his control of Thrace his martial remit already reached to that vast basin's western shore. But his sieges of Perinthus in the Propontis and Byzantium on the Bosporus were oddly unsuccessful: oddly, because siegecraft had been one of his greatest military strengths since very early on in his reign.

Matters were not helped by Athens's declaring for Byzantium, which had been among the six founder members of the Second Athenian League in 378 and controlled the grain route through the

Bosporus. Philip's response was potentially lethal. He intercepted a huge grain fleet of 240 merchantmen in the narrows between the Black Sea and the Aegean; most or all of those ships, all private-enterprise operations, were carrying wheat from the black-earth lands of south Russia and Ukraine to the port of Piraeus, where the Athenians had set up favourable legal and commercial conditions for the mostly non-citizen and even non-Greek traders to operate in.

Philip's action threatened hunger, even starvation for the poor Athenian citizen majority, and Demosthenes was able at last to claim, triumphantly, 'I told you so.' What he had been saying about Philip for the past dozen years had actually come to pass: he really was now manifestly Athens's public enemy number one. The Assembly formally repudiated the Peace of Philocrates and prepared itself in principle for war with Philip. However, it took getting on for two years for the fighting to materialize, and Philip was already much the better prepared for it.

Philip, interestingly, seems not to have been all that bothered by this Athenian demarche; indeed, he seems still to have been looking for a plausible reason, or at least an excuse, to come through the Thermopylae pass again with an army and impose himself on all mainland Greece south as well as north of Delphi. It was probably to try to forestall that eventuality that early in 339 the Thebans occupied the town of Nicaea not far from the Thermopylae pass, although they should have known that it could be turned. As it indeed was later in 339, after the Delphic Amphictyony claimed that the town of Amphissa in Ozolian (western) Locris was illegally cultivating sacred land in the plain of Crisa below Delphi (a trumped-up excuse if ever there was one) and – surprise, surprise – appointed Philip to command the punitive force.

He did not hurry himself unduly. It was not until late in 339 that he at last marched south as far as Phocis. The Fourth Sacred War was on. Quite properly, he spent the next months settling the Amphissa question, using trickery to do so as was his wont, and after expelling its citizens turning Amphissa over to the Amphictyony. For him, however, that was but a curtain-raiser. His real immediate and overriding military-political objective was to get himself in a position of overall control, hegemony if not suzerainty, of all mainland Greece. To achieve that, he knew he would have to take on and somehow deal with Athens. What he did not know when he arrived at Elatea in Phocis, but three days' march away from Athens, was which side the Thebans would take. He assumed it would be his. But for once this superbly canny ruler got it wrong.

Consider the matter from the viewpoint of the – utterly panicked – Athenians. They had by far the biggest trireme warfleet in the Aegean. Philip had none. But there was nothing new in that. That mismatch had existed already in 357, when Philip had taken over control of Amphipolis, and no amount of Athenian naval endeavour had been able to do a thing about that, any more than about his destruction of the Athenians' allies in the Chalcidian cities in 348 or of the cities of their Phocian allies in 346. Conclusions would have to be tried on land, therefore, but for that the Athenians had one serious deficiency: their lack of a decent cavalry. That was a deficiency that only one city or region might conceivably be able to remedy: Thebes and Boeotia.

However, since 370 and especially as recently as 346, Thebes and Athens not only had not been good friends but had actually been enemies. Looking back as far as the late sixth century, indeed, Athens had much more often fought against than fought on the same side with the Thebans. On the other hand, on the other hand . . . in 340, Thebes like Athens was a democracy, and whatever else Philip was for, he was certainly dead against democracy in any form, either at home or abroad. Moreover, the convinced democrat Demosthenes, Athens's – and Greece's – leading champion of resistance to Philip, not only was in the ascendancy in Athens but was also opportunely the official representative, the *proxenos*, of the Thebans there.

It was therefore relatively easy for Demosthenes to deploy all his oratorical skills to persuade the Athenian Assembly of the merits of a Theban alliance, and to have himself appointed to lead a delegation to Thebes to negotiate that alliance forthwith. Much more difficult of course was to persuade the Thebans that it was in their best interests too to abandon their admittedly very one-sided alliance with Philip and take him on in battle alongside the Athenians and their allies. Yet somehow Demosthenes pulled it off, and in the teeth too of representations to the Thebans made on behalf of Philip. Thus it was that the Thebans, who could in principle have 'done an Argos' (which in face of the Persian invasion in 480 had opted for what it claimed was a position of neutrality), instead declared firmly for Athens and . . . the freedom of Hellas.

Yet Philip again saw no cause for hasty action. Possibly he still envisaged some future for renewed diplomacy. However that may be, it was only in high summer, late July, of 338 that he did eventually take up arms and march his army along the road that led to Chaeronea on the western shore of Lake Copais, between Tegyra to the north and Coronea to the south. There the Thebans and the Athenians and their allies awaited him in the broiling sun (I have myself tried, in vain, to find an ounce of shade at midday in high summer at the magnificent prehistoric site of Gla, mentioned in Chapter 2). On 2 August, by our calendar, battle commenced.

The battle of Chaeronea – or perhaps 'this' battle of Chaeronea, since more than one were fought here – took place just over eight years before the battle of Gaugamela in what is today northern Iraq. I mention those two in a single breath, not only because Alexander of Macedon was involved on the winning side in both but also and mainly because both battles were, like Leuctra, extraordinarily decisive. Gaugamela decided that it was only a matter of time before the Achaemenid Persian Empire would be at an end and pass under the dominion of Alexander. Chaeronea in 338 decided that Alexander's father Philip would be suzerain of all Aegean Greece, and so in a position to put into effect his long-meditated plan for the conquest of the Persian Empire (which in the event he was unable to lead, but which his son and heir triumphantly did).

The sides at Chaeronea were probably quite evenly matched in terms of numbers. The Athenians and Thebans and allies from Acarnania, Achaea, Corinth, Chalcis, Epidaurus, and Troezen among others amounted to some 35,000 in all. Philip and his greater Macedonian and Thessalian force numbered 32,000, according to Diodorus – 30,000 infantry plus 2,000 cavalry. But whereas Philip's army, commanded as was usual in such a critical situation by the king in person, was a fully professional force, beaten into shape and kept in top condition for getting on for twenty years, the Theban-Athenian force was pretty much a scratch army, never before having assembled together to fight, even if the newly allied had managed to squeeze in some sort of combined practice. In terms of morale, the Thebans and other Boeotians did have rather more at stake, since the battle was being fought in their own backyard, but they did not have the almost unbroken string of successes to look back upon that the Macedonians and Thessalians did.

We think we know how the anti-Macedonian battle line was disposed. The Thebans, including the famous Sacred Band, were granted, or assumed, the place of infantry honour, on the right wing; the Athenians correspondingly took the second-best place, on the left, with their allies variously placed in between them. However, considerable doubt subsists concerning both the disposition of Philip's line and the evolution of the battle. Granted, there is no doubt that Philip as commander-in-chief followed Greek convention – the convention that Epaminondas had defied at both Leuctra and Second Mantinea – by placing himself on the right wing, opposite the relatively weaker Athenian hoplites. Nor is there any doubt that his eighteen-year-old son and heir presumptive Alexander, son of his northern Greek wife Olympias (just one of his seven 'wives', several non-Greek), was placed in some capacity and in some position of command on the left. There is, however, still room for doubt as to precisely what that capacity was.

I share the view that Alexander fought as a cavalryman, as he always did on every other known occasion, and indeed as commander of the crack Macedonian cavalry unit known as the Companion Cavalry. Eighteen would have been a young age to command the Companions, true, but he had already won his spurs two years earlier when acting as regent of the kingdom and fighting non-Greeks up north, and indeed had had the temerity to rename a town after himself, the first of many 'Alexander-villes' to come. Philip would therefore have been seeking in part to borrow from the playbook of Epaminondas at Leuctra, but he would have been placing not himself but his son in the direct firing line of the best of his opponents' hoplites, the Thebans, and would have been hoping presumably that his best cavalry would sufficiently disrupt their cohesion for his own infantry – some bearing the extra-long lances called *sarissae* – to get in amongst the Thebans. Another view, however, has it that the confrontation on Philip's left wing was essentially an infantry affair, a reconstruction that would leave relatively small credit for Alexander to garner.

At all events, however exactly the battle evolved, Philip ultimately won it hands down. It's estimated that both the Thebans and the Athenians lost more than 1,000 dead and suffered 2,000 captured. But this battle of Chaeronea was not only a huge advance for Philip and his Macedonians. It was also the last gasp of the Thebans' Sacred Band, the crack infantry unit that had been first formed in 378. Philip himself, according to Plutarch's *Life* of Pelopidas, came over from the opposite wing specially to view the corpses of their slain. According to legend, they had died to a man – but actually that might be no more strictly accurate than the myth that all 300 of Leonidas's special bodyguard died with him at Thermopylae in 480. At all events, excavation has uncovered 254 bodies buried compactly on the battlefield in such a way as to suggest they had all belonged to a single unit. Surely these are all members, among the last members ever, of the Sacred Band.

Plutarch adds a curiously authentic touch. Not all Greeks of the fourth century BCE, and certainly many fewer of the Greeks and non-Greeks of Plutarch's own day, the first/second century CE, were equally enamoured of Thebes's – or Sparta's – (homo)sexual mores and practices. That possibly explains why Philip allegedly delivered a backhanded compliment over their corpses, to the effect that they had done 'nothing shameful'. The Thebans themselves certainly agreed. Some years later, in circumstances to which we will return in the next chapter, they erected the famous Lion monument that still – as reconstructed from many fragments – stands proud over the battlefield today (see figure 16). A lion had also been the Spartans' monument of choice to commemorate the feat of Leonidas at Thermopylae, but then his very name was a compound of the Greek word for 'lion' (*leon*).

That commemoration, however, was for later, in a somewhat happier time for Thebes. The immediate aftermath of the battle was, for most Thebans, simply ghastly. Termination of the democracy, a democracy that had voted to ally with Athens against Macedon, went without saying. Likewise, rewards were on offer for those pro-Macedonian, oligarchic Thebans who had been opposed to that decision and were now ready and willing to implement Philip's wishes – or rather mandates. The first of those – shades of the Spartans' intervention in 382 – was the installation on the Cadmea of a Macedonian garrison. The Boeotian federation as such was not, however, abolished, but as with the Spartan domination of 382–79 it will have been 'tamed' in a suitably oligarchic direction. Nor was Thebes alone in receiving a Macedonian garrison post-Chaeronea: that fate was also suffered by Corinth and by the city of Chalcis on Euboea.

Athens, by contrast, got off very lightly from Philip, at least on the surface. Alexander was sent by his father to Athens ceremonially, to accompany the urns containing the ashes of the Athenian slain. That was the only time in his life that Alexander ever visited Athens. (Did he, one wonders, remember Athens's Odeum building below the Acropolis or the Parthenon temple atop it, when he captured and partially destroyed the Persians' palace complex at Persepolis in 330? Both those buildings had Persian echoes.) Philip, so far as we know, never did visit Athens. But he had big plans for the city, despite its Demosthenes-led opposition and despite its democracy. After all, some quite eminent Athenians had been prepared at least to tolerate if not facilitate his hegemony of Greece in the past; and for the future, or so he believed, he actually was going to need the Athenians as his active military allies. As mentioned above, Philip had no warfleet. But Athens did, potentially a huge one of several hundred triremes. It is true that its last big battle during the so-called Social War (the war against its revolted allies) of 357–355 had not been a success, but it could at any rate be called upon to provide vital backup and to convey and convoy supplies and men for the massive military enterprise he had in mind.

For Philip, as noted, had long contemplated some sort of Asiatic campaign of conquest against the Persian Empire before he actually got himself into a position to carry it out. His treatment of Thebes after Chaeronea, though exceptionally harsh, presaged his general attitude to the subordinated Greek cities that he brought together more or less forcibly under the umbrella of an alliance that moderns call the League of Corinth. Philip wanted to be sure that the Greek cities that joined him in swearing (another) common peace and military alliance were suitably tamed and reliable. Delegates from the cities were summoned in the later part of 337 to Corinth – aping and deliberately recalling the Hellenic League alliance sworn there against the Persians first in 481; and a full offensive and defensive alliance was concluded, with him as its *hegemon* (leader).

Unlike in the previous Peloponnesian or Athenian alliances (and of course the Second Athenian League formed in 378 was now formally terminated), these allies were all allied to each other as well as to their mutual *hegemon*. 'League' is therefore for once the proper term, and modern historians speak of the 'League of Corinth', though in ancient parlance it would have been known as just '[King] Philip and the Hellenes'. Allied delegates were to meet in council (*sunedrion*) four times a year, at Corinth. One Greek city, however, stood out and, being weak and divisive, was purposely allowed to stand out:

Sparta. Not only did it pose no threat, but its dissidence would ensure the loyalty of all the most virulent anti-Spartans, such as Messene and Megalopolis.

Utterly predictably, the very first decision made by the tamed catspaw council was to appoint Philip as commander-in-chief of a grand, panhellenic campaign against the Persian Empire. Or, that charged word, crusade. It may be a loaded term, but Philip certainly cloaked his actual political-material, power-and-glory-bringing aims in the language of pious religion. In line with his behaviour in 346, when he had already played the panhellenist card, the expedition was to be construed and realized as an act of *tisis* (Greek for retribution, often in a religious sense). This was to be payback for the sacrilegious crimes committed by the Persians in 480–79, when under Xerxes – the most impious 'barbarian' (non-Greek) man of all (see Herodotus) – they destroyed a multitude of Greek shrines and temples, most conspicuously and notoriously those on the Acropolis of Athens.

Yet who were the 'they' that wreaked this impious havoc? On which side were the Macedonians in 480–479? Yes, that's right: on the side of the Persians. The disunited kingdom of Macedon in 480 and 479 had actually been a sub-province, a vassal state, of the Achaemenid Persian Empire. No matter how hard their even more exceptionally long-reigning king Alexander I (*c.* 494–450) had tried, he could never shake off entirely the taint of subservient treachery; moreover, the supposedly honorific title he acquired of 'Philhellene', friend of the Hellenes, meant strictly that he was not considered to be a Hellene himself (though formally he was, and recognized as such by the authorities from the city of Elis who ran the all- and only-Greek Olympics). Philip's aims therefore, in his crusading propaganda of 337, were above all to disguise that chequered Macedonian (including royal Macedonian) past, and to appeal spuriously to the panhellenic spirit that the wars of 480–479 had (only) temporarily evoked.

Thebes in 337, though garrisoned and non-autonomous, was still

Greek and so part of the Hellenic League of Corinth and a partner in its anti-Persian aspirations. Yet just a couple of years later a like appeal to panhellenist sentiment and solidarity was to be deployed by Philip's – and the League's – successor Alexander *against* Thebes, as we shall soon see. That, after all, was historically consistent, since Thebes too had indeed medized in 480/479. But in 337, Philip was aiming to appeal above all to Athens, for the reasons given above.

In summer 336, Philip began his Persian campaign by dispatching a substantial advance force under his most trusted and experienced Upper Macedonian general Parmenion to secure a bridgehead around the Hellespont in north-west Asia Minor. But then, alas for him (but not for his son and successor Alexander), he was assassinated by a member of his personal bodyguard. Macedonian history was running true to its old regicidal form, or so it seemed. The oppressed Thebans in particular began to dream of a better, Macedon-free future. How wrong they were proved to be.

CHAPTER 11

The Destruction of Thebes, 335

The destruction of Thebes on the orders of Alexander III, King of Macedon (later surnamed 'the Great'), has rightly been classed as one of the most dramatic catastrophes to befall a major Greek *polis*. As we shall see, the adjective 'dramatic' has a peculiarly apt point in this context. The destruction occurred just three years after the disaster of the defeat at Chaeronea by Alexander's father Philip II. It set the seal on Thebes's downfall from a position of great power and influence to one of minor significance.

As noted, shortly before Philip's assassination he had embarked on the conquest of at least part of the Persian Empire. That conquest was to be taken as far as it feasibly then could be by his son Alexander, who in turn succumbed to a premature death. This Macedonian *Drang nach Osten* (push to the east) represented the death-knell of the traditional Greek *polis* as a power-unit in Greek history, though there were some occasional later partial exceptions, such as the island-city of Rhodes, and the federations of Achaea and Aetolia. The Theban federation, however, was once again no exception (see next chapter).

Philip's assassination caused temporary chaos at the heart of his kingdom; at least three or four pretenders either put themselves forward or were backed, including one backed by Athens. But realistically the choice was only ever between Alexander and another son of Philip, who seems not to have been fully capable. Alexander it was who, with the aid of some judicious assassinations, succeeded to the throne, ruthlessly, just as the Macedonian constitution, such as it was, permitted or demanded. This regime was an absolute autocratic hereditary monarchy, tempered only by some conventions of spurious equality, especially between the king and those few elites whom the king was pleased to designate his comrades, or Companions (*hetairoi*).

Wishing passionately to pursue the conquest of Asia (from which, ironically, Philip seems to have wished to exclude him), Alexander's first action outside Macedonia in 336 was to get himself recognized as Philip's successor as *hegemon* of the League of Corinth, and thus as commander-in-chief of its declared Persian war. Alexander therefore continued to treat Athens, unlike Thebes, with kid gloves – no garrison, no interference with its constitution and internal affairs. In return, Athens continued to do nothing overtly anti-Macedonian, although in 336, before Philip's assassination, the Athenian Assembly had sufficiently chafed at Athens's loss of freedom and power, and sufficiently feared a Macedonian imposition of a pro-Macedonian tyrant (as had happened elsewhere under Philip), to pass a famous anti-tyranny law and decree.

The marble stele recording this momentous decision has been excavated in the Athenian Agora. Above the text is placed a bas-relief sculpture depicting Democratia, the goddess personification of democracy, in the act of crowning with a victor's wreath of sacred olive leaves a seated middle-aged male figure representing Demos, the personified Athenian People. This was a powerful way of recalling that the original democracy had been conceived and successively renewed as precisely an anti-tyrannical form of *politeia*.

In fact, the Athenians did nothing concretely anti-Macedonian during the entire reign of Alexander. (For example, they did not follow the Spartans, as several other Greek states did, in their vain uprising in 331 or 330.) In 335, they did institute a formal period of 'national service' for eighteen- and nineteen-year-old citizen *ephebes* (literally, 'those on the threshold of manhood/adulthood'), who were specifically tasked with defending the frontiers of Attica in the name of a whole slew of local and Hellenic gods, goddesses and heroes and heroines. But in that same year, they lifted not a finger to defend their erstwhile partners in resistance in Thebes.

The Thebans, as detailed in the last chapter, had moreover been punished far more harshly by Philip than had the Athenians. In 336 there was some hint of their contemplating overt rebellion, but this was quickly snuffed out. By 335, however, it seems that even the normally 'packed' pro-Macedonian Theban assembly had had enough of Thebes's servitude and effective imprisonment. Rashly, as it soon turned out, it voted to revolt against Alexander, wishfully believing a false rumour that he had been killed on campaign some 500 kilometres off, way up in northern Greece and the peri-Danubian region. Within a fortnight, in harsh reality, the very much alive Alexander was outside the gates of Thebes at the head of an allied army. A bloody battle ensued, which Alexander's forces easily won. The ensuing cost to Thebes of their revolt and defeat was almost without limit.

Alexander's grand sack of Thebes was probably authorized through a formal decree of the League of Corinth, which had been set up by his father to be the instrument of his military-political control of all Greece south of his home territory of greater Macedonia. But the decree had Alexander's name all over it. With his father's treatment of Olynthus as an inspiration and validation, Alexander gave the order for (almost) all Thebans to be either killed or sold into slavery, and for (almost) all the city itself including its fortification walls to be razed, levelled with the ground, physically annihilated. Altogether, some 6,000 Thebans were killed, and many thousands more were sold into slavery abroad in the process known as *andrapodismos* (literally, the casually inhumane transformation of humans into 'man-footed creatures', the legal equivalent of four-footed animals – and so fit for the slaughter).

Woe to the bloody city! It is all full of lies and robbery; the prey departeth not. The noise of a whip, and the noise of the rattling of the wheels, and of the pransing [sic] horses, and of the jumping chariots. The horseman lifteth up both the brightsword and the glittering spear: and there is a multitude of slain, and a great number of carcases; and there is none end of their corpses; they stumble upon their corpses.

This is not actually a description of the sack of Thebes. It is the fulmination of minor Old Testament prophet Nahum in the King James Bible (1611). But, with a couple of significant exceptions, it could have been.

The exceptions are very revealing. Alexander was apparently a remarkably pious man; one might indeed apply to him the Greek term *deisidaimon* (superstitious), as discussed contemporaneously by Aristotle's pupil and successor as head of the Lyceum research institute, Theophrastus, originally from Eresus on the island of Lesbos. Alexander was always desperately keen to keep his own gods and goddesses and heroes and heroines firmly on his side through prayers, vows, massive and expensive animal blood-sacrifices, the interpretation of multiple signs, omens and portents – in short, the whole panoply and paraphernalia of official Greek polytheistic worship. Alexander must therefore have believed either that the destruction of Thebes had positive divine sanction or at least that it was not inconsistent with or contrary to divine will.

He was also always keen to enlist new superhuman powers in his service where available, and they became more and more numerous and more important as he marched with his conquering armies ever further east and south, away from the old centres of Hellenic settlement. His devotion to Egyptian Amun (in Greek Ammon), for example, was quite exceptional. However, Alexander was also a fervent follower of the old Greek gods, and two of those that he especially venerated just happened also to be two of Thebes's most prominent – and native, in a sense – divinities: Dionysus and

Heracles (see Chapter 4). One of the prime motivating forces behind his later Indian (ad)venture, it was said, was his desire to rival, emulate or even outstrip Dionysus and Heracles, both of whom were credited in myth with actually having been there and done that. For Alexander to have effected the destruction of their Theban shrines and sanctuaries would therefore not have been countenanced or even contemplated. So, they at least were religiously spared, along with their priests and priestesses.

Besides religious personnel, other Thebans who were spared included ritual guest-friends (*xenoi*) of prominent Macedonians and members of the families of official representatives (*proxenoi*) of the Macedonians in Thebes, together with any philo-Macedonian Thebans who had opposed the revolt. So far, so predictable. But that leaves one further category of exception to the otherwise almost universal rule of slaughter and destruction: namely, the living descendants of the poet Pindar and the house he had once lived in on the Cadmea.

This was pure Madison Avenue – by which I mean propagandistic window-dressing for external consumption on the eve of Alexander's joining the already underway panhellenic expedition against Persia. At any rate, the exception can't – or shouldn't, logically – have been all about Pindar himself. As rehearsed in an earlier chapter, the praise-poet's loyalties had been by no means impeccably panhellenic in an anti-Persian sense. On the other hand, Pindar had indeed written odes in substantial numbers for victors from many different Greek cities who had been crowned in the four great 'panhellenic' religious festivals, the Olympics, the Pythian Games, the Isthmian Games and the Nemean Games. And one of those four, the Olympics – the original Games, and later the premier Games of what had become an interlocking circuit from the 570s on – had actually been in course of celebration while the Persians were making their original invasion of Greece in August 480.

Who better, then, as an emblematic figure to symbolize Greek resistance and antipathy to Persia than Pindar? Well, actually, there probably was at least one better poet-emblem available: Simonides from the island of Ceos (modern Kea), the original praise-singer par excellence, and Pindar's model. It was Simonides, for instance, who penned the famous epigram about Thermopylae: 'Go, tell the Spartans . . .' However, Simonides was not a Theban nor had he lived in Thebes, so in the circumstances of 335 he simply didn't count. Moreover, Pindar – for all his other pro-aristocratic, less than hellenically patriotic leanings – had not only called Athens the 'violet-crowned' but had written other nice things about the city, which Alexander was then keen to butter up. Hence the sparing of Pindar's house, conveniently located on the Cadmea, something which of course Boeotian Plutarch was no less keen to record and talk up.

The 335 *katastrophe* – destruction – was thus the endpoint of Thebes's most brilliant four or five decades, the origins of which may be traced back to the mid-fifth century. Aeschines, Demosthenes's at first rival and then deadly enemy in Athens, expressed it most memorably, employing the rhetorical figure of *anadiplosis* (doubling): 'Thebes, Thebes, a neighbour city, in the course of a single day has been plucked up from the very heart of Hellas.'

Thebes, the real Thebes of History, was therefore dead. But not for all that long, although its resurrected afterlife as a historical city was to be far less glorious. On the other hand, as if by divine compensation, its afterlife as a city of Myth was to soar as never even in antiquity. Thebes, mythical Thebes, would become all the rage.

PART V

AFTERLIFE:
THE PERSISTENCE
OF OEDIPUS

CHAPTER 12

Thebes Rebuilt

At this point, the idea of counterposing the Thebes of History and the Thebes of Myth suffers temporarily an insurmountable blockage. For some two decades after ground zero, 335 BCE, historical Thebes ceased to exist at all, in any shape or form. But though lost, the city was not altogether forgotten by contemporaries, and well before the end of the fourth century BCE it was resurrected and repopulated.

This was within the period of Greek history following the early death of Alexander the Great at Babylon in 323 BCE that is traditionally known as the 'Hellenistic' Age. Still Greek (Hellenic), yet the Greek world now stretched far to the east geographically, to embrace the vast realm created by Alexander's conquest of the Achaemenid Persian Empire. But the spread was not only geographical but also, crucially, cultural. Greek became the language of administration and high culture, and many new Greek cities were founded more or less permanently, as far east as Afghanistan and the Indus valley. Moreover, besides a certain inevitable amount of top-down Hellenic imposition, there was also considerable cultural melding and fusion, especially in the Nile Valley of Egypt ruled by the dynasty of the Ptolemies from 306 to 30 BCE.

After Alexander's death there ensued a very long series of internecine wars between a succession of rival, mainly Macedonian warlords, all keen for their slice of Alexander's leavings. Some sort of stability finally emerged in the early third century: in Old Greece

the Antigonid dynasty ruled the roost from Macedonian Pella, challenged interestingly by a couple of major federations, the Achaean
and the Aetolian Leagues; in Egypt there ruled the dynasty established
by Ptolemy I, based in its new capital of Alexandria, founded but
not built by Alexander; and in Asia the Seleucids held sway over the
largest chunk of what had been the Achaemenid Persians' empire.
But by the mid-second century BCE the 'cloud in the West' (as one
far-sighted Greek politician put it) – Republican Rome – had occluded
such genuine liberty as the mainland Greeks still then possessed.

From then Greece, despite Rome's propaganda to the contrary,
was no longer free but became a protectorate of Rome under the
pseudo-ancient (Homeric) title of 'Achaea'. Epaminondas's shade
would have mourned. It did not help that the by-then rebuilt Thebes
(see below) was on the wrong side in the decisive civil-war battle of
Actium, 31 BCE, won by Octavian, later Augustus, the first Roman
Emperor, over Mark Antony and Cleopatra (the last of the Ptolemies).
The conventional outer limits of the Hellenistic age are thus the
death of Alexander in 323, and 30 BCE, when Rome under Octavian
absorbed Egypt following the defeat and deaths of Antony and
Cleopatra. During these three centuries, 'Old Greece', the Greece of
our Thebes, grew proportionately smaller, both in size and in significance.

There was, however, a compensation, a very big one, and not by
any means only for the ancient Greeks. As Roman poet Horace (Q.
Horatius Flaccus) memorably wrote in the time of Augustus: 'captive
Greece took its fierce conqueror captive, and introduced [the] arts
into rustic Latium [the region of Italy of which Rome was the capital,
whence our 'Latin']'. The Romans demeaned the Greeks deliberately
by miscalling them 'Graeci', rather than 'Hellenes', as they have
mostly (post-Homer) called themselves. But on the other hand by
thinking of themselves, indeed reinventing themselves, as the Greeks'
cultural descendants and inheritors, and both imitating and preserving
their original works, the Romans have done us – *their* cultural
descendants and inheritors – a very big favour indeed.

And this is not to forget the 'other' Romans: the Greeks whom we now usually refer to as 'Byzantines' but who proudly called themselves 'Romaioi', 'Romans'. Edward Gibbon, historian of the decline and fall of Rome's empire, notoriously considered the Byzantines a disgrace to both the Greek and the Roman name, but opinions on that have altered considerably since the late eighteenth century. Through Constantinople (originally Byzantium, now Istanbul), founded in CE 324 and renamed after Roman Emperor Constantine the Great (313–337), a continuous alternative stream of Classical tradition, literary and otherwise, has flowed to this day (see next chapter).

The date of (what we call) 316/15 for Thebes's refoundation is unequivocally stated in a document of 263/2 BCE from the Cycladic island of Paros, known therefore as the Parian Marble. In the so-called Testament of Alexander, a forgery concocted under the Ptolemaic regime in Egypt some time after 306, it was claimed that Alexander had envisaged the resurrection of Thebes all along, but of course he had not. For one thing, he had had no time to do so, being utterly preoccupied with managing and indeed still conquering a kingdom and empire of his own in Asia right up until his untimely death at Babylon aged only thirty-two.

By 316, after the first round of the bloodletting among Alexander's would-be successors had been completed, Cassander was in command of what we have come to call the Antigonid kingdom of mainland Greece; it is named after its founder, Cassander's father Antigonus Monophthalmus ('the One-Eyed' – like Philip II, he'd lost the other one in war). Any major decision taken within his realm (a kingdom, *basileia*, technically, only after 306 BCE) ultimately therefore belonged to Cassander, and it was he who authorized the rebuilding of Thebes after a horrendous interval of almost twenty years.

Like those Messenians who in the early 360s were in charge of seeing that New Messene was rebuilt as a going concern, the hastily reconvened authorities of Thebes resurgent issued a call for the return 'home' of the wide diaspora of émigré Thebans. Like the priests and managers of Delphi after the terrible fire that destroyed the Temple of Apollo there in the early 340s BCE (and indeed like those currently responsible for the rebuilding of Notre Dame in Paris in our own day), they also issued a proclamation calling for massive financial contributions. As if at the start of a new Olympic Games cycle, envoys were sent out far and wide – appealing both generally on grounds of Thebes's mythical and historical significance within the Hellenic family's collective memory, and specifically on grounds of particular associations and connections, including real or fictive kinship, with individual cities, or on grounds of empathy to cities which had suffered a like fate of total annihilation.

We have long possessed a substantial fragment of the official published record of the financial contributions received (see figure 17); more recently, a new fragment of this record has been discovered, though unfortunately it does not fill the gap in our knowledge caused by the loss so far of the document's opening section. Nor do we know in which *agora* or other public civic space of New-Old Thebes the record was erected. But the new discovery has had one very positive effect. It has prompted a whole host of scholarly reconsiderations, and a much fuller appreciation, of what exactly went into the refoundation of Thebes in 316.

The motives of several of the cities and individuals who are known to have contributed financially are pretty readily explicable: Athens – ally of Thebes when it was destroyed, and harbourer of Theban exiles (as it had been in 382, and as Thebes had been to Athens in 404), perhaps feeling a little guilty for its otherwise supine behaviour in 335; Messene and Megalopolis, cities newly founded just a couple of generations back under the aegis of Thebes and Epaminondas; and Philocles, hellenized king of the Phoenician Sidonians, and some Cypriot individuals – working the Cadmus connection. Aegae, a town of Aeolis in Macedonia, might also have invoked *syngeneia* – kinship (through the Aeolic language family to which Boeotian Thebes belonged). Troas, also in north-west Asia Minor, probably had symbolic reasons (the Trojan War); likewise

Cos – mythology again. Aegina, finally, could have invoked both symbolic and practical reasons.

As interesting but in their way perhaps even more revealing are the cases of three contributing cities and towns that had no previous known, real or fictive, connection with Thebes: Ionian Eretria on Euboea; the (Dorian) Cycladic island of Melos; and – also Dorian – the town of Arcades on Crete. It has been very plausibly suggested that in the first two of those three cases what chiefly motivated them was empathy: they too had suffered total annihilation as cities – Eretria in 490 at the hands of the Persians and Melos in 415 at the equally violent hands of the Athenians. The motives of Cretan Arcades, however, remain inscrutable.

What were these and other moneys spent on? Walls, buildings, land – and people. Land needed to be put back under cultivation; this was an agrarian society. Rebuilding the city's defences was of course also a top immediate priority. But so too were the needs of religion. Alexander's orders had been to spare temples and shrines, but some restoration and refurbishment at least will have been required in many if not all cases after twenty years of neglect.

Quite noticeably, another of the Thebans' very first acts upon their return was to dig into the now surely weed-ridden ruins of the Cadmea, there to uncover, salvage and make a particular fuss of two statues, one secular, one sacred, both involving the resurrection and commemoration of very famous Thebans of the good old days. The sacred statue was a representation of Hermes, protector god of travellers and mediator between the divine and the human spheres. But this particular statue had an added point of significance – an attached inscription which alluded to the famous victory won by their favourite son, *auletes* Pronomus (cited in Chapter 7). The claim that all Hellas had acknowledged Pronomus's primacy was probably an implied dig to expose the hypocrisy of the Macedonians' panhellenist propaganda.

The secular statue was of Epaminondas: no prizes for guessing why *he* had been so selected by his countrymen. It has also been suggested that it was at this same time and in this same spirit of commemorative restoration and reconstitution that two other monuments that we have already encountered were first erected. The first of these is the Theban monument for the famous victory at Leuctra in 371 (see figure 14); it has been variously restored over the years. The other is the equally famous monumental lion sculpture placed on the battlefield of Chaeronea (see figure 16). What the newly re-established Thebans may well not have appreciated, however, is the role about to be played, elsewhere, at about this time by a native-born Theban émigré. It was to have worldwide implications.

Crates, son of Ascondus, was born to a well-off Theban family in about 365 BCE, at the height of the Theban hegemony or ascendancy. All sorts of legends grew up around him later, so it's not possible to say with certainty what moved him to leave his native Thebes for Athens, or when exactly he left. I suspect a combination of intellectual curiosity and Macedonian devastation. For Crates embraced the intellectual side of Athens, the 'town hall of Wisdom', as Plato had labelled it, a city where many philosophies bloomed and blossomed. And we remember that the Thebans Simmias and Cebes had been acolytes of Socrates.

What caught Crates's imagination and devotion was the relatively newfangled Cynic (dog-like) philosophy as practised – very publicly – by Diogenes, a native of Sinope on the southern shore of the Black Sea and another immigrant to Athens. Crates is said to have become a follower of Diogenes, if not in imitation of every extreme manifestation of his frankly antisocial behaviour. What Crates was most concerned to enjoy and advocate was freedom from the slavery of material possessions. He in his turn attracted as a pupil another migrant who had come to Athens from far afield. Zeno was originally from Citium on Cyprus, a Phoenician foundation with – like Herodotus's Halicarnassus – a mixed non-Greek/Greek population.

Zeno himself seems to have been of mixed ethnicity, but the philosophy and philosophical school that he founded in Athens in *c.* 300 BCE was thoroughly Hellenic: Stoicism. It took its name from the Painted Stoa (or Colonnade) in the Athenian Agora, since Zeno and his pupils followed Diogenes's public, outdoors lifestyle and advocated likewise a minimalist, frugal mode of living, though with an infinitely sophisticated substrate of intellectual argumentation to back it up. Crates deserves his honoured place in the Stoic philosophical tradition that was ultimately to capture the minds of many leading Romans, and indeed has a strong following to this day.

The refounded Thebes was soon reintegrated into the renewed Boeotian *koinon*. Federal *archontes* are attested, for example, at Hyettus between 250 and 171 BCE. But Thebes's own *polis* territory was shrunken, and Thebes no longer had any Boeotia-wide reach, let alone the basis for any sort of Greek 'hegemony'. All the same, it was by no means an entirely negligible place. A literary work of the third century BCE, ascribed to one Heraclides of Crete and entitled 'Concerning the *Poleis* in Hellas', has quite a lot of interesting things to say about Thebes. The author estimates the length of the city's rebuilt enceinte wall at 70 stades (about 11.5 km), making it longer even than that of Messene. He reports that Thebes is well watered, which accounts for its many gardens, and – not unconnected – that it has many horses. But he is not very complimentary about the environment and climate. Summer is all right, he concedes, but winter in Thebes is bad: windy, snowy and muddy. He is even more uncomplimentary about the people – or, to be more accurate, the men, who he says are quarrelsome, litigious and violent.

However, he has nothing but praise for the women of Thebes, hymning their elegance, grace and deportment; and he adds that – in public – they went about heavily veiled. He also extols their blond (*xanthon*) hair. Unless this is merely conventional and poetic – Homeric – terminology, it's possible that some of the new post-315 inhabitants had been drawn from outside the usual eastern Mediterranean gene pool. His description (always supposing it's accurate) calls to mind the so-called Tanagra painted terracotta figurines, some of which do indeed depict just such female beauties (see figure 15). Although a comfortable enough place to live in, no doubt, the rebuilt Thebes never recovered anything like its Classical-era political and military significance.

In the post-Alexander Hellenistic period (*c.* 323–30 BCE), even Macedonia became a region of Greek cities, with all the usual amenities and accoutrements of urbanism, including demarcated public central spaces, spacious gymnasia, and the erection of inscribed public documents. The way had been prepared, little though the Macedonians themselves could have guessed it, for expansionist imperial Rome to make of Macedonia in 147 BCE its first eastern *provincia* – unless largely Hellenic or Hellenized Sicily (converted into a province in 241) is also counted as 'eastern'.

The major Greek historian of Republican imperial Rome's post-216 BCE rise to 'world' domination, which included the conquest of Old Greece, is Polybius (*c.* 200–120 BCE). In book twenty of his forty-book mega-history he descants upon the rise but more particularly the fall of the Boeotians. But then he was himself an Arcadian (a native of Epaminondas's foundation of Megalopolis), and his brand of nationalism – or rather regional provincialism – was popular and prevalent in second-century BCE Greece. Polybius was a stickler for historiographical protocols that excluded emotive, 'tragic' history-writing, such as that practised by his bête noire Phylarchus of Athens, but he was prepared to allow local patriotism to compromise strict objectivity when it came to writing up the history of one's own city. That meant in his case that it was OK to be rude about Sparta, which in 223 under its revolutionary king Cleomenes III had inflicted on Megalopolis a minor version of what Alexander had visited upon Thebes in 335.

About the time of Polybius's birth, in the late third or early second century BCE, the city of Messene began the construction of a rather magnificent shrine complex (later re-dedicated and renamed in honour of healing hero-god Asclepius), adorned with images created by the best artisans and craftsmen of the day, including the native-born sculptor Damophon. It's been described as a sort of gallery of public memory for the local residents. Figures depicted included Asclepius and his sons, and Apollo and the Muses – together with the personified city of Thebes flanked by statues of Theban Heracles and (of course) Epaminondas. Altogether, these divinities, personifications and heroized mortals evoked the city's – that is, Thebes's – glorious past; but, above all, they celebrated and commemorated the central event of the founding – or, as the Messenians mythologically preferred, re-founding – of their city by Epaminondas and the Thebans in 369.

In 196 BCE, Roman generalissimo Titus Quinctius Flamininus declared Greece 'free' at a rally staged at – predictably – Corinth. Free, that is, to be a willing subject of the Roman Republic's rapidly growing eastern empire. Greek patriots were not fooled, but their dreams of genuine freedom were just that, pipe dreams. The so-called Achaean War of 149–146, originating in an anti-Roman, liberationist rebellion in the Peloponnese, prompted a massive and decisive military intervention from Rome, from which the city of Corinth received the full Thebes treatment (and was uninhabited thereafter five times as long as Thebes had been). This resulted in the creation in 146 of a Roman protectorate of Greece to the south of Macedonia (itself, as noted, made into a full-blown Roman province in 147) under the title of 'Achaea'. Thebes thus became – again – an 'Achaean' city. Insult was added to injury, in the eyes of some Thebans, when it turned out that one of Rome's principal negotiators of this enforced 'deal' was the aforementioned Polybius. But was there a Boeotian *koinon* post-146? Rome, like Sparta before it, had no use for such multi-state political organizations.

A yet further battle of Chaeronea, in 86 BCE, recalled and reinforced Epaminondas's rueful description of Boeotia as the 'dancing-floor' (*orchestra*) of Ares, god of war. Rome was in Greece to stay, and it did the Thebans no good to follow almost all their mainland Greek compatriots in siding with Mark Antony against Octavian (C. Julius Caesar Octavianus, later Augustus) in the civil war to end all civil wars during the late 30s. For once, Sparta – holdout resister in days gone by against the superior powers of Philip, the Achaean League, and the Rome of Flamininus – made the right call, came out for Octavian and was lavishly rewarded by the newly self-declared *princeps* (chief) of the Roman world, Emperor Augustus, as Octavian became in 27 BCE.

Thebes and Boeotia did not simply fade from the map in the Late Antique Roman and the subsequent Byzantine epochs; there was, for example, a lordship of Athens and Thebes in the high Byzantine era, but it existed under Frankish and Catalan rule (1212–1388). Latin hegemony lasted until 1458, when the Ottoman Turks – masters of Constantinople since 1453 – took Thebes over and renamed it Istefe. Apart from a brief Venetian interlude (1687–1699), Greece ('fair Greece, sad relic') remained under Ottoman domination (the *Tourkokratia*) until 1821.

It was only with the liberation of mainland Greece south of Macedonia and Thrace – and the establishment in 1832 of the new state of Hellas under a Bavarian monarch approved by the Great Powers – that genuine research into the antiquities and history and legacy of ancient Greek Thebes could be seriously undertaken. An early notable example is the *Reisenotizen* (notes on travels) of 1876 and 1877 by the German scholar H. H. Lolling, which were helpfully re-edited and published as recently as 1989. Subsequent archaeological excavations and publications, which have enabled an alternative history of ancient Theban material culture to be written, have been reviewed in Chapter 1.

CHAPTER 13

Mythic Revivals: the 'pigs' bite back

What have the ancient Thebans ever done for us? On the one hand, 'ancient' Thebes is just that: ancient. Evidence for reconstructing and re-evaluating ancient Thebes from a historian's point of view has been transmitted by various means both written and unwritten, visual and textual: through creative literature at one extreme, and through the archaeological spade and trowel at the other. That story is the story of one of the two cities of Thebes examined in this book, the city of History.

On the other hand, though dead in one sense, ancient Thebes does in fact live on most vigorously today, as a city of the imagination, and it does so *via* a quite surprisingly varied range of receptions and inheritances. This is Thebes the city of Myth. Classical 'reception', as it is known, comes in three main shapes or forms. First, there is the movement of an ancient text or myth over time and history from antiquity to modernity, and from one author to the next: what was once famously characterized (by the late American literary critic Harold Bloom) as 'the anxiety of influence'. Second, there is the way or ways in which a post-Ancient author engages with an Ancient author or artefact or group of same. Third, and most complex of all, is the cultural context of historical period or artistic movement within which – or informed by which – Classical reception may either be possible or actually occur. Ancient Thebes brilliantly, triumphantly, offers suitably classic illustrations of all three types or forms of Classical reception.

Given the wealth of available materials, this chapter aims to provide but a series of snapshots rather than a comprehensive overview. It offers, to change the metaphor, a tapestry of many usually independent and diverse threads rather than a narrative with a single underlying or informing thread. It does not pretend to be anything like exhaustive, merely illustrative. But the diverse illustrations are, I think and hope, always at least interesting, and sometimes really quite important, each in their own way. The answer to the question posed in the first sentence of this penultimate chapter is therefore: really rather a lot.

I begin with a musical grace note. It is drawn from one of the most influential of all post-Antique literary productions, the so-called *Alexander Romance* that had its origins in Roman-period Alexandria in Egypt and over the ensuing centuries spread the fame of Alexander within the national literatures of dozens of countries and nations throughout Europe and Asia. The 'Byzantine Alexander Poem' (BAP), for conspicuous example, which was composed in Greek in lines of fifteen syllables in either the thirteenth or the fourteenth century, forms a unique branch of the post-Classical *Alexander Romance* tradition.

In the context of 335 BCE, the BAP imagines a famous Theban singer and *aulos*-player called Ismenias (one recalls the authentic and famous Pronomus, discussed in Chapter 7) attempting to charm Alexander into not destroying Thebes. He does so by rehearsing the great figures of Theban myth, some of whom intersected with Alexander's own personal, myth-historical genealogy. The effect, unfortunately, of the fictional Ismenias's intervention was merely to increase Alexander's irritation with Thebes and inflame his determination to annihilate it. Which meant that, just as the walls of the original Thebes of Cadmus had been erected to the sound of music, so in close harmony and perfect symmetry those same city walls had been brought tumbling down to a like accompaniment.

One of the *Alexander Romance*'s remotest outfalls is to be found in a humorous passage of Shakespeare's *Hamlet*, placed in the mouth of the garrulous gravedigger. We shall return shortly to Shakespeare in another, Theban connection. Literature in English – English English, as it were – is often taken to begin over two centuries earlier, with Chaucer, who lived from the second quarter to the very end of the fourteenth century CE. It is pleasant therefore to record that the cultural memory of ancient Thebes is visible right from the start, in Chaucer's 'Knight's Tale'. Two of its central characters are indeed Thebans – Palamon and Arcite – and the poem's main theme is honour among friends: that is, the two Theban friends who rival each other in their love quest for fair Emily – until Arcite graciously concedes defeat.

Chaucer, as is usually the case with even the greatest of creative writers, did not invent his tale from whole cloth. Far from it. His main source was the 1340/1 *Teseida* (the *Theseid*, or poem about the Athenian Theseus) of the Florentine Boccaccio (1313–75). But whereas Boccaccio had attempted a pseudo-Classical, pseudo-Virgilian manner, Chaucer by way of omissions, additions and condensation (he reduced Boccaccio's nearly 2,000 lines by about four-fifths) contrived something quite new: a medieval romance studded with elements of feudal realism of an English kind. Chaucer thus rendered the tale suitable to be utilized in turn, in their different ways, by both William Shakespeare (*Two Noble Kinsmen*, written in collaboration with John Fletcher) and John Dryden.

That is a not uninteresting development within the context of the English literary canon; but for our Theban-directed purposes no less interesting and important is the identity of Chaucer's secondary source, an ancient – Roman – source: namely, the twelve-book *Thebaid* by the poet he calls (with unintended humour) 'Stace'.

> *Go, litel bok, go litel myn tragedye,*
> *Ther God thi makere yet, er that he dye,*
> *So sende myght to make in som comedye!*
> *But litel bok, no making thow n'envie,*
> *But subgit be to alle poesye;*
> *And kis the steppes where as thow seest pace*
> *Virgile, Ovide, Omer, Lucan, and Stace.*

Chaucer's 'Stace' is Roman poet Statius (P. Papinius Statius), active towards the end of the first century CE. He was the latest in a long line of first-rate Roman poets who had seen the inspirational light shining in the Greek east. As Horace famously put it, *'Graecia capta . . .'*

Horace himself (65–8 BCE), the son of an ex-slave freedman, rose from his humble origins to be patronized by Maecenas, minister of culture to the first Roman emperor, Augustus. He was thus a stablemate of Virgil (P. Virgilius Maro), who composed the great Roman-Augustan epic, the *Aeneid*. Of course, what the Romans did with those introduced Greek 'arts' was another matter, and Horace would have been odd if he hadn't thought that they had been significantly improved by the Romans. Most modern critics would probably concede that Horace has a point, and sometimes, as in the case of Virgil with Homer, it's possible to compare directly the Roman with the Greek original. But in most cases it's not possible to conduct that comparative exercise, since the Greek original of an extant Latin 'imitation' – or derivative – does not itself survive.

Such is the situation of the *Thebaid* of Statius, also rendered like the *Aeneid* in twelve books, and which is thought to have been composed and published in the dozen or so years between CE 80 and 92. The original Greek *Thebaid* epic, several thousand hexameter lines long, survives only in 'fragments' – quotations that may or may not be verbally accurate. Statius's 9,478 hexameter verses do survive. Like other Greek and Roman post-epic composers, Statius did not confine himself to a single 'source', and of course he gave the original myths his own spin – or spins. Statius's work has its own intrinsic interest, though it's not his only extant composition, and many prefer his *Silvae* ('Woods'). It is its reception, however – or rather one very particular reception – that commands attention, one which was created during Chaucer's lifetime (*c.* 1340–1400).

The Chester Beatty Library, now housed and beautifully displayed in its dedicated space in Dublin Castle, contains many rare treasures, written in many languages and scripts with correspondingly diverse visual repertoires employed to – in both senses – illuminate them. 'CBL inv. W 76' is an illuminated manuscript of Statius's *Thebaid*, in its entirety, written on vellum in folio format (see figure 18). The text and initials were completed first, the illuminations followed. Each of the twelve books is illuminated with a miniature image: these 'busy compositions', as the curator F. Croke describes them, combine several of the storylines drawn from the related texts. The identity of the artist is unknown, though the name of the fourteenth-century Veronese painter Jacopo Avanzo has been linked with the manuscript, which is dated *c*. 1380. Altogether, one can see why Chester Beatty's wife Edith was so keen to buy it in 1925, as a fit present for her American industrialist husband, and was also prepared to pay the vast sum of £7,000 (over £400,000 in today's values).

An artist in a very different medium and epoch was the Frenchman Jean-Auguste-Dominique Ingres (1780–1867), a full-on painter in the neoclassical manner. His huge 1806 painting *Napoleon I on His Imperial Throne* is an enduring icon of imperial power and majesty – and a Herodotean-style warning of the inevitable cycle of human affairs, of *peripeteia*. Two years later, Ingres painted his first, student version of his also huge canvas *Oedipus and the Sphinx*, which he enlarged and completed between 1825 and 1827. On either side of the Napoleon and his original Oedipus picture Ingres had painted *Ambassadors of Agamemnon in the Tent of Achilles* (1801) and *Jupiter and Thetis* (1808). In the enlarged *c*. 1826 version of *Oedipus and the Sphinx* Ingres (see figure 19) has painted a brightly illumin-ated landscape in the distanced background, so as to set off and contrast all the more sharply the Sphinx figure crouched on her rock and shrouded in gloom to the viewer's left. Directly in front of her a pensive, smart, enquiring Oedipus places his raised left leg upon a rock and rests his left elbow on his left knee, all the while crooking his index finger up towards the Sphinx. These stunning paintings show just how far the Classical had then interpenetrated the neoclassical in Ingres's aesthetic and artistic repertoire; but so memorably disturbing is his 1808–27 Sphinx image that it prompts further reflection on the original significations of the Sphinx figure in the ancient Greek representational art that inspired the young Ingres (see Chapter 7).

From the outer eye we pass to the inner, the eye of the soul or psyche. Euripides's *Bacchae* has already been referred to (Chapter 7) for what it contributed to the myth of Dionysus's reception (or non-reception) in Thebes, and for what it said about Euripides, about Dionysus, about Athens – and Thebes – in 405 BCE. Here we turn to a peculiarly modern interpretative spin, Freudianism, to which the play may now be subjected, or by which its understanding may be enhanced, according to taste. Dr Sigmund Freud of Vienna and London (1856–1939) was a connoisseur of the Classics and an obsessive-compulsive collector of Greek, Roman, Chinese and especially Egyptian antiquities – now on display in the eponymous Freud Museum in north-west London that was his home after he fled Vienna in 1938 (see figure 21). To aid his thoughts, or complicate them further, a copy of Ingres's *Oedipus and the Sphinx* was hung suggestively beside the couch in his study.

In the course of his long and painstaking case-study researches and through his voluminous writings, Freud discovered – or invented – several psychological 'complexes'. Of these, by far the most famous or notorious was and is the 'Oedipus complex', for which he offered in evidence his case study of 'Little Hans' in 1909. Do we – all males, anyhow – subconsciously/unconsciously seek to kill our fathers (if we know who they are, and even if we don't), and have sex with – 'marry' is a bit of a euphemism in these circumstances – our mothers (whose identity we are more likely to be sure of)? So Freud seemed to want to suggest.

Actually, it quite soon became clear that, even if Freud's own intellectual intentions and ambitions had been vaultingly universal and universalizing, cultures in the anthropological sense were alas far more radically individuated and resistant to homogenization than his theories could possibly cope with. Seeking a universally valid theory of (all) individual human psychodynamics, Freud had in fact come up with a culturally overdetermined hypothesis, the validity of which is now very widely questioned, even though there are still psychoanalysts practising today on both sides of the Atlantic of a self-described Freudian or neo-Freudian persuasion.

For a society's sexual customs and norms are at least as historically determinative of behaviour as its members' individual psychodynamic drives and motivations, conscious or otherwise. One comparative cultural anthropologist, Michael Carrithers, has even gone to the lengths of writing a book entitled *Why Humans Have Cultures* (1992), implying that having a culture was itself an essential and indispensable part of what made us humans in the first place. Likewise, only more so, cultural anthropologist Ruth Benedict's brilliant *Patterns of Culture* (1934), which sometimes makes one wonder how such different cultures as the three that she minutely analyses can all possibly be described under the same common label of 'human'.

Nevertheless, there is still a legitimate case for 'psychologizing', including would-be 'Freudian', readings of literature, if only as subordinate add-ons to more mainstream, all-encompassing or culture-appropriate readings. It was not long indeed before literature and littérateurs were put on the metaphorical couch, as it were, and what more suitable – or obvious – subject for the application of a 'Freudian' analysis than the very play – *Oedipus Tyrannus* – which had prompted the choice of eponymous nomenclature? (There is also 'the Electra complex', the love–hate of a daughter for her mother, but this has had far less traction, either in scientific literature or in practical application. Part of its difficulty is that there are two tragic Electras: Sophocles's proudly single, murderous *revanchiste* is a rather different character from Euripides's no less socioculturally transgressive – she has been forcibly married to a local peasant husbandman – but considerably more mild-mannered eponymous heroine.)

Euripides's *Bacchae* is surely another good case in point. In 2002, the Royal National Theatre staged Colin Teevan's translation, which had been written expressly with a view to its being directed by Peter Hall, who was of the fixed view that, if you are going to do more or less 'straight' versions of Greek tragedy, admittedly in English not ancient Greek, then you have to do them with the actors in full head-masks, and with as few actors – as distinct from chorus-members – as possible, so as to conform to and thereby honour the ancient Greeks' practice of having only three actors (all male) act all the speaking and non-speaking parts.

That view was then and of course still is massively controversial, and it's not clear that carrying it out entirely worked for Teevan's *Bacchae*, despite using such great actors as Greg Hicks (playing Dionysus) – whereas it more obviously had worked, triumphantly, for the great Tony Harrison's version of the *Oresteia* trilogy, which Hall had also directed, in 1981/2, both in London and at Epidaurus. However, the Teevan–Hall version came with a great bonus, offstage, since the printed text was prefaced by a superb introduction from Peter Hall's namesake (no relation), Classical Greek scholar Edith Hall. I quote a telling fragment. After pointing out the post-Antique continuity of interest in the play, she writes:

> *Since Freud, however, it has been possible to interpret the play as a brilliant articulation of the dark unconscious [NB: not 'subconscious'] desires of the human psyche – the erotic, cannibalistic and murderous urges which can scarcely be perceived and yet motor human relationships and experiences of self and other.*

Freud and his theories have generated many and varied but usually vehement reactions, from the bouquets thrown by his more or less sympathetic followers to the slings and arrows loosed off by his rivals and outright enemies. The latter are currently in the ascendant; indeed, all forms of psychoanalysis are in decline, in the wake especially of the neuro-psychiatric revolution (with its emphasis on hard-wired brain function). Nevertheless, the work of Freud and his followers (and enemies) still constitutes one of the most substantial attempts at uncovering the secret springs of individual and collective action.

Two very different, but each in its own way illuminating, scholarly readings illustrate the myth's continuing post-Freudian fertility. Anthropologist Claude Lévi-Strauss (1908–2009) used his structuralist analysis of the Oedipus myth in all its known ancient forms and variations as a way of demonstrating what he argued to be the universal modes of human self-understanding, by way of oppositions and inversions such as the raw and the cooked, and nature and/versus culture (*Structural Anthropology*, English translation, 1963). Cultures in the view of Lévi-Strauss seek to mediate between these, in variously complementary and contradictory ways.

Classical philosopher and historian, and former Resistance hero, Jean-Pierre Vernant (1914–2007) sought to do something similar for the ancient Greeks by means of social-psychological interpretation of their thoughtworld, but minus Freud's notion of 'complex'. By no accident, in his old age he also wrote a lucid account of ancient Greek mythology, translated from the 1999 French original in 2002 as *The Universe, Gods and Mortals*; intended in the first instance for a juvenile readership, it has its distinct adult charms.

Epaminondas's bon mot – that Boeotia was the dancing-floor of war god Ares – has been quoted more than once. In 2019, New York University's Institute for the Study of the Ancient World hosted an excellent exhibition, entitled *Hymn to Apollo*. This was a paean aptly enough to the fact that it was *hommage* to Greek Apollo, lord of the ancient dance, that lay behind the wondrous reinvigoration of the world of modern dance by the Ballets Russes company in the first three decades of the last century. This movement of recuperation was led by the painter-designer Léon Bakst, in association with impresario producer Serge Diaghilev.

The Ballets Russes company was formed outside Russia and made its bow in Paris in 1909. It was Bakst's visit to Greece in 1907 that immediately presaged and inspired a whole host of ancient-Greek-related Ballets Russes dance creations, though he had already in 1902 and 1904 designed productions of *Hippolytus*, *Antigone*, and *Oedipus at Colonus* in St Petersburg. His *Narcisse*, set in Boeotia, was originally performed by the company in Monte Carlo in 1911 and was the first of an ancient-Greek-themed Bakst trilogy. For *Narcisse*, Bakst not only designed the scenery and costumes but also wrote the libretto (see figure 22). Unfortunately – or fortunately – he played fast and loose with Greek or pseudo-Greek mythology.

The story of Echo's unrequited passion for beautiful Narcissus was well known from the hugely influential *Metamorphoses* of Ovid, who seems to have invented it. Echo was a nymph from Boeotian Mount Cithaeron, which presumably was what prompted Bakst's transcultural invention of a shrine in Boeotia of the (very Roman) goddess Pomona, spirit of fruitful fertility. It is to her in the Bakstian version that Echo applies for aid in her suit, only for Narcissus to turn the original selfie and fall in love with his own reflected image. The ballet's main characters are the eponymous Narcissus and Echo, supported by dancers representing bacchantes, young Boeotian women, and nymphs. The Ballets Russes practised total art – music, dance, painting, and costuming all seamlessly intertwined. In that as in many other ways it resembled its ultimate inspiration, the tragic and comic drama of ancient Athens. In England, a little earlier, that same inspiration had taken another, more revivalist form.

In 1883, the first Cambridge Triennial Greek Play was performed, as part of a quite widespread movement to revive performance of ancient Greek dramas in something like their original language – though of course necessarily minus any good or accurate knowledge of their original music, costumes, choreography, blocking, etc. etc. By then, ancient Greek dramas had long been integral to Western cultural consciousness, and indeed it was the recovery and transcription of them in the early Italian Renaissance that lay crucially behind the creation of the new genre of grand opera, in the hands of Claudio Monteverdi and others in the Veneto and elsewhere (see further below).

Thanks famously to the combination of Oxford Regius Professor of Greek Gilbert Murray and theatre magnate Granville Harley Barker, Greek tragedy – in English, not Greek – began to be brought to far wider audiences. For example, in 1911 – during the last summer season of the empire on which the sun never set – Murray produced a translation of the *Oedipus Tyrannus*, for performance, not just for reading, rumination and reflection. This is the famous translation for the production directed by Max Reinhardt at Covent Garden (1912) that became a major plank in the campaign against theatre censorship.

Not long after, Murray was to be a prime mover of the post-First World War League of Nations. Murray it was who thus set the tone and standard for 'engaged' re-performance of ancient Greek – that is, almost exclusively Athenian – tragedies. Which is exactly as it should have been, because, as we have seen (Chapter 7), in their original form and setting, especially after the institution of an early form of democracy in Athens in the decades on either side of 500, the annual performance of tragedies, satyr-dramas and later comedies at religious festivals in honour of Dionysus was an integral element of what it was for the Athenians to 'do' their brand of democracy.

By contrast, Rufus Norris, the current director of London's National Theatre, has recently claimed rather absurdly that by giving Sophocles's *Philoctetes* a 'modern twist' he would be able to show that it was still 'a very valid Greek play'. Someone who didn't need telling that was – well, pretty much anyone who's tried to re-stage a fifth-century BCE Greek tragedy, as many have (among the most successful in recent times being Robert Icke).

Most 'popular' of all for this purpose has been Sophocles's *Antigone*, named for one of Oedipus's two daughters. So popular indeed has it been over the centuries that the critic George Steiner could write a whole book with *Antigones*, plural, as its title. At all events, the phenomenon does certainly require some explanation. Moreover, since that book was first published, in 1984, there has been a veritable torrent, not just spate, of subsequent productions and interpretations, some in pseudo-ancient dress (some even spoken in a sort of ancient Greek!), some in a variety of modern dress, with directors and players competing to bring out and highlight what they take to be *the* defining point or points of the drama.

Yet arguably none of these more or less 'straight' renditions of what, through textual transmission, has come down to us as Sophocles's *Antigone* has caused quite as much notice and controversy as a version – or rather a reworking – of that Sophoclean original by French playwright Jean Anouilh (1910–1987) that was written and first staged in Paris while that city of light was still under the dark gloom of Nazi German occupation, in 1944. Why should the occupiers have permitted such a performance of such a play, with its portrayal of resistance to authoritarianism? What indeed did Anouilh think he was doing – or what was he hoping to achieve – by it? Grist to George Steiner's relentless mill.

Less controversially, but still challengingly, later playwrights in happier political circumstances have taken to writing and staging new plays that rework the old Theban myths/stories. I give just four examples out of the many many possible. Canadian poet-playwright Anne Carson's *Antigonick* does not, in my opinion, show her at her absolute best. It introduces an annoying extra character, 'Nick', who does nothing to enhance and quite a lot to diminish the drama. (Her 'straight' version, that is translation, of *Antigone* was performed very recently at the Barbican in London, and as so often the director, Ivo van Hove, went for an updated, modern, almost bureaucratic repositioning, but it dropped deadly dull from his hands, and the celebrity casting of Juliette Binoche in the title role did nothing to rescue it, since apart from being far too old to play a teenager convincingly she lacked the requisite vocal and other heft.)

Scottish poet-playwright Liz Lochhead's *Thebans* (originally 2003) appears to have been far more successful. ('Appears' because

I haven't been fortunate enough to see a production.) As if in antici-patory response to Rufus Norris, Lochhead was quoted as saying 'There is no time in history when they [the Theban and other ancient Greek plays] didn't seem both prescient and contemporary.'

My third choice is Moira Buffini's *Welcome to Thebes*, which was given its 'world premiere' in the Olivier auditorium (modelled by architect Denys Lasdun on the fourth-century BCE theatre at Epidaurus in the Peloponnese) of London's National Theatre (founded by Laurence Olivier) in 2010. The highly informative, extended programme note provided by Buffini contains a bombshell – or what would have been a bombshell in mid-fifth-century BCE Athens, let alone thirteenth-century BCE Thebes: 'I made Eurydice, Creon's wife, forced in legend to knit as her husband made his mistakes, the elected leader of Thebes.' Elected? What, not divinely appointed and dynas-tically enthroned? And a . . . woman 'President'? It makes all those other thrusting, masculinist Antigones look like participants in the proverbial vicarage tea party.

Lastly, the work of a Nobel Laureate: in 2004, Seamus Heaney had his *The Burial in Thebes* first performed in Dublin's Abbey Theatre. Audiences couldn't help but be reminded – as they were also in his *The Cure at Troy*, a version of Sophocles's *Philoctetes*, and as they were intended to be – of the all too many burials, including mutually murderous kindred burials, caused by the latest vicious, internecine bouts of 'troubles' that have affected and afflicted Northern Ireland, the rest of the UK and the Republic of Ireland for so many years.

Finally, not a play but a novel: Nicolas Nicastro's *Antigone's Wake*. It comes initially as a bit of a relief to learn that this is not to be yet another reworking of the Oedipus–Creon–Antigone–Seven Thebans cycle. But then one finds that it's a novelization of imperial Athens's campaign of suppression conducted over nine months against the revolted, oligarchic island-city of Samos in 440/39 BCE, as seen through the eyes of Sophocles. He might indeed have been one of the Ten Generals involved in that vicious and protracted campaign of suppression, savage punishment and reprisal, as he was certainly the author just a year or two earlier of the original *Antigone*. Besides, Nicastro's Sophocles is probably not the standard current image of the man – as opposed to master-playwright, he is shown here as vain, insecure, and (too) proud of his accomplishments.

Opera, despite its Latin-based name, is in its origins as a modern art form thoroughly Greek, as we have noted. The Florentine musicians who grouped themselves as the Classics-inspired Camerata in *c.* 1580 were soon followed by master-composer Claudio Monteverdi (1567–1643, originally from Cremona, he died in Venice) and his reworking of the myth of Orpheus and Eurydice (1609, 1615).

The complex history of operatic renditions of ancient Theban myths is a full study in itself, and I have to be egregiously selective. The quasi-operatic 'musical drama' *Semele* of George Frideric Handel (originally Händel), with a libretto borrowed from William Congreve (1705/6), caused quite a stir in London's Covent Garden in the Lenten season of 1744, partly for its musical virtuosity but also for its plot, featuring centrally an adulterous sexual relationship. It was first revived in modern times in Cambridge, England, in 1925, and is now regularly performed as a fully staged opera.

The Romanian George Enescu (1881–1935) composed several symphonies and other orchestral works, together with piano music and songs, but only one opera: *Oedipe*, with a libretto by Edmond Fleg (1874–1963). This is widely reckoned to be his masterpiece, and new productions are commissioned, as recently in Salzburg, Austria. What's unusual about its scenario is that its four acts attempt to cover all its mythical eponym's life, *via* the Theban plays of Sophocles, from Thebes to Corinth, then back to Thebes, and finally to Colonus in Athens.

In 1966, the *Bassarids* of Hans Werner Henze (1926–2012) saw its first staged incarnation, with a German translation of its one-act English libretto (by W. H. Auden and Chester Kallman); the original English version was first staged in the States in 1968. Based directly and faithfully on the *Bacchae*, it takes its learned title ('Raving Ones') from an alternative name for the eponymous chorus of bacchantes or maenads ('Madwomen').

More eccentric still, though, is my main exhibit. In 1992, the English National Opera staged what may be – I stand to be corrected – the only opera it has ever permitted to be performed in Greek: ancient Greek, that is. As a rule, the ENO does what its title proclaims, that is, performs its operas in English, even or especially when the libretto of the often far-famed original was written in, say, Italian. But the *Bakchai* or *BAKCHAI* (sic) of modernist English composer John Buller (1927–2004) broke that rule spectacularly. Not only did the opera base itself closely on the Euripidean original (discussed in Chapter 7), but it also proclaimed its source inspiration by its very text. The opera received some exceptionally good notices, too, but I have to say that, as a regular opera-goer and devotee of Mozart, Beethoven, Rossini, Verdi – and Strauss (Richard) – I found the experience acoustically challenging if dramatically effective.

It's undeniable that an ancient Greek tragic drama would have been scored and played and sung with as much complexity and subtlety and expertise as a modern opera, but the ancient idioms, conventions and harmonies seem to me likely to have been desperately foreign, irreducibly alien to most or all of our contemporary operatic modes. To try therefore to mix ancient Greek language and theatrical content with modern musical sensibilities seems predestined to end in something of a cultural mismatch, not to mention mishmash.

From music back to words. The Nazis' occupation of Greece was slightly shorter if no less brutal than their occupation of France mentioned above, but it too had its moments of cultural relief, not exactly light, but lighter perhaps. One of the more unexpected of these occurred in Thebes in 1943. It was remarkable enough that the no doubt classically educated Major Dr Detlef Schleiermacher should have ordered a command performance of the Thucydidean *Epitaphios* (the Periclean Funeral Speech in Thucydides' *History* Book

2) after the unforced death of two of his soldiers in a car accident. But he also had to cope with four cases of illicit homosexual relations among the men under his command. These he neatly sidestepped, indeed exonerated, by reference to the ancient Theban Sacred Band!

The tale is told beautifully by multi-talented German author and *auteur*, Alexander Kluge, in his *Drilling Through Hard Boards: 133 Political Stories* (2017, German original 2011). This fascinating galli-maufry has been rather extravagantly described by a critic as 'a kaleidoscopic meditation on the tools available to those who struggle for power'. Epaminondas at least might have understood.

To conclude, it seems only appropriate to return to the world of Myth. Once upon a time – strictly, before Time was – there reigned chaos, darkness and the void. Then Ouranos (heaven) mated with Ge (earth), and from their cosmic union issued forth an undammable sea of stories about primordial beings of terrifying aspect: male gods with a horripilating propensity to assert themselves by raping at will any fair mortal women who caught their fancy and whom they could catch, and semi-divine heroes covering the spectrum from the some-times feminized, sometimes bestial Heracles to Odysseus, wily master of the civilized word.

In all the main western languages, the genre to which such stories belong and their scholarly study have taken their names from ancient Greece: *muthos/oi*, and *muthologia*, the latter another Platonic coinage like *arkhaiologia*. Mythology and mythography are reasonably well defined and understood genres today, but Italian publisher Roberto Calasso's *The Marriage of Cadmus and Harmony* (1999, as heroically translated by Tim Parks) is harder to pin down, generically speaking.

On one level, it is itself a – new – myth: a postmodern, grunge version of the age-old human yearning for the lost innocence of a paradisal Golden Age. As such, it belongs, despite its rarefied literary provenance, firmly to the sphere of popular culture – nothing wrong with that. But on another level it presents itself as a – critical – retelling of the more widely influential of the ancient Greek myths, and an exploration of their deep structure, thereby complying with the protocols of academic discourse (set by such as Professeurs Lévi-Strauss and Vernant, above).

Calasso emerges as brilliantly learned, a genuine scholar. A glance at the original sources helpfully listed at the back of his book reveals familiarity with all the main ancient Greek myth-mongers, from Homer (eighth/seventh century BCE) to Nonnus (sixth century CE), plus the odd hellenizing Roman sources such as Ovid's *Metamorphoses*. At regular intervals too, Calasso self-consciously punctuates his often poignantly or sexily evocative retellings with more or less straight commentaries.

In these he dwells on the cornucopious multiplicity of the ancient Greeks' world of myth, and on its indeterminacy and refusal of closure (entirely grist to his own mill of course). He revels in that mythic repertoire's rampant superfluity, and he savours the delicious paradox that, in the mythopoetic world, incompatibles become consistent. Once or twice he is prepared even to question scholarly orthodoxy, for example, the notion (accepted by me) that Greek divinities are to be understood as personified, anthropomorphized forces or bundles of powers rather than what you or I might habitually recognize as – admittedly larger-than-life – personalities.

At a third level, Calasso springs a further generic surprise: *The Marriage of Cadmus and Harmony*, on top of its more obvious, superficial aims, functions and contributions, is also a belated contribution to the (seventeenth/eighteenth-century) Quarrel of the Ancients and the Moderns. Edward Gibbon, for instance, for all his determined opposition to dry-as-dust pedantry and sacerdotal obfuscation, was an equally firm believer that the Ancients still had a great deal to teach. Voltaire, on the other hand, though agreeing with his younger English contemporary Gibbon on the rebarbative pedantry of the *érudits* and the obscurantism of his clerical enemies, was no less firm a supporter of the Moderns. Calasso shows himself to be a Gibbonian, more an Enlightenment than a Renaissance man, and moreover a passionate philhellene, despite having been born in Florence and working in Milan. The ancient Greeks are for him the essential, indispensable cultural ancestors.

Speaking musically (or Muse-ically), Calasso scores his freshly composed myth as a symphony of human–divine relations in three movements. First movement: in a universe of familial intimacy, the marriage of mortal Cadmus, founder of Thebes (Chapter 1), to the divine Harmonia symbolizes union, unity and unification. It is crucial to this part of the story that all the Olympian gods and goddesses chose to attend their wedding and that – unlike at some other notorious ancient Greek mortal–divine mythical weddings, especially that of Peleus and Thetis – unbridled disharmony did not break out among the guests.

Calasso almost certainly had other, subtextual or extratextual reasons for making of this aspect an emblem, above all a desire to heal deep east–west rifts. For Cadmus's original motive for leaving his native Phoenicia to settle, he thought only temporarily, in Greece was to rescue his abducted sister Europa. But in rescuing her, and founding the earthly city of Thebes, he united Orient with Occident, and almost (to put it anachronistically) Athens with Jerusalem. For perhaps the most precious legacy that Cadmus was held (quite falsely) to have bequeathed to his – now European – descendants was alphabetic literacy. The idea of an alphabet was originally oriental, but the idea of a fully phonetic alphabetic script occidental. Calasso, typically, redescribes this cultural east–west flow as 'the ineffable milk of books'. Working for Adelphi Edizioni, he knew whereof he spoke.

Second movement: Harmonia was the love-child of (adulterous) Ares and Aphrodite, literally as well as figuratively divine. (It's a mythic peculiarity and anomaly that, apart from sibling spouses Zeus and Hera, Aphrodite is the only other Olympian divinity to be considered married.) But, alas, the outcomes of Harmonia's marriage to Cadmus were the near-total (metaphorical, moral) ruin of Thebes and frequent disasters for their mortal descendants. The royal house of Thebes, known after Labdacus as the Labdacids, included Laius and his son Oedipus. Enough said. In the fluid, post-heroic period, in which the line separating gods from mortals was constantly shifting to the detriment of the latter, the irresistibly superior power of the gods was, according to Calasso, characteristically expressed in the form of divine rapes, although humans eventually fought back symbolically through the ritual of animal blood-sacrifice.

Third movement: our 'post-Christian' epoch has dawned, godless in a twofold sense: no more (worship of) Olympian gods or goddesses, but also – post-Nietzsche – no more the (or a) Christian God, either. Here Calasso is guilty of some considerable chronographic telescopy, but this is mainly because he is the moralizing author of a tract for our troubled times. He never tires of belabouring 'our' unwillingness to evaluate a person's deeds by the measure of the heavens, or even to seek out the divine. And yet, as is apparent to him – and as indeed it has been one of the aims of this book of mine to point out and to emphasize – Apollo and Dionysus are both of them still vigorously at work deep within our collective and individual psyches.

Calasso, in other words, regrets bitterly the disappearance of what my history hero Edward Gibbon – who felt likewise – had called 'the pagan establishment'. But the Italian bookman goes far beyond the historian of the Roman and Byzantine empires in his enthusiastic, possibly even romantic vision of the Olympians as the first divinities who desired to be not merely powerful, but also morally perfect.

CHAPTER 14

Conclusion

The structure and argument of Calasso's book discussed in the previous chapter prompt several, I hope timely, reflections. Whereas a Christian, or other monotheist, might ask 'Where would we be without God – or G-d?', Calasso is of the view that a life in which the pagan gods are not invited to the feast would not be worth living. But where, I ask, would those gods – any gods – be without us? We (to quote the scientist J. B. S. Haldane, brother of historical novelist Naomi Mitchison, author of ancient Greece-set *Black Sparta* and *Cloud Cuckoo Land* among others) are the 'god-makers'. Karl Marx was wrong on many things, but he surely rightly postulated some strong correlation between a society's techno-material base and its imaginary thoughtworld.

So, if Calasso's utopian project is not merely an outburst of aestheticized European *angst*, but is genuinely intended to contribute to moral reconstruction, he ought to have engaged in some considerable amount of mundane cultural history – again, as we have essayed in this present book. Taken overall, however, the ledger of critical appreciation for this richly stimulating and original volume – provoked as it was by a key piece of peculiarly ancient Theban mythology and mythography – must come out massively in the black. Homer's Helen in the *Odyssey* gave sage advice: 'Rejoice in the stories.' We, however, should not just rejoice but also and only connect.

For there's something about those old gods and goddesses of

ancient Greece. It is not just that there are neo-pagans today who still worship them, literally; what is striking is that they seem to exercise an enduring appeal even to presumably totally secular people who otherwise would not be seen dead sacrificing a bull to Dionysus or a heifer to Athena. For glamorous instance: in summer 2019 the fashion design duo of Dolce and Gabbana set up their catwalk, not in Milan or Manhattan, but in the Valley of the Temples at Agrigento (ancient Greek Acragas), Sicily; and – presumably divinely inspired – they there launched their latest collection, displaying models dressed up as 'goddesses', and with Artemis and Aphrodite in the van. The founders of the Greek ready-to-wear label Zeus + Dione (founded 2012) might well have wanted to cite Jesus ben Sirach's biblical trope: 'nothing new under Helios'.

But isn't this all a million miles away from the thoughtworld of Thebes's Dionysus in Euripides's *Bacchae*, an immortal god who lethally melded the promise of ecstatic bliss with actual murderous mayhem. And a million miles away too – or so one would have thought, perhaps even hoped – from the thoughtworld of the early twenty-first century CE, more than 2400 years further on. But is it, actually?

In 2015, Steven Johnston, a professor of political theory at the University of Utah, USA, published a remarkable if also rather chilling book entitled *American Dionysia: Violence, Tragedy, and Democratic Politics*. As the 'American' in the title suggests, this is mainly about modern and contemporary democratic politics, especially but by no means only those of the (pre-Donald Trump) United States. But his choice of 'Dionysia' was neither arbitrary nor merely catchpenny window-dressing; Johnston addresses himself very seriously to ancient Greek, or rather ancient Athenian Dionysiac tragedy.

Here, for example, is a typically thoughtful observation, very much in harmony with my own ancient–modern preoccupations:

In suggesting a new Dionysia, in which the ambiguities attending democratic political life would be prioritized against the backdrop of quotidian commitment, allegiance, and loyalty, I take Athens [the democratic Athens that staged the original tragic dramas: PC] as one model of the tragic, but not the model of the tragic. [emphasis original]

If reading about ancient Thebes in this book has had any measurable effect on my readers, its author would like to hope that it has stimulated reflection of that sobering but also inspirational sort. Of the sort so powerfully put into engaged poetry by German poet-dramatist and revolutionary Bertolt Brecht (1989–1956), to whom shall go almost the last word. He began his 1935 poem 'Questions from a Worker Who Reads' as follows (in a translation kindly supplied by Professor Edith Hall and Dr Henry Stead):

Who built seven-gated Thebes?
In the books are stated the names of kings.
Did the kings drag the boulders up?

That sort of critical questioning is a way of bringing us – and the ancient Thebans – back down to earth, but also a way of reminding us of what those Thebans, real as well as imagined, have done and will continue to do for us.

AFTERWORD

A Tribute to Peter Mayer

Early in the present millennium (which began in 2001) I received a phone call from New York City. It was from Peter Mayer, owner-publisher extraordinary, asking my advice on whether he should buy Duckworth. My *Agesilaus and the Crisis of Sparta*, which had been originally commissioned by Duckworth's then owner Colin Haycraft and published in 1987, had been reissued in paperback in 2000, thanks to Colin's former assistant Deborah Blake (Colin having died in 1994). Duckworth's Classics list was – all modesty aside – altogether impressive, and Peter went ahead with the purchase.

Peter had a soft spot for English and London book publishing. He had been born in London in 1936, to a German Jewish mother and Luxemburg Jewish father. He moved to the States at the age of three, almost by chance, and graduated in English Literature from Columbia University, but returned to England to take a degree in PPE at Christ Church, Oxford, in 1954 – still aged only eighteen. Between 1978 and 1997 he was chairman and CEO of the Penguin Group, Britain's then largest publishers, during which tenure he took the vastly more risky decision to publish Salman Rushdie's *Satanic Verses* and field the consequent, non-negligible death threats.

In 1971, Peter had founded, together with his father, the Overlook Press – its name taken from Overlook Mountain by Woodstock in New York State. In 2007, Peter was deservedly honoured with the Poor Richard Award of the New York Center for Independent Publishers, the generous citation for which included mention of

Overlook's publication of my 'works on ancient history' as 'examples of Overlook's independent spirit'.

One of those was my 2006 book on the battle of Thermopylae, originally commissioned by Georgina Morley for Macmillan through my agent Julian Alexander. In 2006, I was beginning my first stint as Hellenic Parliament-funded Global Distinguished Professor in the Theory and History of Democracy at New York University. Washington Square, in a building off which I both taught under-graduates and collaborated with colleagues in the Classics Department then led by Onassis Professor Phillip Mitsis, is but a few stones' throws north of Wooster Street, SoHo, where Peter ruled the roost in his book-ridden, far from designer-modelled eyrie. There, and in his home loft, also in SoHo, and at the Mercer (Hotel) Kitchen, I enjoyed and profited from many an animated conversation with Peter, mainly on political and broadly cultural matters, including of course discussion of what (he insistently demanded to know) I thought he should or should not publish next. Peter was one of the most cultured as well as the most intelligent people it's been my good fortune to get to know well.

Shortly before Peter's death in May 2018, I was lucky enough to have one final meeting with him, in a London pub near Liverpool Street station. We discussed, of course, this present book, how best to approach and dispose it, and he followed up our drink with typically incisive email messages of support and advice. Duckworth Overlook is no more (Duckworth was sold to Prelude, Overlook to Abrams in 2018), and its Classics list had been bought earlier by Bloomsbury. Deborah Blake, who had come with Duckworth to Peter's new venture from the start, exchanging one demanding boss for another, had likewise already moved on, but she, Julian Alexander and I were all in the packed congregation – or rather audience – for Peter's showy memorial event held in Hawksmoor's masterpiece, Christ Church Spitalfields in east London, on St Nicholas's Day 2018. The old devil would have appreciated the tribute, but I personally was rather sorry that neither at that grand occasion nor in subsequent reportage were Peter's resuscitation of and long association with Duckworth given anything like their due.

This book's dedication may perhaps go some way towards correcting that imbalance: I owe Peter a very great deal, and it is with pleasure and pride tinged with considerable sadness that I dedicate this book to his memory.

Sources and Further Reading
(a selection)

What follows is just a sample of the all-too voluminous – and here almost only anglophone – literature devoted over the past forty or so years to the study of ancient Greece in general and to Thebes in particular. For the most part (there are a couple of exceptions) narrowly and/or purely academic works, above all articles in learned journals or scholarly collections (e.g. conference proceedings), have *not* been listed here – a good range of the latter is to be found in the avowedly 'select' bibliography of Rockwell 2017: 158–66 (see section 1, below).

1. THEBES AND BOEOTIA

General

V. Aravantinos *The Archaeological Museum of Thebes* (Latsis Foundation, 2010): www.latsis-foundation.org/eng/electronic-library/the-museum-cycle/the-archeological-museum-of-thebes [cf. http://thebestproject.gr/index.php/2018/01/09/description-of-the-archaeological-museum-of-thebes/]

K. Demakopoulou & D. Konsola *Archaeological Museum of Thebes* (Athens, 1981)

J. M. Fossey *Topography and Population of Ancient Boiotia* (Chicago, 1988)

J. M. Fossey et al. 'Thebai/Thebae' www.https://pleiades.stoa.org/places/541138/

N. Papazarkadas ed. *The Epigraphy and History of Boeotia: New Finds, New Prospects* (Leiden, 2014)

N. Rockwell *Thebes. A History* ('Cities of the Ancient World' series, London & New York, 2017) [select bibliography: 158–66]

A. Schachter *Boiotia in Antiquity: Selected Papers* (Cambridge, 2016)

Myth

D. W. Berman *Myth, Literature and the Creation of the Topography of Thebes* (Cambridge, 2015)

M. Davies *The Theban Epics* (Hellenic Studies Series 69) (Washington, DC, 2015)

R. Edwards *Kadmos the Phoenician: A Study in Greek Legends and the Mycenaean Age* (Amsterdam, 1979)

T. Gantz *Early Greek Myth: A Guide to Literary and Artistic Sources* (Baltimore, 1993)

A. Kuehr *Als Kadmos nach Boiotien kam. Polis und Ethnos im Spiegel thebanischer Gruendungsmythen* (Stuttgart, 2006)

S. L. Larson *Tales of Epic Ancestry: Boiotian Collective Identity in the Late Archaic and Classical Periods* (Stuttgart, 2007)

Prehistory/Late Bronze Age

V. Aravantinos 'The palatial administration of Thebes updated' in J. Weilhartner & F. Ruppenstein eds *Tradition and Innovation in the Mycenaean Palatial Polities* (Vienna, 2015) 149–210

A. Dakouri-Hild 'Thebes' in E. H. Cline ed. *The Oxford Handbook of the Bronze Age Aegean (ca. 3000–1000 BC)* (Oxford, 2010) 690–711

Y. Galanakis https://www.classics.cam.ac.uk/pdfs/news/prosilio-press-release

S. Symeonoglou *The Topography of Thebes from the Bronze Age to Modern Times* (Princeton, 1985)

Early Protohistory, Archaic and Classical, c. 700–300 BCE

R. J. Buck *A History of Boeotia* (Edmonton, 1979)

—*Boiotia and the Boiotian League, 432–371 BC* (Edmonton, 1994)

J. Buckler *The Theban Hegemony, 371–362 BC* (Cambridge, MA, 1980)

P. Cartledge *Agesilaus and the Crisis of Sparta* (London & Baltimore, 1987, repr. 2000)

—*Ancient Greece: A Very Short Introduction* (Oxford, 2011)

N. H. Demand *Thebes in the Fifth Century: Heracles Resurgent* (London, 1982, repr. 2011)

M. H. Hansen & T. H. Nielsen eds *An Inventory of Archaic and Classical Poleis* (Oxford, 2004) [Thebes & Boeotia: by M. H. Hansen, 431–61]

V. D. Hanson *The Soul of Battle: From Ancient Times to the Present Day, How Three Great Liberators Vanquished Tyranny* (New York, 1999) [one chapter is for Epaminondas; Hanson's other two 'great liberators' are US Generals Sherman (Civil War) and Patton (WWII)]

E. Mackil *Creating a Common Polity: Religion, Economics, and Politics in the Making of the Greek Koinon* (Berkeley, 2013)

E. Occhipinti *The Hellenica Oxyrhynchia and History: New Research Perspectives* (Leiden & Boston, 2016)

J. S. Romm *Love's Warriors: The Sacred Band of Thebes and the Last Days of Greek Freedom* (forthcoming, provisionally 2021)

B. Steinbock *Social Memory in Athenian Public Discourse: Uses and Meanings of the Past* (Ann Arbor, 2013)

S. Tufano 'The beginnings of Boiotian local historiography. Localism and local perspective in Boiotia between the end of the Fifth Century BC and the Age of the Theban Hegemony' *TEIRESIAS* 462.0.05 (2016) 18–23

Hesiod

R. Hunter *Hesiodic Voices: Studies in the Ancient Reception of Hesiod's Works and Days* (Cambridge, 2014)

R. Lamberton *Hesiod* (New Haven & London, 1988)

A. Loney & S. Scully eds *The Oxford Handbook of Hesiod* (Oxford, 2018)

F. Montanari, A. Rengakos & C. Tsagalis eds *Brill's Companion to Hesiod* (Leiden, 2009)

A. E. Stallings trans. *Hesiod: Works and Days* (London, 2018)

Pindar

B. Kowalzig *Singing for the Gods: Performances of Myth and Ritual in Archaic and Classical Greece* (Oxford, 2007)

A. C. Sigelmann *Pindar's Poetics of Immortality* (New York, 2016)

Plutarch

A. Georgiadou *Plutarch's Pelopidas: A Historical and Philological Commentary* (Leipzig, 2014)

C. Pelling *Plutarch and History: Eighteen Studies* (Swansea 2002, repr. 2011)

II. THEBES: RECEPTION AND LEGACY

History/Archaeology

V. Aravantinos *The Archaeological Museum of Thebes* (Latsis Foundation, 2010): www.latsis-foundation.org/eng/electronic-library/the-museum-cycle/the-archeological-museum-of-thebes

K. Demakopoulou & D. Konsola *Archaeological Museum of Thebes* (Athens, 1981)

S. Symeonoglou *The Topography of Thebes from the Bronze Age to Modern Times* (Princeton, 1985)

Freud and the 'Oedipus Complex'

P. duBois 'The persistence of Oedipus' in her *Out of Athens* (New York, 2012) [ch. 9]

C. Lévi-Strauss *Structural Anthropology*, Eng. trans. (London, 1963)

J-P. Vernant 'Oedipus without the complex' in his *Tragedy and Myth in Ancient Greece*, trans. J. Lloyd (London, 1981)

Theatre

M. Anspach ed. *The Oedipus Casebook* (East Lansing & Chicago, 2019)

C. Atack *The Discourse of Kingship in Classical Greece* (Abingdon & New York, 2020)

E. Hall 'Introduction and Notes', *Sophocles: The Theban Plays* (Oxford, 2009)

—*Greek Tragedy: Suffering under the Sun* (Oxford, 2010) [Further Reading: 359–97]

T. Harrison *The Inky Digit of Defiance*, ed. E. Hall (London, 2017)

F. Macintosh *Sophocles: Oedipus Tyrannus* (Cambridge, 2009)

O. Taplin trans. *Sophocles: Oedipus the King and Other Tragedies* (Oxford, 2016)

III. GENERAL: ANCIENT GREECE

Reference

The Barrington Atlas of The Greek and Roman World ed. R. Talbert (Princeton UP, 2000; available also as CDRom) [Thebes: 55 E4 Thebae]

J. Bintliff *The Complete Archaeology of Greece: From Hunter-Gatherers to the Twentieth Century* AD (Oxford & Malden, MA, 2012)

The Cambridge Dictionary of Greek Civilization ed. G. Shipley et al. (Cambridge, 2006)

C. Mee & A. Spawforth *Greece* (Oxford Archaeological Guides) (Oxford, 2001)

Oxford Classical Dictionary [OCD] 4th edn ed. S. Hornblower, A. Spawforth & E. Eidinow (Oxford, 2012, also available online)

Oxford Dictionary of the Classical World ed. John Roberts (Oxford UP, 2007) [an abridged reworking of the OCD]

Princeton Encyclopedia of Classical Sites ed. R. Stillwell (Princeton, 1976) [esp. P. Roesch on Thebes]

Ancient Sources: Texts in Translation

M. Crawford & D. Whitehead *Archaic and Classical Greece. A Selection of Ancient Sources in Translation* (Cambridge, 1983)

M. Dillon & L. Garland *Ancient Greece. Social and Historical Documents from Archaic Times to the Death of Socrates*, rev. edn (London & New York, 1999)

C. W. Fornara *Archaic Times to the End of the Peloponnesian War*, 2nd edn (Cambridge, 1983)

P. Harding *From the End of the Peloponnesian War to the Battle of Ipsus* (Cambridge, 1985)

Pausanias *Guide to Greece*, trans. P. Levi, 2 vols (Harmondsworth, 1971)

P. Rhodes *The Greek City States. A Sourcebook*, 2nd edn (Cambridge, 2007)

Ancient Sources: Archaeology, Language

S. E. Alcock & R. Osborne eds *Classical Archaeology* (Oxford, 2007)

M. Andreadaki-Vlazaki & A. Balaska eds *The Greeks. Agamemnon to Alexander the Great* (Athens, 2014)

A-Ph. Christidis ed. *A History of Ancient Greek: From the Beginnings to Late Antiquity* (Cambridge, 2007)

Modern Works: One-volume Overviews

J. Boardman, J. Griffin & O. Murray eds *The Oxford History of the Classical World* (Oxford, 1986)

R. Browning ed. *The Greek World. Classical, Byzantine and Modern* (Thames & Hudson, London & New York, 1985)

P. Cartledge ed. *The Cambridge Illustrated History of Ancient Greece*, rev. edn, pb (Cambridge, 2002)

C. Freeman *Egypt, Greece and Rome. Civilizations of the Ancient Mediterranean*, 2nd edn (Oxford, 2004) [esp. chs 8–19]

P. Levi *Atlas of the Greek World* (Oxford, 1980)

J. McInerney *Greece in the Ancient World* (London & New York, 2018)

R. T. Neer *Art and Archaeology of the Greek World*, 2nd edn (London & New York, 2019)

R. Waterfield *Creators, Conquerors, and Citizens: A History of Ancient Greece* (New York, 2018)

Modern Works: Historiography

M. Crawford ed. *Sources for Ancient History* (Cambridge, 1983)

C. Fornara *The Nature of History in Ancient Greece and Rome* (California & London, 1983)

J. Marincola ed. *A Companion to Greek and Roman Historiography*, 2 vols (Oxford, 2007)

T. Scanlon *Greek Historiography* (Chichester, 2015)

Modern Works: Epigraphy

R. Osborne & P. Rhodes *Greek Historical Inscriptions to 403 BC* (Oxford, 2018)

P. Rhodes & R. Osborne *Greek Historical Inscriptions 404–323 BC* (Oxford, 2003)

IV. PERIODS

Prehistory, General

O. Dickinson *The Aegean Bronze Age* (Cambridge, 1994)

C. Renfrew *The Emergence of Civilisation. The Cyclades and the Aegean in the Third Millennium BC* (Cambridge, 1972)

Protohistory and Early History, including Archaic to 500

P. Bang & W. Scheidel eds *The Oxford Handbook of the State in the Ancient Near East and Mediterranean* (Oxford, 2013)

H. Beck & P. Funke eds *Federalism in Greek Antiquity* (Cambridge, 2015)

J. Boardman *The Greeks Overseas. Their Early Colonies and Trade*, 4th edn (London & New York, 1999)

A. R. Burn *The Lyric Age of Greece* (London, 1960, rev. edn 1978)

O. Dickinson *The Aegean from Bronze Age to Iron Age: Continuity and Change between the Twelfth and the Eighth Centuries* BC (London & New York, 2006)

M. H. Hansen & T. H. Nielsen eds *An Inventory of Archaic and Classical Poleis* (Oxford, 2004) [Thebes & Boeotia: M. H. Hansen, 431–61]

See also below: Murray 1993, Osborne 1996, Hall 2007, Desborough 1972, Coldstream 2004, and Jeffery 1976.

Classical: 500–300 BCE

M. H. Hansen & T. H. Nielsen eds *An Inventory of Archaic and Classical Poleis* (Oxford, 2004) [Thebes & Boeotia: M. H. Hansen, 431–61]

S. B. Pomeroy et al. *A Brief History of Greece: Politics, Society, and Culture*, 3rd edn (Oxford & New York, 2014)

J. T. Roberts *The Plague of War: Athens, Sparta and the Struggle for Ancient Greece* (2019)

W. Shepherd *The Persian War* (Oxford, 2020)

See also below: Davies 1993, Rhodes 2007

V. MONOGRAPHS: ARCHAIC TO HELLENISTIC

Fontana series (Glasgow, Oswyn Murray ed.)

J. K. Davies *Democracy and Classical Greece*, 2nd edn (1993)

O. Murray *Early Greece*, 2nd edn (1993)

F. W. Walbank *Hellenistic Greece*, 2nd edn (1992)

Methuen/Routledge series (London, Fergus Millar ed.)

S. Hornblower *The Greek World, 479–323* BC, 4th edn (2011)

R. Osborne *Greece in the Making, 1200–480 BC* (1996, 2nd edn 2009)

G. Shipley *The Greek World After Alexander, 323–30 BC* (2000)

B. Blackwell series (Oxford)

R. Malcolm Errington *A History of the Hellenistic World 323–30 BC* (2008)

J. Hall *A History of the Archaic Greek World, ca. 1200–479 BC* (2007, 2nd edn 2014)

P. Rhodes *A History of the Classical Greek World* (2007)

E. Benn series (London)

N. Coldstream *Geometric Greece* (1977; rev. edn Routledge, 2004)

V. Desborough *The Greek Dark Ages* (1972)

L. H. Jeffery *Archaic Greece: The City States 700–500 BC* (1976)

Index